# BRITAIN BEYOND BRE✕

WILEY

# BRITAIN BEYOND BREXIT

*Edited by*
Gavin Kelly and Nick Pearce

Wiley
In association with *The Political Quarterly*

This edition first published 2019
© 2019 The Political Quarterly Publishing Co. Ltd.

John Wiley & Sons

*Registered Office*
John Wiley & Sons Ltd, The Atrium, Southern Gate, Chichester, West Sussex, PO19 8SQ, UK

*Editorial Offices*
101 Station Landing, Medford, MA 02155, USA
9600 Garsington Road, Oxford, OX4 2DQ, UK
The Atrium, Southern Gate, Chichester, West Sussex, PO19 8SQ, UK

For details of our global editorial offices, for customer services, and for information about how to apply for permission to reuse the copyright material in this book please see our website at www.wiley.com/wiley-blackwell.

The right of Gavin Kelly and Nick Pearce to be identified as the editors of the editorial material in this work has been asserted in accordance with the UK Copyright, Designs and Patents Act 1988.

*Library of Congress Cataloging-in-Publication Data*

Names: Kelly, Gavin, 1970- editor. | Pearce, Nick, 1968- editor.
Title: Britain beyond Brexit / edited by Gavin Kelly and Nick Pearce.
Description: Chichester, West Sussex, UK ; Medford, MA : Wiley in association
  with The Political Quarterly, 2019. | Includes bibliographical references.
Identifiers: LCCN 2019009681 | ISBN 9781119572077 (pbk.)
Subjects: LCSH: European Union--Great Britain. | Great Britain--Economic
  policy--21st century. | Great Britain--Social policy--21st century. |
  Great Britain--Foreign economic relations. | Great Britain--Politics and
  government--2007-
Classification: LCC HC240.25.G7 B7464 2019 | DDC 330.941--dc23 LC record available at
https://lccn.loc.gov/2019009681

Cover image © Simon Menges
Cover design by Soapbox, www.soapbox.co.uk

Set in 10.5/12pt Palatino by SPS

Printed in the UK by Hobbs the Printer
1    2019

# Dedication

This book is dedicated to the memory of Jeremy Heywood (1961–2018). An outstanding public servant, colleague and friend.

Published by John Wiley & Sons Ltd, 9600 Garsington Road, Oxford OX4 2DQ, UK and 350 Main Street, Malden, MA 02148, USA

# Acknowledgements

We would like to thank Emma Anderson for expertly handling all the editorial and publication processes necessary to bring this book to completion; Sharon Mah for her cover designs; Sharmina Khanam for organising the seminar for the book's authors and first-class administrative support; and George Bangham and Stephen Clarke of the Resolution Foundation for their incisive research. We would also like to thank all the participants at the inaugural seminar at which the ideas and arguments of the book were first aired and the editors of *Political Quarterly*, Ben Jackson and Deborah Mabbett, for their support and advice throughout the project.

Published by John Wiley & Sons Ltd, 9600 Garsington Road, Oxford OX4 2DQ, UK and 350 Main Street, Malden, MA 02148, USA

# Contents

# Notes on Contributors

**David Adler** is Policy Coordinator of the Democracy in Europe Movement 2025 and a Research Partner at Generation Rent.

**Ben Ansell** is Professor of Comparative Democratic Institutions at Nuffield College and the Department of Politics and International Relations at the University of Oxford and a Fellow of the British Academy.

**Torsten Bell** is Director of the Resolution Foundation.

**Andrew Carter** is Chief Executive at the Centre for Cities.

**Stephen Clarke** is Senior Economic Analyst at the Resolution Foundation.

**Diane Coyle** is Bennett Professor of Public Policy at the University of Cambridge, and researches the economics of digital technologies.

**Swati Dhingra** is Associate Professor at the Department of Economics and Centre for Economic Performance at the London School of Economics.

**Robert Ford** is Professor of Political Science at the Department of Politics, University of Manchester.

**Antony Froggatt** is a Senior Research Fellow, at Chatham House and an Associate Member of the Energy Policy Group at the University of Exeter.

**Andrew Gamble** is Professor of Politics, University of Sheffield.

**Laura Gardiner** is Research Director at the Resolution Foundation.

**Paul Gregg** is Professor of Economic and Social Policy, University of Bath.

**Will Jennings** is Professor of Political Science and Public Policy at the University of Southampton.

**Michael Keating** is Professor of Politics at the universities of Aberdeen and Edinburgh and Director of the Centre on Constitutional Change.

**Gavin Kelly** is Chief Executive of the Resolution Trust and Chair of the Living Wage Commission.

**Matthew Lockwood** is a Senior Lecturer in Energy Policy at the University of Sussex.

**Geoff Mulgan** is Chief Executive of Nesta and a senior visiting scholar at Harvard University.

**Nick Pearce** is Professor of Public Policy and Director of the Institute for Policy Research at the University of Bath.

**Martin Sandbu** is an economics commentator for the *Financial Times*.

**Catherine Schenk** is Professor of Economic and Social History at the University of Oxford and Professorial Fellow at St Hilda's College Oxford.

**Maria Sobolewska** is Professor of Political Science at the Politics Department and Centre for Dynamics of Ethnicity, University of Manchester.

**Gerry Stoker** is Professor of Governance at the University of Southampton and the University of Canberra.

**Paul Swinney** is Director of Policy Research at the Centre for Cities.

**Gemma Tetlow** is Chief Economist at the Institute for Government.

**Duncan Weldon** is the Associate Editor (Economics) of *Prospect Magazine*.

**Simon Wren-Lewis** is an Emeritus Professor of Economics at Oxford University and an Emeritus Fellow of Merton College.

# Introduction: Brexit and the Future of the British Model of Democratic Capitalism

GAVIN KELLY AND NICK PEARCE

## Introduction

BRITISH POLITICS is regularly said to be at a critical juncture. With Brexit, for once this is not hyperbole. It represents the most significant moment of political choice and potential rupture since the Second World War, and in peacetime, possibly since the repeal of the Corn Laws in the nineteenth century.

For four decades, membership of the European Union (EU) and its predecessors has shaped the evolution of Britain's model of democratic capitalism. It has anchored the UK's economic policy framework, governed the UK's trade, restructured British manufacturing and its supply chains and helped attract foreign direct investment into the country. The City of London has been transformed since the 1970s to serve EU as well as global markets. European companies now supply many of Britain's utility needs, from energy to rail and bus transport. EU membership is even built into our hard infrastructure, most obviously through the Channel Tunnel. The supply of migrant labour from the EU, particularly since 2004, has greatly altered the UK's workforce, transforming a number of sectors like retail, hospitality, care and food processing. Other industries like agriculture and fisheries have been fundamentally reshaped by common EU policies.

The impact of the EU extends far beyond economics, however. British society has a different make-up and look and feel due to EU membership. The population, and the places in which it lives and works, has become more European. Several generations' horizons, sense of mobility and travel patterns have been greatly broadened. Social and environmental policies, from annual holiday rights to clean beaches, have rested on EU initiatives. The UK's place in the world and foreign policy has been moulded and moderated by our membership. Our legal system, and the very form of statecraft pursued by the British state, has been transformed. It is no exaggeration to say that the European project has re-made us.

Yet to present this simply as a story of disruption and transformation would be to mislead. There are deep continuities too. There is a UK 'pre-history' to EU membership that has also endured, not least in our political economy, much of which is rooted in the Victorian era. The UK is a liberal market economy with a global financial sector, deregulated labour market,

Published by John Wiley & Sons Ltd, 9600 Garsington Road, Oxford OX4 2DQ, UK and 350 Main Street, Malden, MA 02148, USA

shareholder dominated corporate governance, and an education system with a strong bias against vocational skills in favour of generic ones. Entry to the 'Common Market' in 1973 helped cement the structures of this British liberal market economy, rather than fundamentally reforming it along coordinated or social market European lines. The UK did not leave its economic past behind when it joined the European project.

The role of the state in the economy was significantly reduced as well as reformed in the 1980s, and the postwar growth model of an export-orientated national economy with significant domestic manufacturing, energy and food production was progressively dismantled.[1] But the underlying institutions of the UK liberal market economy remained in large part intact throughout these transformations. They evolved in tandem with a political system dominated by two main parties and a liberal welfare regime of mostly flat rate benefits and significant means-testing, rather than the multi-party politics of proportional voting systems, and social insurance or universalist models of welfare found in Northern Europe.[2]

As it entered the new millennium, the UK was an open, financialised economy, deeply integrated into European markets, with a growth model underpinned by consumption and an oversized housing sector. High value service exports and foreign direct investment helped to offset a persistent deficit in manufactured goods. To be sure, this growth model had formidable strengths: competitive advantages in knowledge-based sectors; a buoyant labour market, drawing in highly skilled migrants; and productivity gains driven by leading edge service companies and world class universities and research. But these were matched by chronic failings: weak investment; entrenched inequalities between people, places and generations; a dystopian housing market; and rampant insecurity in segments of the jobs market, among others.

When the UK was battered by the financial crisis in 2008, it exposed economic fault-lines that had been obscured by the long era of benign growth in the 1990s and 2000s. They became even more visible, and acquired greater public consciousness, following the Brexit referendum. Despite the gains made before the crisis, levels of UK productivity remained comparatively low and, remarkably, have now barely improved for a decade. Real wages are still significantly below pre-crisis levels. And longstanding inequalities of income and wealth, between both the regions of the UK and its social classes, show little sign of diminishing. As a nation, the UK continues to rely, in the words of the governor of the Bank of England, on 'the kindness of strangers' to pay its way in the world.

A new and darker global context also overshadows the withdrawal of the UK from the EU. The protectionist, America First agenda of Donald Trump reverses seventy years of US commitment to an integrated Europe and has already engendered geo-political division over tariffs, the role of NATO, and the EU's relationships with Russia and Iran. In tandem with this we've witnessed the rise of nationalist and neo-fascist parties, both within the EU and outside it, who share a common hostility to internationalism at a time when the looming crisis of climate breakdown demands urgent global action. Brexit arises at a moment when the postwar institutions of the international community are under huge stress.

At the level of domestic policymaking, withdrawal from the EU presents a series of discrete challenges, such as how to handle a range of repatriated powers. Each policy area is important. But if our analysis is narrow, focussing on a set of single issues, we risk missing the bigger shifts. Hence, in this book, we address Brexit in the context of the impending challenges of the 2020s and beyond. We situate the question of leaving the EU and what it means in the larger sweep of the outlook for democratic welfare capitalism in the UK. The leading contributors to this special volume range widely across politics, economics, social policy and democratic and constitutional reform, while the book as a whole seeks to connect the domestic situation of the UK with its external position, both economic and geo-political.

At the time of writing (January 2019), the politics of Brexit remain radically uncertain. A number of scenarios—Theresa May's proposed deal, leaving the EU without a deal, a soft Brexit, an agreed extension of the Article 50 process, or a second referendum with the option of remaining in the EU —are all still possible. For the most part, the contributions to this book are predicated on some form of withdrawal from the EU taking place in the years ahead. But beyond that, the scope for analysis and interpretation remains very wide, and the chapters consequently contain diverse perspectives on what has caused the Brexit rupture in British politics, and what its consequences might be.

## The political causes of Brexit

To make sense of the vote to leave the EU, we need to unpack both the moment in history in which it occurred, as well as the coalitions who supported it. The timing of the vote was inauspicious from a Remain perspective. Not only did it take place amid the worst decade of pay growth since the Napoleonic wars, the deepest austerity in modern times and in the shadow of the eurozone crisis. It also occurred when broadly eurosceptic baby boomers were at their electoral peak, while the more pro-European 'silent generation' of the war years was in steady decline, and their younger more Remain-minded cohorts were yet to reach their full electoral potency. Economically, as well as electorally, it represented a truly reckless moment for a Remain-supporting Prime Minister to seek to settle the European question.

But whatever the timing, the referendum fundamentally pivoted around the creation of an alliance of older, conservative middle class voters and the semi-skilled and unskilled working class—a combination of what David Willets has called 'the insulated and the excluded'.[3] Political discourse about the referendum has been dominated by the plight of so-called 'left behind' voters. Yet in reality, older, relatively prosperous voters were just as significant in number, reflecting the UK's marked inequalities in voter turnout by age.

3

The referendum result, therefore, represented a reckoning with places that have never recovered from the shock of de-industrialisation and Thatcherism, as well as groups who have not been reconciled with the ascendance of ever greater social liberalism and the cosmopolitan remaking of Britain, or the European remaking of the British state.

For those reasons, the outcome of the vote is difficult to explain in terms of the dominant political economic interests in the productive economy. The City of London, the major business organisations and the trade unions all supported Remain, as did the main political parties. The Leave vote disproportionately came from interests outside the labour market—older voters with a foundation of housing and pension wealth, or the state pension and pensioner benefits—and those struggling precariously within it, like the low skilled and self-employed. Its campaign was led by a political and economic elite—even if it was an unconventional one, drawn from beyond the organised pillars of the economy—but it successfully channelled an eruption of politics against the established political economy. It shook to its core the world-view that the big contours of the UK's economic policy were firmly set and resided outside the reach of democratic contest. And it forced attention—if not public policy—upon an economic trajectory that had so unevenly distributed the gains of growth over the last four decades.

Other drivers of the referendum vote are perhaps easier to grasp. The young and middle aged, and the better educated, were far more inclined to vote Remain. These are the social groups most comfortable with immigration and the diversity of modern Britain. The geography of the referendum reflected this, pitting most of the major urban centres and university cities against the towns, countryside and coastlines. Majorities in Scotland and Northern Ireland voted Remain, while most of England and Wales opted to Leave. This political geography is new: in 1975, none of the UK's constituent nations voted 'No' to EEC membership, and England and Wales recorded the largest supporting majorities.

While these headline territorial patterns are striking, consideration needs to be given to differences within regions and how they interact with the effects of age. Look, for instance, at retired voters in a strongly 'Remain' region like London and we see that they backed Leave in similar proportions to the retired of Yorkshire, the north-west or Wales. Equally, if we just consider those in work, we see that Remain won in more nations and regions of the UK than Leave. Brexit has certainly fractured the electorate in important ways, but it is a far more complicated picture than London, Scotland and Northern Ireland versus the rest of England and Wales.

The Brexit juncture comes in a new era of UK politics. It marks the first real crisis of politics in the post-devolution era in which the UK has become formed as a multi-national state, not just in terms of its governance, but in its identity too. Formal decisions concerning Brexit reside with the Westminster Parliament, but the consequences ripple across the UK's nations and their assemblies, parliaments and civil societies. The European question has layered another deep cleavage onto the already fractious territorial politics of the union.

## The consequences of Brexit: political economy

Over the last forty years, Britain has sought consistently to entrench its liberal market model within the EU, pursuing the creation and completion of the single market, while (for the most part) resisting Delorsian ambitions to embed European capitalism in a pan-European social democracy. Its period of membership may have often been grudging, but it has also been consequential. The decision to leave the European project can therefore be expected to alter the future trajectory of the EU. But what might it mean for the future political economy of the UK? Will it essentially be a story of continuity or should we see dislocation? Will it be the same but worse, or is this the start of something very different?

When it comes to the UK's growth model, it is hard to see where a significant re-orientation will come from. The major devaluations of sterling over recent years (one following the 2008 crisis, the other after the Brexit vote) have not spurred export growth but have reduced real wages. If nothing else, they have exposed the contemporary hollowness of the age-old hope that a weaker currency will prove to be an elixir for British manufacturing. A surge in export-led growth in the years ahead seems highly unlikely: if the UK ends up outside the single market and customs union, there will inevitably be new frictions in trade with Britain's biggest market, while any new trade deals with other countries will be time consuming, involve sharp trade-offs and are likely to generate only negligible gains in GDP compared to the expected losses arising from diminished access to the EU. Financial services, on which the UK relies heavily for export performance, are likely to shift a significant proportion of business to the EU. Gravity is not so easy to defy.

A new era of wage-driven growth feels unrealistic too. Even now, at a mature stage of the economic cycle and in the face of a tight jobs market, pay rises remain anaemic by postwar standards. Without a turnaround in productivity, wage growth will remain weak, as will household income growth, all of which is a major constraint on the consumption-led UK growth model.[4] Business investment, too, is not well placed to come to the rescue. The UK's long-running problem of weak investment has, if anything, intensified in the post-crisis era and now Brexit uncertainty represents a major additional drag on business sentiment. Public investment is increasing substantially, but not at a rate sufficient to transform the overall outlook.

The engines of demand in the UK economy have been slow to recover since the financial crisis and have been further weakened by the prospect of Brexit. This will place more strain on macro-economic policy. It is unlikely the UK will return to anything like 'normal' monetary policy in the immediate future. Fiscal pressures are set to ease relative to the deep austerity of recent years, but this is only likely to mean that spending keeps up with inflation rather than recovering any of the ground lost after 2010. And history suggests that before too long—even leaving aside any disruptive shocks—we should anticipate another recession or slow-down. A new phase of policy activism may well be needed before the last phase has been wound down.

## Brexit and the welfare state

Between 1997 and 2010, New Labour pursued a social investment strategy: fleshing out the UK's liberal welfare state with new spending on tax credits, childcare, investment in education and skills, and a major expansion of higher education. Poverty fell, inequality levelled off and income mobility rose. These were major social achievements, though for many post-industrial towns and cities, they never amounted to the creation of a viable new economic future. What appeared for a while to be a durable electoral coalition of the working class and middle class socio-cultural professionals underpinned this policy shift, but has since fragmented.

This period of growth in our welfare state was followed by sharp retrenchment after 2010, with deep cuts in support for those of working age and a pronounced reshaping of spending in favour of pensioners. By the time the Brexit referendum took place in 2016, public opinion had already begun to turn against further cuts to social security—a trend that is likely to continue in the years ahead—rendering the politics of 'welfare savings' ever more intractable.[5]

The fiscal pressures on the welfare state will only grow. All ageing societies like the UK face significant challenges financing their welfare states, particularly because of rising health, social care and pension costs. This shrinks the space for fiscal generosity and sharpens trade-offs between the welfare preferences of different sections of the electorate. The UK has already aggressively pursued the 'orthodox' repertoire of strategies for mitigating long-term fiscal pressures of ageing on the welfare state: migration has grown, the employment rate is at a record high, punitive working-age welfare conditionality has been imposed, and the state pension age has been hiked. On each score the limits have been reached.

Any version of Brexit will serve to intensify these fiscal constraints, not only because of the damage done to tax revenues, but also because of additional pressures on spending. Since the referendum, there have been repeated calls from across the spectrum for increased spending to respond to the popular demand for change, and shore up Britain's domestic and international frailties: we've seen this on issues ranging from industrial and regional policy, to training, housing, farming and defence. There is little sign that Brexit points towards a smaller state.

All told, the Brexit penumbra will make the already difficult politics of moving to a sustainable twenty-first century welfare settlement far harder. The postwar welfare expansion was funded on the back of major switches in spending priorities, historic broadening of the tax base and a prolonged era of productivity growth. Any post-Brexit welfare adjustment will have to put more of the strain onto higher taxes.

There will, however, be clear limits to the tax rises that a wage-squeezed public will bear. Ultimately, the future of the welfare state—and the social contact that depends on it—will require a rekindling of productivity growth. If our liberal market economy cannot achieve this, then political pressure will grow for the state to pursue far more *dirigiste* strategies. These will have to encompass the 'everyday' or 'foundational' economy of private sector and publicly procured low wage service jobs in which millions of British workers are employed, not just the leading edge of high valued export sectors that industrial strategy typically embraces.[6]

## Politics after Brexit

The marked age divide in British politics that has emerged in recent decades acted as a midwife to the Brexit vote and was consolidated at the 2017 general election. Age has not ended the importance of social class, nor have voters' 'values' become somehow detached from any relation to their material circumstances or the wider institutions of the economy. But it is certainly true that navigating the demographic schism has become the *sine qua non* of political management in the UK.

If the Brexit cleavage remains central to British politics in the decades ahead—and 'Remain' *vs* 'Leave' become entrenched in the long-term political identities of large swathes of the electorate—this will only serve to magnify existing intergenerational tensions. Political parties seeking paths to electoral majorities will need strategies—including public policies for tax and spend, and social cohesion—that can plausibly overcome or at least ameliorate these divisions and command cross-generational support.

Population change will, of course, alter the make-up of the electorate over the long run. But recent experience from the UK, EU and US politics shows that demographic destinies can take a long time to arrive: in the meantime, politics can be contingently and rapidly reshaped as parties re-orient their strategies to meet electoral demands made by 'declining' or marginalised social groups.[7]

The playing out of the shift towards increased ethnic diversity will remain a feature of British society and its politics. On the one hand, public opinion since the referendum shows a marked weakening of hostility to immigration. And, more generally, Britain remains a relatively cohesive society compared to some European counterparts. However, levels of inward migration are likely to remain high in the future, albeit rebalanced away from the EU to the rest of the world because of the probable curtailment of free movement.

And experience in much of the rest of Europe shows that discontent about migrants (and refugees) can quickly be channelled into support for far-right and nativist parties. Britain's majoritarian electoral system has insulated but not inoculated it from these strains of politics. One of the biggest questions of post-Brexit politics is whether this remains the case.

Just as demography will remain a defining divide in post-Brexit politics, so too will territorial politics. One of the paradoxes of recent years is that the post-1998 institutions—the Good Friday Agreement and 1998 Scotland Act—have at a deep level shaped our constitution. Yet, surface level political debate (if not the substantive nature of the deal finally reached with the EU) has often proceeded as if we still inhabited some bygone era of unitary-state, Westminster-centric politics. This contradiction and its consequences—not just in terms of its impact on nationalist sentiment in Scotland and Northern Ireland, but also on the future trajectories of pro-union parties within each of our nations, in particular Scottish Conservatives and the Scottish Labour party—will be one of Brexit's legacies. It is also possible—though difficult to predict—that the politics of Englishness, and the place of England in the union, will remerge as an important vector of politics in the UK once the intense focus on Brexit and the institutional form it takes diminishes.

All of this will reverberate through our party system for decades to come. To date, much of the focus of political debate has been on whether there might be a formal realignment in our party system—either through a new centrist party or the emergence of an insurgent English nationalist alternative to UKIP that folds in a swath of Conservative Leave supporters, as well as some traditional Labour voters.

Whether or not this party realignment comes to pass is moot: the hurdles to it are high in a majoritarian electoral system. Either way, the aftershocks of Brexit will continue to cause flux within and between the existing parties, not least because devolution and the proportional voting systems of the devolved parliaments and assemblies create space for political insurgency that can profoundly influence the major UK parties. Political identities have been shaken up, if not completely broken, by the Brexit convulsion. It will be years before they settle down and when they finally do, it will affect not just who voters trust and the issues they gravitate to, but the political coalitions they might join.

## After the Brexit storm

The Leave vote was not simply an exercise in imperial nostalgia, as some have claimed. But, as we have shown, there are deep continuities between Britain's present and its past that will shape its future. The dominant role of the City in the UK economy and the liberal framework of its political economy have endured over decades, as has the nature of its welfare state. Even the newly emergent forces that are restructuring the institutions of the union and the relationships between its nations have deeper historical roots.

But a political moment as large as Brexit will, without doubt, bring change too—some of it directly related to leaving the EU, but much of it rooted in other long-standing failings—whether on regional inequality, housing, or economic insecurity—that now have greater political potency. Add to this the newer societal challenges that any government has to face up to in the decades ahead: switching to low-carbon production and transportation systems, meeting the escalating care costs arising from ageing, and supporting the workforce to transition to longer working lives. And then consider the pent-up problems caused by the austerity decade that will trouble our public realm in the years ahead: councils and school-chains going bust, hospitals needing bailing out, demands for the Universal Credit roll out to be halted, and so on.

In addition to these burdens on state capacity will be the return of EU responsibilities to the UK amid a period of uncertainty. Whether it is forging a new trade policy in a protectionist age, a competition policy fit for the era of big tech, or a migration framework suited to a greying society, the British state will be learning to read a new map in a fast shifting landscape.

The confluence of these pre-existing pressures with the new and urgent imperatives of Brexit will put strains on the state that have not been experienced since at least the mid-1970s. It is hard not to see government becoming more involved in key aspects of our national economic life—certainly as a result of necessity, and possibly ideology too.

Will, however, this greater involvement give rise to any fundamental shift in our political economy? In part, the answer will, of course, come down to political choice. No variety of democratic capitalism is immutable. For the first time in recent memory, the momentum in both main political parties simultaneously lies with those favouring radical economic rupture: whether through leaving the EU without a deal if necessary and pivoting towards a low tax, deregulated 'Singapore of the West' model; or restoring public ownership and state-financed and directed growth. The politics of the moment would suggest the British model is set for profound upheaval.

Yet if there is a lesson from twentieth century history, it is that some core features of our political economy are hard to shift: they have survived multiple changes of government, world wars, contrasting philosophies of economic management and profound shifts in the structure of the global economy. Anyone assuming that the political tumult of Brexit will inevitably give rise to some fundamental re-ordering of our capitalist model—whether for good or ill—may well be waiting in vain.

What is certainly true, however, is that the constellation of pressures facing the UK means that a key feature of the post-Brexit era will be learning to navigate vulnerability. In the macro-economy the UK will live with levels of public debt that are far higher than the recent norm for decades to come, at the same time as interest rates seem likely to sit close to the floor. Reduced policy space means the risk of greater exposure to shocks.

A sense of heightened economic exposure will also be the norm for the British worker, and not just because of their weak bargaining position and the continued decline of unions. Workers are likely to remain exposed to the risk of further exchange rate devaluation—which, as recent years have shown, feeds through directly into lower real wages. The risk that mobile employers decide to uproot production and leave the UK, or downgrade their operations here, is also likely to be heightened for years to come.

At the constitutional level too, precariousness will prevail. No one can know how Brexit will play out on the forces pushing for Scottish independence—though it is not unreasonable to think that the shock of a hard Brexit might set back the independence cause in the short to medium term, while strengthening it beyond that. Either way, the issue will remain at the fore, as will the status of Northern Ireland and, most probably, the governance of England within the union. Far fewer of these issues are settled than seemed the case just a few years ago.

The governing challenge is not just the technical task of successfully negotiating these risks. If there are reasons to hope that the resilience and flexibility of the UK's economy will help it to adjust to life outside the EU, albeit with weaker rates of growth and less dynamism than in the past, the same may not be true of our politics. The political challenge of forging a coalition of electoral support that could undergird any sustainable governing programme is a profound one. As various contributions to this volume show, post-Brexit politics is likely to remain deeply divided along a number of connected fault-lines: generational, geographical and identity cleavages that cut across the support bases of the two main parties. Crafting a political agenda that spans these divides sufficiently to allow tough governing choices to be made would require remarkable leadership by the standards of any age, let alone one in which the main parties are so visibly struggling to rise to the level of events.

Whatever the chain of events in the months and years ahead—a soft or hard Brexit, or remaining in the EU through a second referendum—there will be a legacy of rancour and bitterness that will be hard to contain within the existing party system, and which may even challenge the basic norms of conduct of democratic politics. And even if the UK does leave the EU, the European question will endure as a major vector of British politics, for as Switzerland and others have found, any country that is a close neighbour to a large and powerful bloc like the EU is likely to be in permanent negotiation with it.[8] All the more so if, as seems highly likely, the UK remains a regulatory rule-taker in one form or another. Politics, more than economics, may be the UK's undoing.

We should, however, exercise caution about the gloom. In the heat of a crisis, it is always tempting to foresee an age of continued tumult. That case is easily made in Brexit Britain. But there are also countervailing forces, too. The consequences of breaking trading ties with the EU are so dire that one way or another the UK will seek to navigate its way towards a relatively close relationship with it. The strengths that have given the British model momentum will hardly fade overnight, even if they now face great strain. Our high value services, world leading university sector, and job-rich labour market, all provide grounds for optimism. The British state has shown itself capable of strategic purpose and organisational ingenuity in the last century. And—however unfashionable it may be to point this out in the current moment—there remains a residual resilience in the democratic politics of the UK.

Declinism is often overwrought and overstated in British public life—that, too, is a part of our tradition. But history suggests powerful new directions can be forged in public policy even in times of adversity. They have many times before, and no doubt will again.

## Acknowledgements

The authors would like to thank Mike Kenny, Andrew Gamble, Torsten Bell and David Willetts for their insightful comments on a draft of this chapter.

## Notes

1 D. Edgerton, *The Rise and Fall of the British Nation*, London, Allen Lane, 2018.
2 P. Hall and D. Soskice, eds., *The Varieties of Capitalism: the Institutional Foundations of Comparative Advantage*, Oxford, Oxford University Press, 2001; T. Iversen and D. Soskice, 'Distribution and redistribution: the shadow of the nineteenth century', *World Politics*, vol 61, no. 3, 2009, pp. 438–486.
3 R. Colville, 'David Willetts on Thatcher, Brexit and the generational divide', 22 June 2017; https://capx.co/david-willetts-on-thatcher-brexit-and-the-generational-divide/ (accessed 3 January 2019).
4 L. Baccaro and J. Pontussen, 'Rethinking comparative political economy: the growth model perspective', *Politics and Society*, vol. 44, no. 2, 2016, pp. 175–207.
5 R. Harding, *A Backlash Against Austerity?*, British Social Attitudes, report 34, Key Findings, 2017; http://www.bsa.natcen.ac.uk/latest-report/british-social-attitudes-34/key-findings/a-backlash-against-austerity.aspx (accessed 3 January 2019).
6 R. Reeves, *The Everyday Economy*, 2018; https://www.scribd.com/document/374425087/Rachel-Reeves-The-Everyday-Economy (accessed 3 January 2019).
7 P. Manow, B. Palier and H. Schwander, eds., *Welfare Democracies and Party Politics: Explaining Electoral Dynamics in Times of Changing Welfare Capitalism*, Oxford, Oxford University Press, 2018.
8 Full speech: Sir Ivan Rogers on Brexit, University of Liverpool, 13 December 2018; https://news.liverpool.ac.uk/2018/12/13/full-speech-sir-ivan-rogers-on-brexit/ (accessed 3 January 2019).

How to cite this article: G. Kelly and N. Pearce, 'Introduction: Brexit and the Future of the British Model of Democratic Capitalism', in G Kelly and N Pearce (eds.), Britain Beyond Brexit, *The Political Quarterly*, Vol 90, Issue S2, 2019, pp. 1–11. https://doi.org/10.1111/1467-923x.12644

# The British Model and the Brexit Shock: Plus ça Change?

## DUNCAN WELDON

FOR MORE than four decades, membership of the European Union and its predecessors, the European Community and European Economic Community, has been an anchor of Britain's economic model. Increasing the size of the market available to UK firms, exposing firms to greater competitive pressure, and ensuring access to wider supply chains and skilled labour have all been important drivers of productivity growth.

More broadly, membership of the EU's customs union, conformity to the rules of the European single market and political engagement with a widening circle of European partners since the mid-1980s have acted as a policy anchor for Britain's economic policy making elite, ruling out both some of the more interventionist policies favoured in the past by the left (impeded by single market procurement rules and restraints on state aid) and also some of the deregulatory agenda favoured by the right (constrained by European social and environmental legislation and trade agreements). The original 'Brexit referendum' of 1975 foreshadowed this—with the then No campaign uniting Tony Benn on the left with Enoch Powell on the right. Both saw that membership of the EEC would limit the ability of policy makers to advance their own favoured agendas.

Leaving the EU therefore knocks away a core foundation stone of economic policy making. After a rough performance in the 1970s and shock treatment in the 1980s, a broad consensus formed on how the British economy should be run—one which drew in not only the technocrats of Whitehall and Threadneedle Street, but also the leadership of both major political parties, the leading voices of British capital and, in many important ways, much of the leadership of the labour movement. By the mid-1990s, there was considerable agreement on important contours of the debate: the primacy of monetary policy as a way of stabilising the business cycle; the need to remain competitive internationally (although the definition of competitiveness of course varied across the spectrum); and the importance of structural drivers of productivity growth, such as skills, training and economic openness. Whilst there were important disagreements over the exact size of the state, the generosity of the welfare system and the appropriate level of taxation, the central tenets of the British model were widely accepted.

Post-Brexit, that consensus is falling away, with many on the right now arguing for a 'Singapore on Thames' model of deregulation and further tax cuts to boost a buccaneering, free trading 'Global Britain', whilst many on the left have moved towards supporting a far more *dirigiste* approach to

Published by John Wiley & Sons Ltd, 9600 Garsington Road, Oxford OX4 2DQ, UK and 350 Main Street, Malden, MA 02148, USA

economic policy making, involving state investment banks, renationalisation of key utilities, and greater political control over central banks. The irony, of course, is that whilst leaving the EU may (or may not depending on the eventual final deal) give the British political elite the illusion of 'taking back control' and the ability to set policy in a much less constrained manner, in reality, the likely damage to already weak productivity growth will lead to a smaller economy, weaker public finances and, in all likelihood, less freedom of action for domestic authorities.[1]

Viewed in this way, leaving the EU is an enormous shift in the nation's political economic framework, perhaps every bit as large as the two major shifts of the twentieth century—the Keynesian revolution of the 1930s and 1940s and the monetarist/neoliberal counter-revolution of the 1970s and 1980s. But unlike those two shifts, it is much harder to explain purely in terms of traditional political economy analysis. Indeed, on closer inspection, Brexit may represent not so much an actual change in Britain's political economic paradigm, as a significant worsening of economic performance, but without radical paradigmatic change: a negative shock to the current framework, rather than a transformative shift to a new one.

## Paradigm change

In the political economist Peter Hall's categorisation,[2] a shift in the economic paradigm requires a third order of change. A first order change is a simple resetting of economic policy instruments—be that the adoption of tighter monetary policy or a looser fiscal policy. A second order change is the adoption of new policy instruments, such as the active use of fiscal policy for demand management. By contrast, a third order shift requires not just a change in the instruments used or available to policy makers, but a change in the very goals of policy itself.

The policy paradigm adopted in the 1940s saw full employment (or at least full male employment) as the central goal of economic policy making. Starting in the mid-1970s, this was replaced by the logic of discipline—a striving for more balanced budgets and lower inflation. Both changes were far more sweeping than the decisions taken in, say, the 1960s, to supplement traditional Keynesian demand management policies with an active programme of supply side measures—in that case, the essential aims of policy remained unchanged: what was new was the addition of novel instruments to the policy makers' toolkit.

Whilst the extent of the 'Keynesian revolution' remains disputed—as does the exact dating—there can be little argument that the model of the UK economy underwent a substantial transformation between the early 1930s and the late 1940s. Active demand management (via both fiscal and monetary policy) came to the fore, full employment was adopted as an explicit policy aim, the size of the state grew substantially and it took an increasingly active role in whole swathes of national life previously left to the

13

voluntary and private sectors. The gradual extension of the franchise coupled with the poor economic performance of the 1920s, the patchy economic performance of the 1930s (broadly, a booming south of England and decline of the areas associated with the old staple industries) and the experience of total war in the Second World War, reconfigured Britain's political economy.

The counter-revolution arose out of the seeming failure of the previous Keynesian era: an economy that appeared to be stuck in a stop/go cycle, marred by balance of payments problems, suffering a relative (although perhaps inevitable) decline against its European peers, and high inflation. Inflation hit middle class savers particularly hard and undermined their buy into the system as a whole. Beginning in the mid-1970s, control of inflation came to be seen as a more pressing immediate goal than preserving full employment (although in theory of course, low and stable inflation would itself drive better growth and employment). Alongside this, and accelerating in the 1980s, the state began to step back from many of the roles it has assumed in the decades before. Strategic industries and the utilities were privatised, taxes cut and the labour market deregulated. Many of the policy instruments seized by policymakers in the 1930s and 1940s were given up and the whole aim of policy itself shifted.

Economic policy paradigm shifts can often appear to be something of a black box. In a development of Hall's work, Oliver and Pemberton argued that a paradigm shift tends to follow a pattern.[3] The initially stable paradigm is first challenged by a rising series of 'anomalies'—for example, the rising inflation and weaker growth of the 1960s. Policy makers respond with a bout of experimentation, which in Hall's analysis would be characterised as first and second order changes—the changing of existing policy setting and the trialling of new ones. Staying with the 1960s as an example, fiscal policy was regularly tightened in response to rising inflation, whilst new supply side quasi-planning experiments sought to boost longer-term productivity growth. Only if these experiments fail to quash the anomalies does a state of paradigm crisis develop, opening the door to a more radical third order shift.

Whether or not such a third order shift occurs depends on political contestation, the availability of new ideas and, crucially, the interaction of politics and ideology. During a period of failed experimentation, the marketplace for economic ideas widens—but whether or not they are adopted depends on raw politics. It is never simply the case that 'good' ideas succeed. Keynes may have written that 'it is ideas, not vested interest which are dangerous' but ideas rarely get put into practice without the support of some vested interest or another.

## Brexit and the varieties of capitalism

In this context, it is instructive to look at these transformations of the British economy in the twentieth century—and indeed Brexit—through the lens of the so-called 'Varieties of Capitalism' literature.[4] This distinguishes between national varieties of capitalism, placing the UK in a liberal market economy (LME) grouping, typically alongside a cluster of other Anglo countries such as the USA, Australia and New Zealand. In the 'ideal type' LME, we find shareholder rather than stakeholder corporate governance and finance, limited coordination of business and labour interests, competition on price over quality, lightly regulated labour markets, and strong general education rather than vocational training. Throughout the twentieth century, the UK remained, despite the building of some corporatist machinery in the middle decades, an LME rather than a co-ordinated market economy (CME), of the kind found in central and northern Europe.

Viewed through this lens, the policy innovations of the 1930s/40s and 1970s/80s were no doubt significant, but they did not fundamentally call into question the liberal nature of Britain's political economic framework. Product and labour markets remained, in the main, relatively decentralised, and so crucially did wage bargaining (and attempts to move towards more centralised wage bargaining were fiercely resisted and ultimately unsuccessful). The skills and education systems showed similar levels of continuity and the welfare state that gradually developed over the twentieth century was complementary to this model of capitalism.

Entry to the EEC—and exit from the EU—in this light could be viewed as similar to the shifts in demand management policies in the 1940s or 1980s: important to economic outcomes, but not a fundamental change in what could be called the 'constitution of the economy'—its wage bargaining set-up, training systems, corporate government arrangements, and so on. The essentials of the LME framework would remain in place.

A further argument against Brexit as a fundamental transformation in Britain's political economy is to be found in the lack of a 'battle of ideas' before the Brexit referendum. The literature on the previous shifts suggest that a major change requires not just a period of poor economic performance, but for the right alignment of revisionist policy ideas, discontented interest groups and the political economy alignments, to drive through series movement. For there to be a new paradigm there also has to be a coalition of potential economic winners capable of securing major change.

Class politics and class interest played a major role in both of the UK's two previous paradigm shifts. The Keynesian revolution was not simply the adoption of the ideas of Keynes and Beveridge, but the triumph of the organised working class. Similarly, the counter-revolution was not about the technocratic adoption of the ideas of Friedman, but about the organised fight back by the interest of capital, coupled with the middle class losers of higher inflation—all of which is what makes Brexit so inexplicable from a traditional political economy perspective. In the decade before Brexit, the UK no doubt suffered what might, politely, be termed a series of 'economic anomalies'. The banking crisis of 2008 destroyed a major engine of growth, denuded the public finances and left the UK with its worst decade of growth in over a century, and its longest real wage squeeze in two centuries. With productivity essentially stagnant, the policy experiments of the Cameron era ultimately failed to stabilise the old paradigm.

But the usual ingredients for a major shift appear still to be missing. It is hard to find many examples of serious analysts arguing that the solution to Britain's economic ills could be found in leaving the European Union. The battleground of ideas in the run-up to 2016 had focussed mainly on fiscal policy rather than the UK's international trading and regulatory arrangements, or its place in the single market. The traditional political economy producer interest groups in 2016 were firmly lined up in favour of a Remain vote. The leadership of the trade union movement alongside most major unions and the majority of the Labour party argued for Remain, as did the vast bulk of British business—across almost all sectors of the economy—alongside the leadership of the Conservative party.

Many were indeed arguing for change in 2016, but few for the sort of change the UK is now embarking on. The contrast with the intellectual tumult of the 1930s or the 1970s is stark. In both those cases, a fierce battle was fought over the aims and instruments of economic policy management. Both organised labour and capital—alongside the political parties—took active positions.

It is tempting to try to describe the Brexit vote as a revolt by the losers of globalisation—communities that had experienced de-industrialisation and stagnating wages simply voting against what the elite desired. One could argue that the Labour party and the leadership of the trade unions have been disconnected from their traditional support bases and that class politics (despite appearances) actually drove the Leave victory. Innumerable newspaper opinion columns have indeed attempted to make this case. But the evidence suggests otherwise. Despite the popular image of Brexit being something which finds its loudest proponents in a stereotypical northern working men's club, the reality is that the most hardcore Brexiteers are usually to be located in the bar of a southern golf club. Age and education, rather than class or politics, drove the real cleavages of the Brexit vote. Indeed, the young voted overwhelmingly for Remain, despite having suffered the worst excesses of the last decade in terms of unemployment, falling wages and precarious work, whilst older voters—protected from the worst of austerity and most likely to have enjoyed a period of rising asset values—voted Leave.

Neither class analysis nor the battle of ideas offers many clues to what drove the vote of June 2016. This is something new—a potentially large shift in the economic policy, driven by neither ideas nor by major interest groups. That may offer clues to how the political economic pieces now in flux may eventually settle.

## National economy redux?

An alternative way of viewing the whole debate is to use a different frame entirely, most clearly argued in the recent work of the historian, David

Edgerton,[5] which recasts the terms of the battle. For Edgerton, British history should not be seen as continuous. His central thesis is to recast UK history into a struggle between 'the global' and 'the national'. He argues that early twentieth century 'Britain' was, both economically and politically, a uniquely global and open polity, that it was only from the 1930s and 1940s that a cohesive political and economic 'national Britain' really existed and that from the mid-1980s onwards that national Britain was once more subsumed into a more global existence.

For much of the British left, the Attlee government will forever be a high-water mark of British social democracy. But Edgerton argues that the view of that administration as being focussed on 'welfarism' is fundamentally incorrect. It was far more concerned with national productionism—with the building of a British-focussed economy, coupled with a renewed warfare state. As he writes: 'I think, for example, that the actual post-Second World War United Kingdom was in some ways better prefigured in the programme of the Tories and the British Union of Fascists than that of the Liberal or the Labour Party. Although explicit nationalist political economy was a rarity, it was implicit in much economic commentary, concerning everything from the balance of payments to research policy'.[6]

In this version of the national story, the 1930s and 1940s indeed saw a paradigm shift—but it was more driven by a turn away from the global towards the national, than by a shift from a *laissez-faire* model to one of active demand management. Similarly, Edgerton argues that the changes of the 1970s and 1980s, and entry to the EEC, make at least as much sense if viewed as a way of re-globalising the UK economy than when seen as a simple turn back towards market mechanisms.

Perhaps an argument can be made that Brexit is the third act of Edgerton's drama—an attempt to renationalise the economy? Certainly, that view is popular in 'Lexit' (or left-wing fans of Brexit) analysis. The great irony would be if supporters of a free trading, buccaneering 'Global Britain', also saw Brexit mark a step back away from a globalised Britain. Indeed, all but the very softest of Brexits would likely mean less immigration, less foreign capital flows and less trade intensity. The pendulum would indeed move back from 'global' and towards 'national'. But it is very difficult to see it swinging by a great deal.

As Edgerton himself has argued, Thatcher may have talked of recharging and unleashing British capitalism, but it is hard to describe the capitalism that dominates the British economy today as especially 'British'. What were once called the 'commanding heights' are dominated by either foreign owned firms or parts of complex international supply chains. Finance and the City may be a traditional British strength, but many of the dominant firms are foreign owned and even the 'British' banks, insurances companies and asset managers are dependent—in most cases—on overseas earnings and funding.

The manufacturing sector is in the main, if anything, even more internationalised. The Mini might be an iconic British brand still made in Oxfordshire, but it is owned by BMW and most sales are to Europe. The engine shanks are manufactured in Warwickshire, but sent to Germany for assembly before being returned to the UK to be added to the vehicle, which is then just as likely to be sold in the Netherlands as in the UK. There are components of the car which will cross the North Sea four or more times before final sale. Non-resident buyers of British homes have become a political flashpoint in recent years, but the very construction force that builds them is disproportionately from EU accession countries, whilst much of the capital funding these developments ultimately comes from East Asia.

Even in the non-tradable sector, it is hard to find large swathes of 'national British capitalism'. The workforce in low wage, non-tradable sectors such as hairdressing or restaurant work is, once again, disproportionally imported. The utilities and railways are mainly foreign owned and often rely on imported capital goods. Fishing, and the return of control over the UK's national waters, was a key calling point for the Leave vote in certain communities, but the majority of fish caught in British waters are consumed overseas.

The UK has run a current account deficit, often a large one, every year since 1998 and in reality, for most of the last four decades. Few parts of the British economy have been left untouched by international capital flows. In the years since 2008, the global economy has seen some—depending on how one measures it—'deglobalisation', or at the very least, a pause in the process. Cross border capital claims are below the level they were a decade ago for the first time since the 1930s—mainly the result of banks pulling back on cross border lending, whilst the share of trade in global GDP (which grew continuously throughout the 1980s, 1990s and 2000s) has been fairly steady over the last ten years. But even if the pace of globalisation has slowed or even, by some measures reversed, this is still a far cry from the 1940s.

The deglobalisation/nationalism of the British economy that occurred in the 1930s and 1940s was a product of another time. Manufacturing supply chains—and even finance—were still more obviously national. Britain, as the hyper globalised country of the day, was something of an outlier and the moves in those two decades brought it back into line with its European peers. Attempting to 'renationalise' an even more globalised twenty-first century UK economy is a much steeper challenge.

The history of Britain's political economy, then, provides few clues to how Brexit will unfold. In many ways, it is just too different to what has come before. It is, of course, hardly surprising that a long period of economic semi-crisis will provoke an attempt at change. It would be more unusual if there wasn't a counter-reaction. What is novel, however, is the UK embarking on a major shift in its core economic relationships without the support of any major economic interest group and without a preceding battle of ideas on what a new paradigm will look like. In an inversion of the usual chain of events, the battle of ideas has now been joined *after* a major decision has been taken. Presented with a (rather unspecific) call for change from the electorate, politicians are now arguing over exactly what that change should look like. Leaving the EU, in its harder forms (not aligning with the EU's regulatory state) appears to offer more freedom to domestic policy makers. The Labour party has adopted its most radical programme since the 1980s, with talk of a major state investment bank, a large programme of domestic investment and a deliberate attempt to rebuild British domestic supply chains and take back ownership of key economic infrastructure. In many ways, it is a familiar programme—much of it rings true to Edgerton's analysis of the programmes of the 1930s and 1940s. Meanwhile, important voices in the Conservative party are pushing an agenda of global free trade, deregulation and tax cuts—a doubling down on the initial programme of the Thatcher years.

And yet, whilst the battle of ideas has widened, the core economic interest groups of organised labour and organised capital are, in the main, arguing for the least disruptive and the softest Brexit possible—something incompatible with the programmes of the left or the right. Creating the nirvana favoured by either the vocal left or the vocal right seems impossible in the short term. Both ignore the damage done by tearing up the existing framework under which capitalism in Britain operates. It is hard to create a productionist, national model for the UK economy when most of its industry relies on foreign sales and foreign components. Equally, for all the talk of embracing free trade on the right, the first act of 'Global Britain' would be to leave the deepest and most integrated cross border market the globe has yet seen. In terms of the traditional model, the 'anomalies' that drove the challenge to the existing paradigm are likely to continue, and experimentation as envisioned by both the left and the right are highly unlikely to end the period of crisis.

## Plus ça change

Perhaps, then, Brexit cannot be explained in terms of a traditional model of economic policy paradigm shift because it is *not* a paradigm shift. The flaws in the old model of growth were exposed by the financial crisis of 2008 and led to what might be termed 'extreme anomalies'—stagnating productivity, weak growth and a squeeze on real incomes of historical proportions. But whilst policy makers did indeed respond with experimentation—a particular combination of tight fiscal policy and ultra-loose monetary policy—the case was never really made for a major regime shift. Neither at the level of ideas, nor interest groups, was a serious case made for Brexit as a solution to Britain's economic woes. The foundations of Britain's liberal market economy survived both the Keynesian revolution and the neoliberal counter-revolution. It doesn't seem unreasonable to expect they will also weather the leaving of the EU.

For all the talk of a radical change in the economic policy set-up, it is just as likely that the end result is a very British attempt to 'muddle through' with a model which itself is not working and of which one of the key props (EU membership) has just been kicked away. The implication of this is that Brexit will not generate a new model for the UK, but simply an inferior version of the existing one.

The past two years of British political economy have been unprecedented and confusing in equal measure. For the first time, a major economic experiment is beginning without the support of any of the traditional political economy interest groups and without a preceding intellectual debate. Policy makers, who themselves mainly supported Remain in the referendum, find themselves arguing for a harder Brexit than their traditional economic supporters in key interest groups. The battle for ideas feels, in terms of potential scope, more open than it has for three decades. But this wide-ranging debate all too often ignores the reality of a slowing economy and damaged public finances. Much of the left and the right is arguing about how to reform a British capitalism without really ever engaging in how 'British' it is. The results are likely to be messy.

## Notes

1 N. Campos and F. Coricelli, 'How EEC membership drove Margaret Thatcher's reforms', Vox CEPR Policy Portal, 10 March 2017; https://voxeu.org/article/how-eec-membership-drove-margaret-thatcher-s-reforms (accessed 2 December 2018).
2 P. Hall, 'Policy paradigms, experts and the state: the case of macro-economic policymaking in Britain', in S. Brooks and A. Gagnon, eds., *Social Scientists, Policy and the State*, New York, Praeger, 1990, pp. 53–78.
3 M. J. Oliver and H. Pemberton, 'Learning and change in twentieth century British economic policy', *Governance*, vol. 17, no. 3, 2004, pp. 415–441.
4 P. Hall and D. Soskice, eds., *Varieties of Capitalism: The Institutional Foundations of Comparative Advantage*, Oxford, Oxford University Press, 2001.
5 D. Edgerton, *The Rise and Fall of the British Nation*, London, Allen Lane, 2018.
6 Ibid., p. xxvi.

How to cite this article: D. Weldon, 'The British Model and the Brexit Shock: Plus ça Change?', in G Kelly and N Pearce (eds.), Britain Beyond Brexit, *The Political Quarterly*, Vol 90, Issue S2, 2019, pp. 12–20. https://doi.org/10.1111/1467-923X.12625

# Brexit and the Future of Trade

## SWATI DHINGRA

THE UNITED KINGDOM is one of the most open economies in the world. Its exports and imports were over £600 billion (30 per cent of UK GDP) each last year. It is 'extremely open' from an investment perspective, both its outward and inward foreign direct investment (FDI) stocks, equivalent to 55 per cent and 46 per cent of GDP in 2015, are higher than the UK share in OECD GDP. Given their importance for the economy and the dependence on EU policy in these areas, international trade and investment are the biggest areas of economic policy that the UK will need to decide on as it prepares to exit the European Union.

Despite all the concerns about the upheaval Brexit will cause, it will nonetheless present a once in a lifetime opportunity to re-define Britain's role in the world economy.[1] New economic and political developments—rising economic marginalisation, trade wars, a weak world economy and new forms of globalisation—must be taken into account as the UK decides on its post-Brexit policy. This chapter explains key developments that determine the economic challenges the UK needs to address through its future trading relationships. It examines the best possible ways of addressing these challenges through its future trade policy with the EU and the world economy, and its domestic policies for inclusive growth.

The Brexit vote in June 2016 revealed the extent of political polarisation within the country, much of which can be traced back to decades of marginalisation faced by economically declining areas of the country. Political developments outside Britain, like the economic policies and trade wars of President Trump, have further revealed the fragility of the existing trading system. Many have understood these events as a backlash against the world trading system and a rejection of policies which have perpetuated years of economic neglect of large sections of society.

This apparent backlash against globalisation has come at a time of sluggish income and productivity growth in the world economy. The global financial crisis has deepened the economic hardship faced by many people. Wage growth in almost all advanced economies is much lower than before the crisis. Productivity growth continues to be slow, even negative, after the crisis. The UK has fared worse than many advanced economies. Since the global financial crisis, UK real wages have fallen by more than in other OECD countries and relative wage growth is just above that of Greece.[2] The modest real wage recovery that started in 2014 has recently been eroded by higher price inflation from the sterling depreciation that followed the vote to leave the European Union. Productivity has also fallen after the financial crisis and is recovering more slowly than in France and Germany.

Published by John Wiley & Sons Ltd, 9600 Garsington Road, Oxford OX4 2DQ, UK and 350 Main Street, Malden, MA 02148, USA

A small open economy like the UK has more at stake than most other nations from the backlash against globalisation and weakened world economy. Reduced trade and investment can exacerbate the negative trends in wage and productivity growth by reducing the level of economic activity with foreign markets. The UK must therefore seize this difficult yet historic moment to create agency for a modern trade policy that strives to support inclusive growth.

## The UK's relationship with the EU

We need to start with realism. The EU is the UK's largest trade partner. Around a half of the UK's trade is with the EU. As a member of the EU, the UK is in a customs union with member states, and conducts its trade policy collectively with them. A customs union means that all tariff barriers have been removed within the EU and members charge the same tariffs to countries outside the EU. Membership of the Single Market means eliminating non-tariff barriers that apply across goods and services and accepting common standards and regulations.

The main economic issue generated by Brexit is that the UK is highly integrated with the EU and its separation will increase the costs of doing business with member states. To take just one example, outside the customs union, all goods sold to the EU would need to satisfy rules of origin checks, which can add between 4 and 15 per cent to the cost of a good.[3] In the event of a 'no deal' Brexit, cars would incur a 10 per cent tariff rate, which the head of European manufacturing at Nissan stated would be a 'disaster' for the UK automotive industry. Furthermore, there may be divergence in regulation between the UK and EU such that regulatory checks will be required for goods, services and investments.

State-of-the-art models of international trade, using comprehensive trade data, estimate that a 'no deal' option would lead to a large reduction—about 40 per cent—in trade with the EU over the next ten years.[4] Reduced trade alone would imply a 2.9 per cent reduction in income per capita (or 2.6 per cent net of changes in budget payments to the EU). In a 'no deal' scenario, a decade of higher trade barriers would translate into a reduction of £1,890 in household income every year after Brexit relative to the UK's existing relationship with the EU. These costs would be halved if the UK followed a Norway-style relationship with the EU (inside the Single Market but outside the EU customs union). Overall, there is a *consensus* among economists that UK's trade and investment with the EU will fall substantially after Brexit, and the extent of these costs will depend on Britain's post-Brexit trade policy (although it should be noted that the UK could stay in a customs union for some time as a consequence of the Northern Ireland 'backstop' provisions of the proposed Withdrawal Agreement between the UK and EU).

The Global Britain campaign is banking on the prospect of new Economic Partnership Agreements (EPAs) with China, India and the USA to cushion this fall. But evidence suggests that the UK stands to lose more by diverging from the EU than it is likely to gain from new deals. Throughout history—and even in this new age of services, complex supply chains and the 'death of distance'—countries trade the most with their biggest, closest neighbours. This is by far the most robust fact about international trade—it is true across a range of countries, time periods and sectors (goods, services, e-commerce and foreign investments). Estimates of economic models that replace EU membership with a free trade agreement with the United States or with uni-lateral zero tariffs in the UK estimate that these will barely make up for a fraction of the losses from reduced economic ties with the EU after Brexit.

The so-called 'Chequers' statement of UK government policy recognises this economic reality, and proposes a single market for goods between the UK and EU, and a customs arrangement that allows the UK freedom to decide its own external tariffs. The proposal tries to minimise trade frictions in goods, but it contains limited details on how to implement a customs arrangement that has not been tried before on this scale by any country. Importantly, it remains vague on services, which make up 80 per cent of the UK economy and where Single Market membership provides greater market access than even the most ambitious EPAs of the EU (such as with South Korea and Canada). Over the long term, Brexit is clearly expected to reduce economic activity and living standards in the UK relative to the status quo.

Early indicators provide worrying evidence that this has already started happening since the Brexit vote. Immediately following the referendum, ster-ling suffered its biggest one-day loss since the introduction of free floating exchange rates in the 1970s—a bigger drop than Black Wednesday and the height of the financial crisis. In fact, the Brexit sterling fall is the biggest drop that has ever occurred in any of the world's four major currencies since the collapse of Bretton Woods. The sterling depreciation from the Brexit vote was expected to benefit UK exporters and improve the earning potential of domestic workers. But new research from the Centre for Economic Perfor-mance shows that wages and training of workers have fallen since the refer-endum. The rise in the costs of imported inputs have led to lower wages and fewer training opportunities for workers in the UK, which could rein-force the trends of anaemic wage and productivity growth.

The UK is deeply integrated in global value chains and access to the EU market is a key driver of its position in the world economy. Given the EU is the UK's closest trade partner in terms of geographical proximity and is a large market with a GDP of almost $20 trillion (double that of China), find-ing any equivalent size replacement is effectively impossible. Importantly, what makes this relationship unique is that when one compares the EU's standards on goods, services and labour these seem far more aligned to those of the British people than those in the US, China and India. This is why securing deep trade deals that reduce non-tariff barriers without com-promising domestic standards would be far harder with these countries. The next section discusses how this might be best approached.

## A new generation of trade deals

Early trade agreements, until the 1990s, focussed on easing trade and investment by reducing tariffs. Today, tariffs are low in most industries and the services sector—which has no tariffs—dominates economic activity in many countries. Modern trade agreements have therefore moved beyond tariff reductions: the bulk of modern trade policy is about reducing the costs of doing business across borders. This includes streamlining customs procedures and port inspections, rules of origin checks, cross-country differences in regulations over things like product standards and safety, easing eligibility requirements for foreign service providers and investors, and settling disputes that might arise with foreign partners. Deep trade deals increase trade volumes by reducing these non-tariff barriers (NTBs), creating an integrated market where domestic and foreign businesses play by the same rulebook.

While deep trade deals raise economic activity and competition by granting market access to one another's businesses, they come with an inevitable trade-off between integration and national sovereignty. Countries involved in deep trade deals or EPAs need to agree similar rules, standards and oversight policies so that businesses compete on a level playing field. If partner countries have similar preferences, it's easy to agree on these rules without giving up much sovereignty. For instance, the UK gives up some sovereignty when it applies the EU's Toy Safety Directive on its businesses. But the loss in sovereignty is small because the safety concerns of UK consumers are similar to those of EU consumers. Many non-tariff barriers, though, reflect a clear difference in preferences between countries rather than an unnecessary impediment to be shaken off. For example, UK consumers differ from US consumers in their tastes for hormone fed beef and chlorine washed chicken, so harmonising safety standards for these products would be undesirable for some consumers. EPAs aim to balance market access for businesses with the need to maintain high standards in products, services, environmental, labour and consumer rights. But they have not always been successful in getting the balance right, and this has culminated in strong anti-globalisation sentiments.

EPAs have not grappled with the profound pressures that new forms of globalisation have placed on the rules-based trading system, such as the dominance of multinationals, the centrality of supply chains, and the growing importance of intermediate inputs and services. Nor have they generally upheld the spirit of equitable rights across stakeholders, which is the purpose of a rules-based trading system. Dani Rodrik of Harvard Kennedy School argues that the regulatory standards in EPAs—covering health and safety rules, investment, banking and finance, intellectual property, labour, the environment—tend to empower politically well-connected firms, including international banks, pharmaceutical companies, and multinational firms.[5] Many who are left behind by recent waves of globalisation share this view.

They feel that they have little say in the rules governing globalisation and seldom have access to notional protections enshrined in EPAs to balance the rights of different stakeholders.

The UK has an opportunity to help shape a model trade policy that recognises the new realities of the rise in global value chains, services and multinationals and that takes on board the concerns of those who have been left behind by the growth of the last few decades. Despite the fact that the UK hasn't been running its own trade policy over recent decades, if we cast back further, we see it has historical experience to draw on. Along with the United States, the UK was a key actor in laying down the rules for a trading system that would prevent countries from engaging in mutually damaging trade wars which arose in response to the Great Depression. Building on this legacy, the UK could seek first mover advantage by drafting a new generation of EPAs that promotes inclusive growth.

This will be necessary if the UK chooses to pursue an independent trade policy, especially under the existing challenges of a weak world economy. But if the UK opts to conduct its trade policy in a customs arrangement with the EU, it will still have influence over the content of deep provisions in EPAs. The European Court of Justice has already ruled that EU member governments have a vote on deep provisions in EPAs, such as investment clauses, so the UK is unlikely to be bound by EU rules on these under a customs arrangement.[6]

Whichever post-Brexit course it takes, the UK should be pushing for a generation of EPAs that reflects public concerns. Many citizen groups are concerned that the existing imbalances in EPAs will exacerbate the race to the bottom on domestic standards, especially when the UK embarks on new trade deals with large countries that have very different standards. The UK can alleviate these concerns by drafting a modern EPA, which ensures that the same rules and rights apply to all stakeholders—domestic or multinational businesses and workers, consumers or investors.

Non-discrimination across stakeholders has always been the fundamental principle underlying EPAs, but it has been eroded by the fragmentation of production across borders. For example, Rodrik argues global disciplines on tax-and-subsidy competition have not been addressed in EPAs because they serve the interests of foreign investors, and ultimately rob tax payers by enriching corporations in a harmful race to the bottom. The rise of new forms of globalisation has created violations of the spirit of equitable rights across stakeholders, which is the essence of a rules-based trading system. The litmus test of the success of a post-Brexit policy will therefore be the extent to which it reinstates the principles of 'national treatment' for all businesses and non-discrimination across all stakeholders, which are now discussed in turn.

## Reinstating national treatment for all firms

National treatment is a fundamental principle of most EPAs, which ensures that countries do not discriminate against foreign companies. The underlying motivation is that businesses must compete on a level playing field to ensure the greatest economic benefits are realised from EPAs. The UK could take a leadership role in advocating national treatment by applying the same rules on the opposite side—multinational enterprises (MNEs) should be accorded the same treatment as smaller businesses and domestic firms.

MNEs directly account for half of global exports, a third of world GDP and a fourth of all employment. They have the ability to source inputs and credit from different countries and to shift profits across different tax jurisdictions. This amounts to MNEs facing different business conditions than firms that might be smaller or purely domestically oriented. Tax shifting is the most striking example of this. About 40 per cent of multinational profits are shifted to tax havens globally, and non-tax haven EU countries, like the UK, are estimated to suffer the greatest revenue losses as a result.[7] The ratio of taxable profits to total assets of foreign multinational subsidiaries in the UK is 12.8 percentage points lower than similar domestic firms (that belong to the same industry and have a similar asset size).[8]

Parliament and government have been at the forefront of plugging loopholes that enable MNEs to shop around for tax benefits and other cost reductions. For example, the UK has previously negotiated tax treaties and data sharing with a number of countries, including with Liechtenstein after the 2008 tax scandal. One approach for reinstating national treatment is through multilateral bodies, such as the OECD and the G20, that are proposing international tax reform. This enables coordinated action, but many would argue that their multilateral provisions are weak because they are non-binding guidelines. They also argue that it does not tackle the fundamental issue that individual governments engage in a race to the bottom by offering attractive tax breaks to MNEs at the expense of other countries. The UK can continue supporting these multilateral efforts. But it would set an exemplary precedent if it followed up with unilateral action given the opportunity to do so.

There aren't ready-made solutions to do this, but some of the possibilities include taxing all MNEs that *sell* in the country and enforcing equal treatment of all domestic firms and MNEs in terms of profits. Treating MNEs that sell in the UK at par with MNEs that locate in the UK would avoid penalising firms that create jobs here. This is one of the motivations for the US proposal to tax incomes based on the country where the income is generated. Taxes based on sales destination prevent the flight of footloose capital, but not profit shifting to exploit the best tax concessions globally. This can be contained if the UK takes the stance of benchmarking MNEs with purely domestic firms or by extending similar benefits to domestic firms. Any action would need to carefully weigh the potentially conflicting commitments in previous tax or investment treaties with the objective of maintaining real competition. A post-Brexit reset in trade policy is an opportune political moment to have this overdue discussion.

## Reinstating non-discrimination for all stakeholders

A second fundamental principle that the UK needs to reinstate is non-discrimination, which has been eroded because many EPAs give greater rights to investors over other stakeholders. Since 1975, the UK has negotiated over ninety bilateral investment treaties, almost all of which include provisions to enforce investors' rights. Until now, the bulk of these treaties have been with countries that are net recipients of investments from the UK, so the investment agreements were largely designed to protect UK investors from expropriation of assets in developing countries with politically unstable conditions.

With the fragmentation of supply chains, most EPAs today contain provisions regarding settlement of disputes brought by investors against host governments. These are often referred to as Investor State Dispute Settlement (ISDS) clauses. They give foreign firms the right to bring claims against the host country if they have not been given fair and equitable treatment. ISDS clauses are increasingly being used by investors to challenge developed country governments. Many challenges have been in sensitive policy areas like public health and environmental safety, and include cases such as the plain packaging of tobacco and the withdrawal of operating licences for nuclear power plants.

The main contention with ISDS clauses is that the language of what constitutes a violation of investor rights is too vague. This constrains governments from changing laws and can lead to a regulatory chill owing to the fear of expensive litigation from foreign investors. Furthermore, the settlement procedure is typically opaque and costly. And there is a growing recognition that ISDS confers rights to foreign companies that are not available to domestic companies. There still isn't a standard solution to balancing the rights of foreign investors for fair compensation and the right to regulate for host governments. In fact, ISDS clauses have been contentious even between developed countries with advanced legal systems, like Germany and Sweden. These problems are expected to become more acute as developed countries get into EPAs, like a transatlantic partnership between the EU, UK and USA. Typically, the US insists on an ISDS mechanism to settle disputes between foreign firms and host governments—indeed, cases brought under US-style ISDS procedures have been some of the most controversial.

New solutions for balancing investor rights with regulatory discretion are being proposed, and the UK can join these efforts to develop workable proposals. For example, New Zealand has signed side letters with several countries in the newly revived Comprehensive and Progressive Trans-Pacific Partnership to opt out of compulsory ISDS. It has also instituted a review of all foreign investments in sensitive areas and proposed safeguards for areas like public health, education and social services, where investors cannot challenge governments.

The UK could go further in ensuring that its public services and domestic standards are not compromised through ISDS procedures. One way that many EPAs do this is by including chapters on social clauses—environment, health and labour rights. Typically, these have been motivated by concerns that developing countries are likely to have lower standards in these areas, and including social clauses in EPAs would induce them to comply with higher standards. But this has meant that the language of these social provisions is weak and they often have limited legal enforceability or compensation for damages. In contrast, investor rights are legally enforceable and the areas that can be challenged under these provisions is much wider.

The UK could seek to redress this imbalance by tightening the language of investor protections and by granting to stakeholders, like workers and consumers, similar rights and dispute settlement procedures as are given to investors. For example, since 2007, the US upgraded labour disputes from a separate sanction to the status of dispute settlement procedures that apply to other commercial disputes.[9] Enforceability of stakeholder rights would also promote the spirit of sustainable development that the UK has championed for the developing world when they have negotiated with developing country trade partners.

Reinstating national treatment and non-discrimination would be big steps towards redressing imbalances in EPAs. But ultimately, trade policy can only do so much in fostering inclusive growth. As Barry Eichengreen of University of California–Berkeley highlights, there is no easy solution to long-term economic problems.[10] To undo the years of economic stagnation faced by many, a post-Brexit economic policy would need to commit to investing in skills so that people face lower risks of being left behind in the future.

## Conclusion: instituting a new social compact

Wages have decoupled from productivity and many working families in the UK have never really shared in the prosperity that globalisation has brought to many global firms and their workers in the last few decades.[11] While redistribution of economic gains can provide compensation to workers who are hurt by economic changes, it is difficult to achieve when the gains are concentrated on one side of the border. There are no good worldwide redistribution systems and these are highly unlikely to arise in the current context of trade wars. Domestic policy will have to continue to fill this gap.

As a starting point, what's needed is an adjustment assistance fund that compensates people who are displaced by economic changes. A post-Brexit UK would be more inclusive of ordinary working families if they had access to an enforceable mechanism to compensate them for job losses induced by broad economic changes. The evidence on the effectiveness of such programmes, like the trade adjustment assistance in the US and EU, has been mixed. For example, these programmes often have stringent eligibility criteria and are heavily under-used, leaving workers exposed to hardship from changes in their economic environment. The UK will therefore need to learn from the improved provisions that countries are putting in to make these programmes more effective. These include higher levels of funding, systematic monitoring and evaluation mechanisms, less stringent eligibility criteria and streamlined application procedures.

But compensation alone will not solve the problems of the constant churn to which workers are exposed. Ultimately, wage and productivity growth require re-training and upskilling of the workforce. High productivity, low inequality economies like Denmark and Sweden commit over 1 per cent of GDP to investments in skills, while countries with greater inequality, like the US and the UK, invest substantially less than that. Going forward, if private investments in skills fall, as is happening already in the UK, public investments would need to step up further to protect workers from permanent income losses.

The UK can ensure these policies are supported along with market access provisions in EPAs. For example, the US brought about companion treaties on labour rights and standards under the North American Free Trade Agreement (NAFTA) and has subsequently included labour rights in other EPAs. The UK can follow a similar approach of linking labour rights, compensation and rehabilitation policies to EPAs, and by learning the lessons from the inadequacies that plague existing provisions. For example, the NAFTA labour side agreement pledges to enforce effectively national labour laws, but it does not provide for effective sanctions. On the positive side, it has a complaints and arbitration procedure that has led to developments, like reforming Quebec's anti-union laws and enforcing health and safety standards in Mexican *maquiladoras*. But sanctions to remedy non-compliance apply to just a few of the labour standards set out in the accord. The UK should take on board the relevant suggestions: specifying rules for accepting or rejecting cases, following up on issues raised by petitioners, deciding what constitutes an appropriate government response to violations and creating oversight bodies to pursue violations.

Anticipating exactly who will be hurt from a particular policy is always difficult—it can take years before the link between job displacements and economic policies becomes apparent. Worryingly, the Brexit vote is already deskilling UK workers and reinforcing the trends of anaemic wage and productivity growth. Whether the UK operates its post-Brexit trade policy independently or via a customs union with the EU, it should be pushing for EPAs that deliver market access without compromising the UK's high standards on labour, products, services and safety.

It will be exceedingly hard to replace any loss of access to the EU market and to find trade partners that share the high quality standards that the UK has always maintained. Any new EPAs with China, India or the US need to respect these high quality standards. If it ends up outside the EU customs union, the UK's best strategy would be to pioneer a new generation of trade deals that balances the rights of different stakeholders and addresses the new economic reality of global value chains and multinationals. The three rebalancing provisions—national treatment, non-discrimination and a new social compact—would be the first steps towards an inclusive economic model. In the current era of strong anti-globalisation sentiments, a post-Brexit trade policy must be re-geared to truly serve British society, not just free trade.[12]

## Notes

1 Department for International Trade, *Preparing For Our Future UK Trade Policy*, foreword, Cm 9470, October 2017; https://assets.publishing.service.gov.uk/gove rnment/uploads/system/uploads/attachment_data/file/654714/Preparing_for_ our_future_UK_trade_policy_Report_Web_Accessible.pdf (accessed 15 January 2019).
2 R. Costa and S. Machin, 'Real wages and living standards in the UK', CEP Election Analysis Series, paper EA036, June 2017; http://cep.lse.ac.uk/pubs/down load/ea036.pdf (accessed 15 January 2019).
3 Department for Business, Innovation and Skills (BIS), *Trade and Investment Balance of Competence Review*, project report, prepared by the Centre for Economic Policy Research, ref. P2130054BIS, November 2013; https://assets.publishing.ser vice.gov.uk/government/uploads/system/uploads/attachment_data/file/2717 84/bis-14-512-trade-and-investment-balance-of-competence-review-project-report. pdf (accessed 15 January 2019).
4 S. Dhingra, H. Huang, G. Ottaviano, J. P. Pessoa, T. Sampson, J. Van Reenen, 'The costs and benefits of leaving the EU: trade effects', *Economic Policy*, vol. 32, iss. 92, October 2017, pp. 651–705.
5 D. Rodrik, 'What do trade agreements really do?', *Journal of Economic Perspectives*, vol. 32, no. 2, 2018, pp. 73–90.
6 Opinion 2/15 of the Court of Justice of the EU on the competence of the Commission to conclude a Free Trade Agreement between the European Union and the Republic of Singapore, 16 May 2017; http://curia.europa.eu/juris/docume nt/document.jsf?text=&docid=190727&pageIndex=0&doclang=EN&mode=req&d ir=&occ=first&part=1&cid=415687 (accessed 15 January 2019).
7 T. R. Tørsløv, L. S. Weir, G. Zucman, 'The missing profits of nations', NBER working paper series, no. 24701, June 2018.
8 K. A. Habu, 'How aggressive are foreign multinational companies in reducing their corporation tax liability? Evidence from UK condential corporate tax return', Oxford University, mimeo, May 2017.
9 F. Giumelli and G. van Roozendaal, 'Trade agreements and labour standards clauses: explaining labour standards developments through a qualitative

comparative analysis of US free trade agreements', *Global Social Policy*, vol. 17, no. 1, 2017, pp. 38–61.

10 B. Eichengreen, 'What explains Britain's Brexit shocker?', Berkeley blog, 24 June 2016; http://blogs.berkeley.edu/2016/06/24/what-explains-britains-brexit-shocker/ (accessed 15 January 2019).

11 J. P. Pessoa and J. Van Reenen, 'Decoupling of wage growth and productivity growth? Myth and reality', CEP discussion paper No 1246, October 2013; http://cep.lse.ac.uk/pubs/download/dp1246.pdf (accessed 15 January 2019).

12 R. Baldwin, P. Collier and A. Venables, 'Post-Brexit Britain should cotton on to an opportunity to transform global trade', LSE Brexit blogs, 21 April 2017; http://blogs.lse.ac.uk/brexit/2017/04/21/post-brexit-britain-should-cotton-on-to-an-opportunity-to-transform-global-trade/ (accessed 15 January 2019).

How to cite this article: S. Dhingra, 'Brexit and the Future of Trade', in G Kelly and N Pearce (eds.), Britain Beyond Brexit, *The Political Quarterly*, Vol 90, Issue S2, 2019, pp. 21–31. https://doi.org/10.1111/1467-923X.12645

# The City and Financial Services: Historical Perspectives on the Brexit Debate

CATHERINE R. SCHENK

AMONG THE MANY uncertainties about the nature of the Britain's international economic relations after Brexit, the role of the City of London as a financial centre is among the most difficult to predict. The financial services sector in London is globally competitive, with a long history of innovation and adaptation to change. The geographical distribution of global banking and finance has been remarkably stable—at least at the top, where London and New York have jointly hosted the major global markets for the past 100 years. However, there are legitimate fears that the locus of European finance will shift away from London with the repeal of EU passporting rights that facilitate the EU-wide services trade. Brexit threatens to disrupt the London-New York duopoly if the bulk of European business migrates to within the eurozone after 2019. The City will need to draw upon all of its competitive strengths—in labour cost, skills, and the agglomeration of services—to retain its global pre-eminence.

Since the 1990s, financial services in the UK as a whole have contributed 5.5–6.5 per cent of GDP a year (rising to almost 9 per cent in 2010), of which about half is generated in London.[1] In 2016, financial services generated 1.1 million jobs, 3.2 per cent of total jobs. Financial services exports amounted to £61 billion and imports of £11 billion in 2016, generating a surplus of £50 billion that helps to pay for imports of manufactured goods. This trade is focussed strongly on Europe; in 2016, 44 per cent of financial services exports went to the EU and 39 per cent of financial services imports came from the EU. It is clear that cross-border business with the EU is an essential part of the business generated in the City of London so the implications of Brexit could be profound for the British economy.

While Britain's financial activity is dispersed around the country, it has always been dominated by London, which has also been the country's major commercial centre. The financial services sector benefits from economies of scale and scope so that financial firms tend to be located in close proximity. This arises from the interdependency of services ranging from insurance, banking, legal, accounting, media and other ancillary business services. The demand for specialised skilled labour also tends to create economies of scale and scope in financial services, for finance at its heart relies on networks, reputation and constant innovation based on human and social capital. The dynamic, interactive and often personal relationships that underpin modern

Published by John Wiley & Sons Ltd, 9600 Garsington Road, Oxford OX4 2DQ, UK and 350 Main Street, Malden, MA 02148, USA

finance thus benefit from centralisation, even in an age of digital communication. As a result, entrenched international financial centres have proved difficult to dislodge in the absence of war or sudden economic collapse.

Brexit poses particular challenges for the City of London. Membership of the EU and, therefore, the common regulatory frameworks, have allowed London firms to provide services to European customers even though the UK is not part of the eurozone. But if we examine the long run historical record, and the evolution of London as an international financial centre, we can clearly see the City's resilience and potential for innovation that could enable it to meet these Brexit threats.

## The City of London: emergence and resilience

The British model of economic development has had finance and financial agglomeration at its core at least since the industrial revolution of the eighteenth century, and in the twentieth century, the City of London proved resilient to a range of political and economic shocks and to the transformation of the structure of the global financial system. During the interwar global economic depression, sterling lost its dominance to the US dollar (albeit temporarily), free trade was abandoned and capital controls marked the Great Reversal of globalisation. After the international economic system was restored in 1947, a new model prevailed: the emphasis was the promotion of freer trade, combined with pegged exchange rates that were supported by national controls on cross-border financial flows. The floating exchange rates and volatile capital markets that characterised the 1930s had ended the enthusiasm for open capital markets. But even in this hostile environment for international finance, the City of London was not restricted merely to the domestic market.

First, the sterling area and the international role of sterling provided continuing opportunities for the City through the Bretton Woods era of capital controls in the 1950s and 1960s. Capital flows to sterling area countries (for example, Australia, New Zealand, South Africa, Malaya, Singapore, Hong Kong) were allowed on a preferential basis. Britain also joined the European Payments Union that allowed more multilateral trade among western European states and sustained demand for commercial services in London.

London also benefitted from tighter exchange controls imposed by other European states. Thus, the development of financial markets in Paris and Frankfurt were hindered by regulations that discouraged inflows and outflows of short-term capital in order to protect their respective exchange rates. Similar controls on flows of sterling were imposed by the British Treasury, but financial institutions in London soon found ways to circumvent them. The most important innovation of this period—and one that may have important lessons for the Brexit era—was the eurodollar market, which revived the City of London merchant banks and attracted an invasion of banks from around the world.[2] The eurodollar market comprised bank deposits, loans and bonds issued in London for customers from around the world, denominated in US dollars. The use of the dollar as the main currency of the City of London demonstrates the ability of British finance to innovate around regulatory obstacles. The toleration of the eurodollar market by the Bank of England and Treasury in turn demonstrates the official commitment to the advantages of the City for the British economy, particularly in this instance its capacity to earn scarce foreign exchange by exporting services. Other European governments pushed such offshore markets out of their own jurisdictions and this helped to launch London into an unrivalled position in the international financial system in the 1960s and 1970s, while exchange controls persisted in New York and European centres.

During the 1970s (in common with other centres) London was rocked by a series of fraud scandals as bankers struggled to cope with newly floating exchange rates and huge opportunities for speculative trading (and losses).[3] Supervision of international banking in London was tightened up somewhat and the leading industrialised economies turned their attention to prudential supervision of an increasingly international market with the launch of what became the Basel Committee on Banking Supervision in 1975. By this time, New York was the largest global banking market in terms of size of assets, but London remained a premier centre, particularly for Europe. Unhindered by the restrictions of the US Glass-Steagall Act, and benefitting from close access to a large European customer base and a time zone five hours ahead of New York, London remained an important host for global financial institutions.

By the 1980s, the City was again lagging behind New York and faced its next existential crisis. In 1974, 'May Day' in New York eliminated minimum commission charges, making trading more competitive particularly for larger traders. From 1979, the final exchange controls in London were abandoned, which opened up New York for British investors in US, UK and international equities. This time the pressure to increase competition was prompted by the state. Margaret Thatcher's Conservative government led the attack on the restrictive self-regulation of the London Stock Exchange (LSE) by challenging the traditional Rule Book under the Fair Trading Act.[4] By 1983, a compromise was reached whereby the LSE agreed to increase competition among brokers, take foreign members into the LSE and combine brokering and jobbing. The Big Bang of 1986 also included a computer-based trading system to rival the NYSE. Although the LSE never again challenged New York in terms of scale, it retained its position as the main equity market for Europe.

But the really lasting and profound transformation of the City arising from Big Bang was the rush of international banks into mergers and acquisitions to seek the scale and scope in order to enter proprietary trading and take on the booming securities business. The mid-1980s regulatory changes heralded the arrival of global financial conglomerates spread across London and New York, with offices in other centres across the world's time zones. Banks' business models shifted from interest income to fees and trading income and raising liquidity through money markets rather than attracting deposit liabilities. Money markets grew rapidly as innovations in securitisation and asset management came to dominate global investment banking.

An important advantage during the 1980s and 1990s was the culture in the City. London combined close geographic links to Europe with a business model for finance that more closely approximated the US culture. Innovation, competition, low personal and corporate tax rates, performance related compensation, quick and short lines of management and decision making were all part of the 'Anglo-American' model that underpinned the growth of major global investment banks in the 1980s and 1990s. Many European financial institutions sought to emulate or acquire these attributes in a rapidly changing market through acquisition both of institutions and teams of professionals and traders. In this context, Deutsche Bank provides a cautionary tale. Unable to find the expertise and skills to embark on investment banking in Germany, Deutsche Bank looked to London to acquire these attributes through a takeover of Morgan Grenfell in 1989. But the cultural gulf between Frankfurt and London proved extremely difficult to bridge. The German model of matrix management structure ensured cross-cutting regional and functional interests for board members and reinforced the governance by consensus that marked the German universal bank. But investment banking, with its need for quick decisions, short lines of management and performance-related rewards was ill suited to this format. The result was prolonged battles between Frankfurt and London over the management and structure of the investment banking business of Deutsche Bank in London. In 1995, the difficult decision was finally taken to move control of Deutsche Bank's investment banking business to London from Frankfurt. This was a clear recognition that the talent, networks and business practices in London were superior. At this point, New York was a difficult market for European institutions to breach, but Deutsche Bank acquired Bankers Trust in New York in order to get a foothold there in 1999. Deutsche Bank's global investment banking business, however, continued to be led from London.

During the 1990s, another existential threat to London emerged: the introduction of the single currency in Europe and the European Central Bank (ECB). How would London fare outside the euro and beyond the reach of the ECB? At this time, there were widespread predictions that Frankfurt would overtake London as the main European financial centre. But London persisted, moving into euro- as well as dollar-business. This time, the benefits to European customers of the agglomeration of services and expertise in London, the regulatory framework and governance structures that promoted revenue-seeking and short-term returns, outweighed efforts in Frankfurt or Paris to rival London as the leading European financial centre. In June 1999, six months after the introduction of the euro, the Bank of England reported that 'There is quiet confidence among international market firms that London has been maintaining its market share'.[5]

Frankfurt was considered the main potential rival at the time and indeed it had many benefits. It was the centre for postwar German finance and banking, the strongest European industrial nation and the host for the new European Central Bank. In 1991, Helmut Kohl's German government launched their plans for *Finanzplatz Deutschland* to enhance the financial services offered there, which included reforming regulation, modernising the stock exchange, promoting new sectors of the industry and championing German financial firms.[6] Key characteristics of the traditional German system, as opposed to the Anglo-American model, were the cross-holding of bank-industry-insurance companies and the operation of the *hausbank* system that secured the bank-based financial system rooted in long-term relationships. This internalised the financial flows for large companies and secured loan finance for the successful *mittlestadt* firms that were at the core of the German industrial success. It also reduced the demand for money market facilities that were resisted by the Bundesbank and also side-lined the stock exchange as a source of capital.

The German system contrasted with the more competitive, fluid and fickle markets of New York and London but left gaps in the financial markets in Germany, particularly in lucrative corporate bonds and equities, pension fund management and money market financing. Lower taxes on securities trading in 1991 were followed by the relaxation of regulations over money market funding instruments in 1994.[7] But while this changed the business model for German banks and firms, Frankfurt did not eclipse London. The agglomeration effects of breadth and depth of expertise, flexible labour markets and lower tax structure were sustained. These advantages in London were especially important as the global financial markets entered a period of instability during the emerging market crises in the late 1990s and early 2000s.[8]

Now, Frankfurt is again a clear rival to London, with German officials calling for euro-clearing to be moved from London to Frankfurt and some banks shifting parts of their clearing operations there.[9] This poses a direct threat to the London Clearing House that deals with about €1 trillion per day. Other European financial centres are also jockeying for position—particularly Paris and Amsterdam—and some activities will inevitably increase their presence there after the UK leaves the EU. While many European banks are poised to open offices in other centres, jobs and activity in London will not necessarily decline in the short term. In most cases, the announcements have been accompanied by reassurance that activities in London will not necessarily be scaled down, or jobs moved away. But in the longer term, it is likely that London will share more of its business with centres elsewhere in Europe. This in turn many undermine the gravitational pull of London that has supported the range of finance-related business.

## What will keep finance in London?

While regulation is clearly key to the location of international financial services, the historical record of governments deliberately 'creating' financial centres is not strong. The City of London grew organically and has adapted to a variety of international environments over the past 100 years. This is not just historical determinism, but also the strong centripetal effects in the range of financial services which are interdependent and rely on a flexible workforce with particular specialised skills. Efforts to promote Paris in the 1960s or Frankfurt in the 1990s have faced obstacles either from competitive advantages of incumbents or recognition of the costs to hosting a global financial centre, including the need for low taxes, low barriers on movement of key workers, accepting flexible labour markets. Moreover, the concentration of financial activity contributes to income inequality and vulnerability to external shocks and this does not suit all political economy climates.

Hosting an international financial centre carries with it risks and burdens as well as advantages. From the nineteenth century, when London was in its most dominant global position, there were frequent complaints that the financial services sector concentrated in the south-east inhibited industrial and manufacturing growth in the country as a whole. The geographic distance between finance in the south and manufacturing in the north, it was argued, made it more difficult for factory owners to raise capital. With its outward, global focus, scarce capital resources were instead directed to foreign investment that built up British industry's competitors in Europe, the Empire and the USA. This critique of the City of London's role in British relative industrial decline became an important focus of academic research in the 1980s.[10] As is often the case, the trends in historical research mirrored the time in which it was written.

The historic model of the cultural and geographic gulf between the City and the domestic economy seemed particularly apt in the decade after the de-industrialisation of Britain accelerated and when Margaret Thatcher's Conservative government waged war against trade unions in the north. At the same time, the image of the City trader finishing business in the early afternoon before retiring to the champagne bar seemed to re-emphasise the dislocation in the British economy and society. Whether these tropes are legitimate, they reinforced a sense that hosting a global financial centre increases income inequality and contributes to social and housing problems in London. This distortion is less important for New York because of the huge scale of the US economy both in terms of output and geographic size compared to London's position in the UK.[11]

What were the sources of London's competitive advantage in a globalised world of the 1990s and 2000s? Agglomeration effects induce a kind of inertia, but there is more to it than this. The advantages of London are perhaps felt most strongly now in the large pool of skilled labour available to

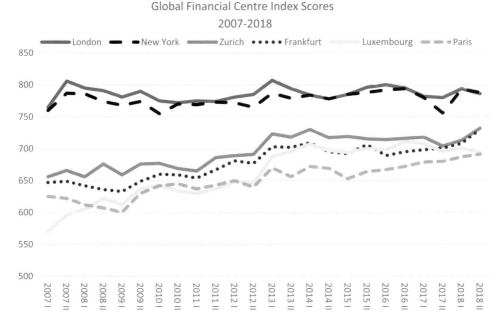

**Figure 1:** Global Financial Centre Index (GFCI) scores, 2007–2018. Note: The GFCI are published mostly on a half-yearly basis in Spring and AutumnSource:Z/Yen Partners. For methodology see http://globalfinancialcentres.net/explore/

employers in London. This has long loomed as a major advantage for London over other European centres. Linked to this advantage are language and legal transparency. It is the ability not only to hire talent, but also to fire in the wake of downturns in the market that help London's competitiveness. No continental European centre made the top ten international financial centres in the category of human capital in 2018, but London ranked second in the world (after Hong Kong).[12] Figure 1 shows the persistently high ranking of London and New York since the Global Financial Centre Index (GFCI) began to be compiled in March 2007. The methodology includes a wide range of secondary data, as well as a questionnaire of about 2,200 individuals, of whom 40 per cent are located in the Asia-Pacific region. It scores the centres across a range of features, including business environment, human capital, reputation, infrastructure and financial sector development. It is striking that London's position has not fallen significantly since the Brexit vote, although other European centres have gained ground. But the figure also indicates that the catch-up is a longer-term process than just a reaction to opportunities arising from Brexit.

Certainly, London's position relative to New York is about equal and this has been the case since 2007.[13] The September 2018 edition marked some changes, with New York narrowly overtaking London and increases for

Frankfurt and Zurich. Zurich is persistently the second ranked European financial centre, although well below London, but other European centres have been catching up since 2007. With different methodologies, *The Banker* ranking has somewhat different outcomes for European centres other than London (for example, Amsterdam and Paris come above Zurich), but it also puts London well ahead of any European centre, particularly with regard to inward foreign direct investment and new firms opening in 2016/17.[14] Furthermore, the City's financial services cluster is expanding, with 1,208 new firms launching operations in London between June 2016 and early May 2017, according to data provider Dun and Bradstreet, bringing the total to 49,185. But this status should not necessarily create complacency about the changes to come after 2019.

'Passports' allow financial institutions based in London to offer a range of services to customers in the EU—either directly from London or on preferential terms through a branch. In 2017, 5,476 UK firms used passports into the UK and 8,008 European Economic Area (EEA) firms used passports into the UK.[15] Without this, UK firms would not have the right to market their services, although they could supply services if a customer approached them (unsolicited).[16] Losing the passports will require financial institutions under the UK regulatory bodies to establish regulated businesses within the EU and to apply for a licence to trade in each EEA country. In August 2018, the UK Treasury announced that the government was committed to continuing inward flows of services from EEA resident firms to UK customers for three years after March 2019, even if there is no transitional 'deal' for Brexit by this time. But the reciprocal rights are not being offered by the EU.[17]

The government's 2018 White Paper on the exit from the EU and future relationship with Europe dropped the automatic regulatory equivalence for services. While stressing that 'In our new strategic partnership agreement we will be aiming for the freest possible trade in financial services between the UK and EU Member States' the White Paper stressed mutual cooperation arrangements and pledged that 'As the UK leaves the EU, we will seek to establish strong cooperative oversight arrangements with the EU and will continue to support and implement international standards to continue to safely serve the UK, European and global economy'.[18] This provoked considerable disappointed angst in the City of London, because of the lack of specifics on the transition for existing contracts, or certainty about the pursuit of mutual recognition of regulations that would facilitate the continuation of relationships.[19] The relationship between the City and the state has always been complex, and James and Quaglia demonstrate that the relationship between the financial services sector and the UK government has waxed and waned during the negotiations with the EU.[20]

The main route to mitigate the effects of the loss of passporting (and the most likely) is through regulatory equivalence in London for some businesses: but this process is bilateral and not fully secure, so it is not a substitute for existing arrangements. Most importantly, equivalence can be unilaterally revoked by the EU at short notice. There are eleven areas listed in the equivalence decisions by the European Commission and over 200 decisions on thirty partner country jurisdictions (including the USA) have been taken under this instrument.[21] In April 2018, Michel Barnier, the main EU negotiator, asked 'Why would the equivalence system, which works well for the US industry, not work for the City?'[22] The draft Brexit agreement in November 2018 accepted that the EU's system for determining regulatory equivalence would be the likely solution for the City of London's access to EU markets.

As financial regulation conforms to a global standard through the G20, Financial Stability Board (FSB) and Bank for International Settlements (BIS) initiatives, then equivalence might be easier to achieve—or at least has less opportunity cost. The UK is a 'rule-taker' from the BIS and FSB as well as from the EU. The review of the European Commission experience published at the end of 2017 noted that a lighter touch was possible where the exposure of the EU to the country was small and that preponderance was deployed in these contexts. This suggests, conversely, that achieving equivalence in London could require a higher threshold of compliance than many of the existing agreements. Moreover, the Commission from late 2014 introduced periodic reviews and monitoring into the equivalence decision, which might be onerous for London.[23] The decision can also be reversed 'at any moment', which creates costly uncertainty. But markets cope with a range of uncertainties and risks and London should be resilient if it is able to offer competitive services to its customers.

In April 2018, Barnier concluded a speech to Eurofi High-level Seminar with optimistic remarks about the future of the City and its relationship to Europe, but he also dashed hopes that the UK might get a special and more permanent equivalence deal as proposed by Philip Hammond, the Chancellor of the Exchequer.[24] One possible adjustment strategy would be to develop strategic partnerships between UK and EU financial firms. This was how British, American and European banks responded to the prospects of European integration in the 1960s, through the creation of consortium banks and banking clubs. But here the lesson of history is less optimistic. In the 1970s, it proved impossible to sustain these cooperative structures: their interests diverged, the new entities competed with their 'parents' and there was costly duplication. Within a decade, most had been abandoned and banks returned to traditional cross-border branches and subsidiaries.[25]

In the past, London has responded to challenges through innovation and it is possible that new advances in financial technology (fintech) will undermine the importance of regulatory boundaries in some markets. There may also be opportunities to deregulate in London to make it more attractive for global business in some areas, although there will need to be compliance with global BIS and FSB standards.

Certainly, new barriers between London and other European financial capitals will induce changes in the geographic distribution of activity. But this may not necessarily lead to a withering away of the influence and centrality of the City of London, but may (in a more optimistic outlook) disperse activity among European centres in order to conform to regulatory barriers. To some extent, this process has already begun due to high property costs in London and the outsourcing of some back-office IT and accounting tasks that ICT innovation made possible in the 1990s and 2000s. The challenge for London is to retain its traditional advantages in quality of labour supply, communications, ease of business, and legal infrastructure for the high value-added parts of financial services.

## Conclusions

London as a financial centre has been resilient to a series of seemingly existential crises over the past century and London's markets have a long history of innovation and adaptation. Core strengths continue to include the agglomeration of services, the pool of skilled labour and flexible labour market. The reliance on breadth and agglomeration means that losing part of the high value-added sectors of the financial industry may undermine the attractiveness of London. Meanwhile, London's exceptional talent pool relies on continued open access for migrant labour from the EU and the rest of the world, a key feature challenged both by the Brexit referendum and the government's long-standing immigration policy.

All told, the challenge of Brexit is important and dangerous. The clearest route to mitigation is through equivalence. This has advantages (institutions are likely to continue to be able to access EU customers), but also disadvantages (London will be a rule-taker from EU and may lose competitiveness vis-à-vis New York). While some lower grade functions are liable to be dispersed, this may also leave City institutions providing some high-level services through subsidiaries in the EU. It is not clear, however, that other European financial centres yet have the infrastructure to replace London in the short term. The optimistic outcome, therefore, is greater complementarity rather than complete eclipse.

## Notes

1 C. Rhodes, 'Financial services: contribution to the UK economy', Commons Briefing Paper SN06193, April 2018; http://researchbriefings.parliament.uk/ResearchBriefing/Summary/SN06193#fullreport (accessed 6 June 2018).
2 C. R. Schenk, *The Decline of Sterling: Managing the Retreat of an International Currency 1945–1992*, Cambridge, Cambridge University Press, 2010.
3 C. R. Schenk, 'The regulation of international financial markets from the 1950s to the 1990s', in S. Battilossi and J. Reis, eds., *State and Financial Systems in Europe and the USA: Historical Perspectives on Regulation and Supervision in the Nineteenth and Twentieth Centuries*, Farnham, Ashgate, 2010.
4 R. Michie, *The London Stock Exchange: A History*, Oxford, Oxford University Press, 1999.

5 Bank of England, *Practical Issues Arising from the Euro*, June 1999, p.14.
6 N. Walter, 'Finanzplatz Deutschland: modernisation and regulatory reform', *Journal of Financial Regulation and Compliance*, vol. 6, no. 4, 1998, pp. 351–356; J. Story, 'Finanzplatz Deutschland: national or European response to internationalisation?', *German Politics*, vol. 5, no. 3, 1996, pp. 371–394.
7 S. Konoe, *The Politics of Financial Markets and Regulation: The United States, Japan and Germany*, Berlin, Springer, 2014, pp. 81–88.
8 HM Treasury, *The Location of Financial Activity and the Euro*, London, HMSO, 2003.
9 'Two big UK banks shift some euro clearing from London to Frankfurt', *Financial Times*, 12 June 2018; 'Germany backs call for shifting euro clearing from London', *Financial Times*, 8 June 2018.
10 S. Pollard, *Britain's Prime and Britain's Decline: The British Economy, 1870–1914*, New York, Edward Arnold, 1989; P. J. Cain and A. Hopkins, *British Imperialism—Innovation and Expansion 1688–1914*, New York, Longman, 1994.
11 New York City (including Newark and Jersey City) comprised about 8–9 per cent of US GDP in 2016 (Bureau of Economic Analysis, US Department of Commerce), while London contributed about 23 per cent of UK gross value added (GVA) in 2016. Of this about 12 per cent was generated by the City of London itself (City of London Corporation).
12 Human capital included availability of skilled personnel, flexible labour market, education and development, quality of life. London came second after Hong Kong and before New York on this measure.
13 Global Financial Centres Index 23, March 2018; http://www.longfinance.net/Publications/GFCI23.pdf (accessed 6 June 2018). This is based on instrumental factors published by a range of institutions and a survey of 2,340 banking and financial related professionals of which 42.5 per cent were from Asia/Pacific and 25.5 per cent were from Europe. The Index was first compiled in 2007.
14 S. Pavoni, 'Brexit-bound London retains top slot in 2017 IFC rankings', *The Banker*, 2017.
15 European Research Centre for Economic and Financial Governance, report for European Parliament's Committee on Economic and Monetary Affairs, *Implications of Brexit on EU Financial Services*, Brussels, 2017, p. 48.
16 British Banking Association, Brexit quick brief #3, 'What is "passporting" and why does it matter?'; https://www.bba.org.uk/wp-content/uploads/2016/12/webversion-BQB-3-1.pdf (accessed 6 June 2018).
17 HM Treasury, guidance, 'Banking, insurance and other financial services if there's no Brexit deal', 23 August 2018; https://www.gov.uk/government/publications/banking-insurance-and-other-financial-services-if-theres-no-brexit-deal/banking-insurance-and-other-financial-services-if-theres-no-brexit-deal#financial-market-infrastructure-fmi (accessed 29 November 2018).
18 HM Government, White Paper, *The United Kingdom's Exit from and New Partnership with the European Union*, London, February 2017.
19 C. McGuinness, Policy Chairman, City of London Corporation, 12 July 2018; https://news.cityoflondon.gov.uk/commenting-following-the-publication-of-the-brexit-white-paper-today-12-july-policy-chairman-of-the-city-of-london-corporation-catherine-mcguinness-said/ (accessed 29 November 2018).
20 Schenk, *Decline of Sterling*; H. Thompson, 'How the City of London lost at Brexit: a historical perspective', *Economy and Society*, vol. 46, no. 2, 2017, pp. 211–28;

S. James and L. Quaglia, 'The Brexit negotiations and financial services: a two-level game analysis', *Political Quarterly*, vol. 89, no. 4, 2018, pp. 560–567.

21 European Commission, 'Recognition of non-EU financial frameworks (equivalence decisions)', Brussels, February 2018; https://ec.europa.eu/info/business-economy-euro/banking-and-finance/international-relations/recognition-non-eu-financial-frameworks-equivalence-decisions_en (accessed 29 November 2018).

22 Speech by Michel Barnier at the Eurofi High-level Seminar, Sofia, 26 Aril 2018; http://europa.eu/rapid/press-release_SPEECH-18-3569_en.htm (accessed 6 June 2018).

23 European Commission, 'EU equivalence decisions in financial services policy: an assessment', SWD(2017) 102 final, Brussels, 27 February 2017; https://ec.europa.eu/info/sites/info/files/eu-equivalence-decisions-assessment-27022017_en.pdf (accessed 6 June 2018).

24 Speech by Michel Barnier at the Eurofi High-level Seminar 2018.

25 D. M. Ross, 'Clubs and consortia: European banking groups as strategic alliances', in S. Battilossi and Y Cassis, eds., *European Banks and the American Challenge*, New York, Oxford University Press, 2002, pp. 135–60.

How to cite this article: C. R. Schenk, 'The City and Financial Services: Historical Perspectives on the Brexit Debate', in G Kelly and N Pearce (eds.), Britain Beyond Brexit, *The Political Quarterly*, Vol 90, Issue S2, 2019, pp. 32–43. https://doi.org/10.1111/1467-923X.12624

# Macroeconomic Policy Beyond Brexit

SIMON WREN-LEWIS

## Introduction

IF YOU ask a macroeconomist how macroeconomic policy should change as a result of Brexit, the chances are they will reply by saying it is a daft question. Leaving the Single Market and Customs Union of the EU will have a negative effect on UK productivity and, therefore, inevitably living standards, that the conventional tools of monetary and fiscal policy can do nothing to prevent or reverse. In this chapter I want to suggest this is rather old-fashioned thinking. What the global financial crisis (GFC), austerity and now Brexit have shown us is that sharp negative shocks to the economy can have additional permanent effects if they are not offset quickly and strongly by macroeconomic policy. One reason the UK has had a poor productivity performance since the GFC is that macroeconomic policy tools have failed to do this. To the extent that Brexit itself will reduce growth in living standards, it is imperative that we do not compound this by repeating the macroeconomic policy mistakes of the last decade. This chapter looks at where we have gone wrong and how we can do better after Brexit.

## Productivity

Unless we stay in both the Customs Union and Single Market, Brexit will make trade with the EU substantially more difficult. Brexiters talk about making new trade agreements with countries outside the EU, but in reality, we are likely to lose more agreements with those countries by leaving the EU than we are likely to gain. Even if trade with third countries did increase, gravity equations—empirical relationships that look at the extent of bilateral trade—tell us that trade with third countries will never compensate for the trade lost to the EU simply because the EU is on our doorstep. That is what the government's own analysis tells us, and it reflects every serious academic study.

Less trade with the EU means that the UK economy becomes less open. That reduces productivity (how much output you get from a given labour force) because you lose some of the gains of specialisation. There is also good evidence that less open economies (in terms of goods and migration) have slower productivity growth than more open economies. Productivity growth is the main determinant, in the medium and long run, of growth in living standards.

Published by John Wiley & Sons Ltd, 9600 Garsington Road, Oxford OX4 2DQ, UK and 350 Main Street, Malden, MA 02148, USA

All this is about resources available to the economy, rather than how those resources are utilised. The macroeconomics of monetary and fiscal policy is about resource utilisation: how to avoid booms that bring higher inflation and busts that increase unemployment. Therefore, the conventional view argues that monetary and fiscal policy can do nothing to counteract the trade lost as a result of Brexit and the productivity decline that produces. There may be many other ways of trying to compensate with policies to boost productivity, but all of these policies could have been done without Brexit, and their impact will have little to do with Brexit.

This conventional view misses an important point which more and more macroeconomists are beginning to take seriously. Following shocks like Brexit, if you get your macroeconomic policy seriously wrong this can make the permanent impact of those shocks worse. This is illustrated by what has happened to UK productivity since the GFC. The literature on what is called the UK productivity puzzle is huge, and I cannot do justice to it here, but I can give you my own interpretation of the evidence.

If you look at productivity growth across the globe,[1] it started slowing in the 1980s and the slowdown gradually intensified until and perhaps beyond the GFC. The UK managed to buck this international trend. Many factors could explain the UK's relatively good performance, such as the Thatcher governments' labour market reforms and the impact that joining the Single Market had on our service exports. The UK continued to experience productivity growth above our European neighbours under the Labour government.[2] This relatively good performance was across the board, and not an artefact of a financial sector bubble. Government policy may have had some role in this, by strengthening competition policy, supporting innovation, expanding university education, improving regulations and possibly higher immigration.

While our productivity performance was better than France and Germany before the GFC, the opposite has been true since then. By some accounts, UK productivity growth over the last decade is worse than it has been for a century. Why this reversal of fortunes? A lot of discussion treats this poor UK performance as something that has been constant since the Great Recession. But if we take a closer look at growth in each quarter compared to a year earlier (see Figure 1), a more interesting pattern emerges.

UK productivity growth did recover after the recession, but growth was lower in 2011 and was then negative in 2012. Growth began to pick up in 2014, but then came to a halt again at the end of 2015. We can make sense of this pattern if we stop thinking of productivity growth as something that is independent of major policy changes. Productivity growth is normally strong in business cycle recoveries because demand grows rapidly, forcing firms to invest in new technology to meet that demand. However the UK recovery after the Great Recession was unlike any other for the last hundred years: we hardly saw any output growth before 2013. A big factor behind this poor recovery was austerity. Why would austerity reduce productivity

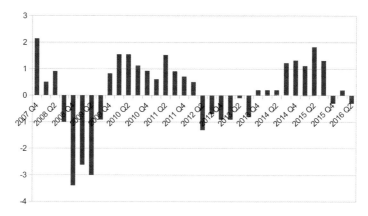

**Figure 1:** Growth in UK output per hour, quarter on previous year's quarter, %

Source: ONS

growth? Austerity reduced the growth in demand, which in turn reduced the need to invest in new techniques to meet that demand. Once the economy finally started growing again in 2013, productivity growth began to pick up.

So what led productivity growth to stall at the end of 2015? The obvious answer is uncertainty about the EU referendum: the unexpected Conservative win in 2015 raised the possibility of Brexit. In my view, at least part of the story behind weak UK productivity growth is uncertainty about the UK recovery because of austerity and Brexit uncertainty.

The implication of our recent experience is that if you screw up macroeconomic policy you will have lasting negative effects on the UK's productivity growth and therefore, inevitably, its prosperity. But the reverse should also be true. If macroeconomic policy puts the emphasis on sustainable growth and tries to minimise disruptive shocks, it will create an environment that encourages productivity growth and therefore growth in living standards.

So where did macroeconomic policy since the GFC go wrong? Why did it fail to combat the negative demand effects of the GFC and Brexit uncertainty, such that levels of productivity are now permanently lower than they might have been? I will start with monetary policy, because according to what I call the 'consensus assignment',[3] it is the stabilisation policy of choice.

## Monetary policy

If you ask many monetary policy makers, including those at the Bank of England, how well monetary policy has been conducted over the last decade, they will typically say their performance has not been too bad. In the context of a slowest recovery in centuries and a deviation compared to previous output trends currently exceeding 15 per cent and growing, that seems an extraordinary response. They will justify that response by referring to inflation, and saying that the decline in output was beyond their control, which I have already argued is incorrect. This suggests that having inflation as the primary target has made UK macroeconomic policy worse over the last decade, with apparently permanent costs.

We can see that happening at specific instances in time. A clear example was when the European Central Bank raised interest rates in 2011. The recovery from the recession caused by the GFC had hardly begun, but a temporary uplift in inflation largely caused by higher oil prices led them to raise interest rates. The same almost happened in the UK, with three out of nine Monetary Policy Committee members voting for a rate increase. The US did not make the same mistake (even though core inflation briefly rose above 2 per cent), but it is notable that the US central bank has a dual mandate (inflation and employment).

This suggests that to continue with inflation as the primary target could jeopardise a macroeconomic policy that focusses on strong growth, and quickly offsets any negative shocks. There is a danger that the Bank of England will overreact to temporary increases in inflation, which will blunt a recovery and cause a permanent loss in productivity. However, a simple dual mandate of the US type gives insufficient indication of where the central bank's priorities should lie. I would favour changing the Bank's mandate to be

*to maximise output growth subject to maintaining inflation within 1 per cent of its target by the end of a (rolling) five-year period*

This mandate allows the central bank to ignore temporary increases in inflation, and focus on sustainable output growth. This can be rationalised by thinking about what the costs of inflation are. Modern macroeconomics examines how, if prices are sticky, inflation can lead to distortions in the allocation of resources because sticky prices are changed at different times. According to this reasoning, inflation in flexible prices, like exchange rates or commodity prices, is not costly. So it seems to make sense for monetary policy makers to ignore temporary movements in inflation, and instead focus on medium term inflation which will reflect changes in sticky prices.

There are other microeconomic arguments for allowing greater variability in inflation compared to output variability. Inflation a per cent or two above target inconveniences everyone a little, but falls in output can have relatively little impact on most but can mean spells of unemployment for a few. There are standard economic reasons why we should care about large costs for a few over small costs for the many, even if on average those costs are the same.

There is another argument for shifting the emphasis from inflation to output. When the inflation target is low, like 2 per cent, this leads to asymmetric risks for monetary policy makers. Running the economy too hot will lead

47

to higher inflation, which can be dampened quite quickly with higher nominal rates. However, running the economy too cold can be much more serious, for two reasons. First, because wages are rigid downward (few like giving or receiving negative nominal wage increases), it is often unclear that the economy is running cold. Second, even if it is recognised, the existence of a lower bound for nominal interest rates means that the central bank's ability to deal with this can be impaired. Putting the emphasis of the central bank's mandate on growth rather than inflation is one way of counteracting that asymmetry.

What should the inflation target be? Another lesson from the GFC is that a low target like 2 per cent risks central banks hitting the lower bound for interest rates quite frequently. A number of economists have suggested raising the inflation target to 4 per cent to ensure this happens less often. While it is hard from a political point of view to raise an inflation target (because many people think it implies lower real incomes), the form of rule suggested above will in effect raise average inflation to above 3 per cent even if the formal target stays at 2 per cent.

I would augment this rule if nominal interest rates hit their lower bound in a way suggested by ex-Fed chair Ben Bernanke.[4] When rates hit their lower bound, it is advantageous to promise lax monetary policy in the future, because this will lead forward-looking firms to spend more or cut prices less today. This could be achieved by converting the inflation target into a path for the price level, so that any undershoot in inflation today requires an overshoot later. Thus

*when interest rates hit their lower bound the mandate should be to maximise growth subject to not exceeding by more than 1 per cent a price path consistent with the inflation target.*

Although higher average inflation and this additional clause reduces the chances of hitting the lower bound for interest rates, that possibility still exists. Proposals to avoid the lower bound completely, such as negative interest rates or helicopter money, require a lot more analysis before they will become acceptable to the academic or central bank communities.

The main instrument central banks currently use when rates are at their lower bound, quantitative easing (QE), is just too unreliable compared to either interest rate changes or fiscal policy. To maximise the pressure on fiscal policy makers to stimulate the economy when rates are at their lower bound, I would take up the suggestion from Ed Balls and colleagues and require the Bank to send quarterly letters to the Chancellor indicating the stimulus they think is needed when rates are at their lower bound.[5]

## Fiscal policy

Fiscal stimulus in response to interest rates hitting their lower bound happened in 2009, but went into reverse in 2010. Ostensibly, this reverse was because of worries about whether the markets would continue to buy government debt. For a country like the UK that has its own currency, this fear was and continues to remain groundless. The fact that the UK has a central bank that can buy government debt means that the UK government can never be forced to default. One thing QE shows clearly is that creating money to buy debt is not inflationary in a recession. The evidence we have suggests there was no impending crisis in 2010. Comment by City folk is not evidence. This is why macroeconomic textbooks say you should have fiscal stimulus in a recession, with no qualifications about the level of debt. There is no consensus macromodel which says that governments with their own currency should be cautious about using fiscal expansion in a recession. Instead, there is a general view that demand-induced recessions can always be ended using a combination of monetary and fiscal policy.

This is not to say that we should be unconcerned about government debt. Instead, it is about priorities and timing. In a recession, the priority is to end it as soon as possible. That may lead to a substantial increase in government debt, but it is absolutely the right thing to do. The reason is very simple. In a recession, trying to cut debt (austerity) wastes resources. Earlier, I suggested that it may also stop productivity increases because firms no longer need to invest in better production techniques. The time to worry about debt is when cutting spending or raising taxes need have no impact on demand and so waste no resources, because its impact on demand can be offset by cutting interest rates. The one time that cannot be done for a country like the UK is when interest rates are at their lower bound.

That was why Jonathan Portes and I suggested that any fiscal rule should have what you could call an interest rate lower bound knockout.[6] As soon as interest rates were likely to hit their lower bound, the normal rule should be suspended and fiscal policy should do whatever it takes to boost demand such that the central bank is able to raise rates again. That could raise government debt substantially, but once interest rates are at more normal levels, debt can be reduced. Basic economic theory suggests the optimal way to reduce government debt is slowly. This means that the fiscal rule outwith zero lower bound periods should target the deficit over a rolling five-year period.

Another argument we make is that public investment should be independent of the main fiscal rule. In other words, the fiscal rule should focus on current rather than capital expenditure. One reason for doing this is that otherwise, it is politically attractive to try and meet deficit targets by cutting investment rather than current spending, and this will lead over time to a deterioration in the supply side of the economy. It is especially important that public investment is not artificially constrained in a post-Brexit future, because public investment is an important means of both directly improving productivity and also facilitating private investment.

The fiscal rule I describe here is similar to the Labour party's fiscal credibility rule. Labour's rule targets a current balance of zero over a moving five-year period (assuming the knockout does not apply), which is similar to the coalition government's original rule (although in that situation the knockout should have applied!). However, Labour's rule also targets a falling debt to income ratio over a five-year period. My own view is that this last target is unnecessary, and could put unnecessary constraints on public investment. With the extent of recovery highly uncertain, a terrible recent record of productivity growth and very low interest rates, now is not the time to constrain public investment because of some arbitrary debt ratio target.

Above all else, it was reversing fiscal stimulus in 2010 (austerity) that prevented a strong and quick recovery from the GFC and helped create the UK's productivity slowdown. Much the same can be said about Brexit uncertainty that began in 2015. This uncertainty was bound to reduce demand, because investment would be put on hold. Yet, rather than offsetting this impact using a fiscal stimulus, we had further austerity instead. (Interest rates were cut after the vote, but only slightly because they were already close to the lower bound.) As a result GDP per head actually fell in the first quarter of 2018.

Many on the left want to go much further than I have suggested, and abandon fiscal rules altogether. I have heard these rules called neoliberal. Fiscal rules (and subsequently fiscal councils like the Office for Budget Responsibility) became popular to counteract what economists called deficit bias: the tendency before the GFC among many economies (but not the UK) to gradually increase the debt to income ratio over time.

There are sound economic reasons for wanting to avoid deficit bias. For example, rising debt needs higher debt interest payments to service it, which in turn increases taxes which have disincentive effects. Fiscal rules are a restraint on governments either cutting taxes, or raising spending to gain political popularity, or to satisfy interest groups, much as Donald Trump has done recently. But this is a medium/long term problem, and it is never a problem that should stop the government doing all it can to end a recession.

## Nominal wages as a macroeconomic instrument?

There are two ways in which governments could, directly or indirectly, put upward pressure on nominal wages beyond influencing aggregate demand. The direct instrument is the minimum wage. This had been set by the Low Pay Commission under Labour, but George Osborne in 2015 decided to increase the minimum wage by more than the Commission had recommended. The indirect instrument is to encourage greater unionisation by various means.

Why would you suggest using either as a macroeconomic policy instrument? The background has been a period of unprecedented decline in real wages in the UK. Many have blamed the currently weak position of the workforce and declining unionisation for this. However, we can almost completely account for low real wages with three factors: stagnant productivity already discussed; two depreciations in sterling which raises the price of imported goods; and rises in indirect taxes associated with austerity. The profit share of corporations has remained relatively static over the last fifteen years.

Many might find it counter-intuitive that weak nominal wages are not responsible for weak real wages. However, this may simply reflect that firms are passing on low nominal wages into low prices to maintain competitiveness. There may nevertheless be a route by which low nominal wages could cause low real wages, and that is if low nominal wages encourage firms to substitute labour for capital, or put off productivity improvements.

There is some evidence that increases in minimum wages can encourage automation.[7] At first sight this seems to contradict the idea that low nominal wages have simply been passed on into lower prices. But raising the minimum wage, or growing unionisation in a few sectors, is different from an increase in wages across the economy. Some firms may be reluctant to raise prices in the former case because it raises their relative price against goods not subject to this wage push, and so may choose to automate instead.

However, we have to be cautious here. The received wisdom, in the UK at least, is that a moderate minimum wage does not lead to significant declines in employment, which appears to imply no labour-saving productivity gains. Significantly higher minimum wages may increase productivity, but they are also likely to raise inflation, and thereby effectively raise the NAIRU (the level of unemployment at which inflation stays constant). It is possible to argue that any new restrictions on migration from the EU, by creating labour shortages, will itself encourage growth in labour-saving productivity. However, an alternative for any such firm is to simply move production abroad.

My own view is that stimulating demand in a high employment but low productivity environment is a far more effective way of stimulating productivity growth than trying to engineer higher nominal wages. In other words, the best way of stimulating wages is through additional demand making the labour market tight, which will provide a strong incentive for firms to invest in productivity improvements, improvements that would then lead to higher real wages. There are other and better reasons to have a minimum wage and stronger unions than an attempt to boost productivity.

## Conclusion

I have argued that the last decade has exposed serious flaws in the way macroeconomic policy is done in the UK, and have suggested how to remove those flaws. Implementing these proposals will not reverse the damaging impact of the loss of trade that Brexit will bring, but they could allow the UK to return to having reasonable growth and productivity levels rather than the stagnation we have experienced since the GFC.

There is one final political economy link between past macroeconomic policy failures and Brexit that it is important to note. The biggest macroeconomic policy failure I have discussed is austerity, and there is some evidence of links between austerity and the rise in UKIP, which helped influence both the decision to hold a referendum and the referendum result itself.[8] More generally, the links between economic stagnation and the rise of populism and xenophobia are clear.[9] Brexit will reduce future UK productivity growth, and therefore future UK living standards. The political health of the UK may also depend on not compounding the impact of Brexit by repeating the macroeconomic policy mistakes of the last decade.

## Notes

1 R. Jones, 'Innovation, research and the UK's productivity crisis', SPERI paper no. 28, University of Sheffield, 2016.
2 D. Corry, A. Valero and J. Van Reenen, 'UK economic performance since 1997', Centre for Economic Performance, London School of Economics, 2011.
3 T. Kirsanova, C. Leith and S. Wren-Lewis, 'Monetary and fiscal policy interaction: the current consensus assignment in the light of recent developments', *Economic Journal,* vol. 119, 2009, pp. 482–496.
4 B. Bernanke, 'Temporary price-level targeting: an alternative framework for monetary policy', Brookings blog post, 12 October, 2017; https://www.brookings.edu/blog/ben-bernanke/2017/10/12/temporary-price-level-targeting-an-alternative-framework-for-monetary-policy/ (accessed 14 January 2019).
5 E. Balls, J. Howat and A. Stansbury, 'Central bank independence revisited: after the financial crisis, what should a model central bank look like?', M-RCBG associate working paper no. 67, 2016.
6 J. Portes and S. Wren-Lewis, 'Issues in the design of fiscal policy rules', *Manchester School,* vol. 83, 2015, pp. 56–86.
7 G. Lordan and D. Neumark, 'People versus machines: the impact of minimum wages on automatable jobs', *Labour Economics,* forthcoming, 2018.
8 T. Fetzer, 'Did austerity cause Brexit?', working paper 381, Economics Department, Warwick University, 2018.
9 A. de Bromhead, B. Eichengreen and K. O'Rourke, 'Right-wing political extremism in the Great Depression', VoxEU blog post, 27 February 2012; https://voxeu.org/article/right-wing-political-extremism-great-depression (accessed 14 January 2019).

How to cite this article: S. Wren-Lewis, 'Macroeconomic Policy Beyond Brexit', in G Kelly and N Pearce (eds.), Britain Beyond Brexit, *The Political Quarterly*, Vol 90, Issue S2, 2019, pp. 44–52. https://doi.org/10.1111/1467-923X.12647

# The Prospects for the UK Labour Market in the Post-Brexit Era

STEPHEN CLARKE AND PAUL GREGG

OVER THE last fifty years, the main challenges facing the UK labour market have shifted. In the 1970s and early 1980s, high wage and price inflation and a wage-price spiral were central concerns, before inflation and wage growth slowed dramatically from the mid-1990s. Mass unemployment became the central concern of the late 1980s and early 1990s, yet this too has given way as the UK now has the highest employment rate in its history. For nearly two decades up until 2007, earnings inequalities between the highest and lowest paid grew sharply; now this too has declined in salience. The financial crisis ushered in today's problems: stagnant wages and the (re-)emergence of insecure and casualised work.

These shifts reflected changes in the wider economy, such as the end of the OPEC oil price hikes, but also changes in policy which responded to concerns. In the 1980s, governments allowed unemployment to rise in order to curb wage growth along with the emasculation of trade unions. The chronic worklessness of the mid-1990s (partly a result of the previous policy shift) induced a response of minimum wages, the extension of tax credits and subsidised childcare to make work more financially attractive, especially to (single) parents. Minimum wages and the rapid growth in the supply of graduates partly addressed earnings inequality.

The post-Brexit era is likely to be another critical juncture in our jobs market. The decision to leave the European Union has already had profound effects. Some are obvious: sterling's depreciation after the vote has reduced real (after inflation) wages by around 4 per cent. Net migration has fallen, even before any change in the country's immigration system. Others shifts, such as lower investment by businesses unsure about the future, are more opaque. Looking forward, the key questions now are: has the Brexit-shock largely played out, or does it have much further to go, with further pressures arising until a final post-Brexit settlement is finally reached? And how will any Brexit-related pressures interact with pre-existing trends that are changing labour markets across advanced countries? In this chapter we will focus on three such trends: international migration, job polarisation driven by technological change, and the shifting of risk from firms and the state onto workers. First, however, we analyse recent developments in the UK labour market.

Published by John Wiley & Sons Ltd, 9600 Garsington Road, Oxford OX4 2DQ, UK and 350 Main Street, Malden, MA 02148, USA

## Brexit and recent developments in the labour market

Wages (after inflation) have been experiencing an unprecedented period of stagnation, with the last decade being the worst on record since the 1860s. As of June 2018, average wages were still 2.6 per cent below the pre-crisis peak, which equates to £680 a year for the typical (median) worker. Wage growth slowed before the financial crisis (from around 2002) and the post-crisis decade of stagnation has included two periods of falling pay. Each followed a major devaluation of sterling: first, soon after the recession hit, and the second, after the Brexit vote. Even outside the periods affected by the devaluations, (real) wage growth appears to be subdued at approximately 1 per cent a year.

Wages used to respond to inflation shocks; in the 1970s oil price hikes resulted in a wage-price spiral. This no longer seems the case: following the two recent devaluations of sterling, import prices rose, thereby boosting inflation and eroding real wages. The post-referendum devaluation of 12 per cent pushed up prices by 4 per cent over 2017 and 2018, with no response from earnings. This is now unwinding and underlying real wage growth is still only around 1 per cent a year. This weakness reflects longer-run forces that determine wage growth: productivity and unemployment.

One view is that the UK's poor productivity growth since the crisis, combined with imported inflation shocks, sent wages into negative territory. In this story, weak productivity drives weak wages. However, the post-2007 fall in productivity was driven by the fact that—unlike the experience in other countries or indeed in the UK in the 1980s and 1990s recessions—employment barely fell after the crash. Real wages fell sharply and so labour became cheaper, making the squeeze on profits negligible. So, poor productivity growth has, in part, been driven by weak wages. The lack of wage pressure has dulled the incentive for firms to invest and improve efficiency, which in turn would boost wages. The virtuous circle of rising wages incentivising firms to invest in labour-saving technology, and in turn boosting pay, is the real engine of rising living standards, but it has stalled, with the weakness of sterling playing a large part.

One thing that could restart the virtuous circle would be further falls in unemployment. The lesson of the late 1990s fall in unemployment was that unemployment movements are an important driver of wage growth. Yet the recent falls in unemployment do not appear to be having the expected effect.[1] This might be a temporary abeyance of normal patterns, but there is also evidence that having a large number of workers in insecure employment (discussed below) might have a similarly chilling effect on wages as higher unemployment.

The flipside of the awful performance of wages since the crash has been the spectacular jobs growth, with the proportion of the working age population in work at an all-time high. Employment growth has been very pro-poor, bringing into work groups who normally have low participation rates, such as the less well educated, those with disabilities and single mothers. There are still significant gaps to close—in particular for people with disabilities—but the improvements for these groups remain a feature of the UK labour over the past couple of decades worth celebrating.

While jobs are relatively plentiful, insecure forms of employment have grown. Agency working, zero hours contracts and, the most important in terms of numbers, self-employment have all risen substantially since the 2008 crash. Increased self-employment represents one in four of the 3.3 million jobs added since the onset of the crisis and, although the rate of the increase in zero hours contracts has been more dramatic, such contracts still only affect 2.4 per cent of the workforce. Growth in 'atypical' forms of employment have recently halted as the labour market has tightened, but it remains to be seen how far they will unwind.

It's possible these concerns may fade if the labour market continues to strengthen, no further serious devaluations occur, and policy-makers respond to public anxieties about insecure employment. Yet there are deeper-seated forces that have shaped the UK labour market over the past two decades which are unlikely to disappear.

## Post-Brexit challenges

### Migration

Until the late 1990s, net migration flows into the UK were relatively small. In the 1960s and 1970s more people left the UK than migrated to the country and even in the 1980s and 1990s, net migration averaged just 30,000 a year. The accession of the A8 states to the EU in 2004 increased immigration dramatically. On the eve of the Brexit referendum, the number of EU citizens working in the UK had reached 2.3 million, and in many sectors, such as food manufacturing, hotels, logistics and scientific research, migrants formed over a quarter of the workforce.

The vote to leave the EU brought a significant shift. Net migration has fallen from 336,000 in the year to June 2016, to 282,000 in the year to December 2017 and the number of EU nationals in employment fell in the year to June 2018 for the first time since 2010. This has happened without any new restrictions on EU migration. Not all of the recent decline in migration is the (direct) result of the decision to leave the EU, though: the value of sterling and the improving economic situation in countries of origin will have both played a role.

It is not clear what will happen when the country leaves the EU. Although the government is yet to decide on the key dimensions of the post-Brexit migration system, the Migration Advisory Committee (MAC), following a commission by the government, has outlined how it believes the system should change. The MAC calls for an end to free movement and that any future migration system should prioritise higher-skilled migrants. To this end, it recommends that there should be no specific route for low-skilled migrants (other than in agriculture), more mid-skilled roles should qualify for working visas and that the current £30,000 salary threshold be retained. If the government follows the MAC's recommendations, it will bring about the biggest change in the UK's immigration system for a generation.

Whether or not the MAC's proposals are introduced in whole (unlikely) or in part (more likely), numbers will probably continue to come down, and the government is also likely to permit sectors such as health, construction, education and others that rely on skilled labour, to access the workers they need. Indeed, in the case of the NHS it has already done so. The government will also pilot a revival of the Seasonal Agricultural Workers Scheme (SAWS) over the next two years. If other lower-paying sectors are not granted similar bespoke arrangements, the slowdown in migration will be felt in parts of the economy that have become reliant on a steady supply of foreign workers. These include low-value manufacturing, domestic services, hospitality and logistics. EU migrants account for a large share of employees in these sectors, staff turnover is high, and the vast majority of these workers would not qualify for a visa under the UK's current points-based immigration system for non-EU migrants.

A decline in lower-skilled migration is unlikely to have much effect on the wages of native workers. There is a broad consensus that migration has had no significant impact on wages for the average or typical native employee, and although there is some evidence that migration may have reduced the earnings of some groups of lower-paid workers, the impacts have been small.[2] In part, this is because minimum wage rates dictate the pay of a significant number of low-skilled employees and the National Living Wage (NLW) is rising rapidly.

The real impact of lower migration is that it will affect *how much* the UK economy produces, *where* things are produced and *how* they are produced. While migration increases GDP, low-skilled migration (so leaving aside the role of migrants in filling skills shortages) has little impact on GDP per capita. Less output is likely, but is not unduly worrying. More interesting is the possibility of substantive change in how firms operate, which may spur improvements in productivity. So far, there is little evidence that firms are ready to change their business models. Despite the fact that three-quarters of firms in low-paying sectors believe that a fall in migration would affect their business, the majority think that after the UK leaves the EU, there will be either no change to freedom of movement, or all migrants with a job offer will be allowed to work in the UK.[3] Furthermore, the majority of firms do not believe that lower migration would encourage them to automate or change the way their business operates. This may change with time as firms realise the scale of the recruitment problems they face.

## Artificial intelligence and technological change

Technological change profoundly affects the work we do, often in unpredictable ways. Since the industrial revolution, technological innovations have usually been considered to be skills-biased—that is, technological change increases the demand for high-skilled workers. Pioneering research has established that the rise of digital technologies worked against those with routine jobs, because computers are good at performing repetitive routine physical and cognitive tasks.[4] Across developed countries, mid-skilled (often mid-paid) occupations such as plant and machine operatives, secretarial and administrative roles, have declined as a share of all jobs from the mid-1970s onwards.

In the UK, there is a strong relationship between the decline in the share of hours worked in the economy between 1993 and 2016 and the extent to which an occupation involves doing routine tasks.[5] However, the UK experienced an occupational 'upgrading' rather than a 'hollowing out' or 'polarisation'. Strong growth in some lower-paying occupations (such as in caring, personal service occupations, where the share of hours worked has increased by 45 per cent since the millennium) was combined with growth in mid paid roles in health and social care, culture and the media, as well as a significant rise in higher-paid professional and technical roles.

Recent advances in artificial intelligence (AI) have led people to suggest that many of the tasks that economists previously classified as non-routine may now be within the grasp of computers. AI systems can now successfully diagnose lung and heart cancer more accurately than doctors; they can review simple legal documents for risks and errors more accurately, and around 200 times faster than lawyers.[6] Some have even estimated that 47 per cent of jobs in the US are at high risk of automation,[7] though other more fine-grained studies suggest a far smaller share of the workforce is under threat.[8]

Indeed, recent data from the UK suggests remarkably little change. Of the occupations that were expanding or contracting between 2001 and 2007, two-thirds were still expanding or contracting between 2014 and 2017, and the pace of change was actually *slower* than before the crisis. Furthermore, workers with higher levels of education are still less likely to be in a shrinking occupation, as are higher earners. What has changed, though, is that younger workers are now more likely to be in lower paying and shrinking industries than in the past, with declining working hours for younger, lower-paid, men. There are some parallels with recent research from the US that shows a marked slowdown in the progression of recent graduates into higher paying occupations, suggesting that demand for skills has shifted and that this has had most impact on younger workers.

Given the large-scale increase in overall employment levels since the crash, there is no evidence of technological change leading to lower levels of employment. Robots may not be taking all our jobs any time soon. But technological change is reducing opportunities for lower-skilled workers, though this may be offset at least partially by lower migration. In essence, there is a race between changing demand for skills and the changing supply, which is shaped heavily by policy decisions. Technological change requires an ongoing policy response to boost skills and their utilisation by firms. But —and it's a big but—the expansion of the skills base in Britain has slowed dramatically. The growth in the share of each cohort attending higher education has slowed and other educational routes have not picked up the slack. Technological change appears to be reducing well-paid opportunities for less-skilled young people, at the same time as human capital accumulation among young people has slowed.

## Shifting risk onto workers

The cumulative effect of the underlying changes in the labour market over the last twenty years, an effect likely to be exacerbated by Brexit, is that workers are shouldering ever more risk. This comes at a time when younger workers, in particular, are likely to be less able to do so. One of the results of the fact that wages no longer respond to imported inflation shocks is that the risks associated with currency volatility and commodity (oil) price movements now fall immediately onto labour. Workers should be paying close attention to exchange rate shifts, not just because they affect the price of a Spanish holiday, but because they increasingly determine real living standards. Large exchange rate movements (a 10 per cent appreciation or depreciation) are relatively common—since 1990 they have occurred approximately once every three to five years—and moves of this size will move real wages by 3 per cent upwards (appreciation) or downwards (depreciation) compared to what otherwise would have been the case. Until recently, real wage falls were almost unheard of (outside of wartime or through government wage controls), yet we have had two periods of falling wages in the last decade after the two large depreciations. Going forward, we may well experience more, particularly as on-going Brexit uncertainty makes the likelihood of such exchange rate moves more likely.

In the last recession, wages fell but few jobs were lost because of a large depreciation. The depreciation occurred because the UK was more heavily affected by the banking crisis than other countries. There is no reason, however, why the next recession need be the same. If the UK is less affected by the next recession than other countries, then an appreciation of sterling is likely and we would expect a return to the norm of past UK recessions, where the main adjustment is in the form of job losses rather than wage falls. Should this occur, the higher prevalence of atypical forms of work now than in the past is likely to exacerbate both the scale of job losses and the fall in working hours, as firms can easily pass lower demand onto workers. The result is likely to be greater earnings volatility for lower-paid workers—due to changes in hours of work more than hourly pay. New research shows that for someone earning £25,000 a year and remaining with the same employer throughout the year, the average change in earnings from month to month was 8 per cent in 2016–17, but for those earning around £10,000 it was closer to 12 per cent.[9] The next recession could markedly amplify this type of income insecurity.

Risks around today's living standards are not the only ones increasingly borne by workers. The closing of defined benefit pension schemes to new members means that all pension risk from movements in stock markets and interest rates will also be borne by the workforce. Over a lifetime, these may even out, but shocks close to, or after, retirement, will become very significant. Finally, the welfare state no longer offers much insurance against unemployment, and cash transfers for those on low incomes are less generous than they used to be. All of the above, along with declines in assets, home ownership, and savings net of debt—particularly for the younger generation—mean that the normal buffers against adverse shocks look weaker than in the past. British workers in the post-Brexit era will be exposed. Almost a decade since the last one, we are due a recession in the relatively near future and a more vulnerable workforce will amplify its effects on the economy.

## Where next?

There is a lot that policy makers can do to respond to these challenges. First, addressing new forms of casualised work (zero hours contracts, low-paid self-employment) would reduce the chance that when the next recession hits, it disproportionately affects those at the bottom of the labour market, with both hours worked and employment falling rapidly for those on casual contracts. Greater protection for these workers would help spread the impact of any adjustment. Addressing atypical work would also benefit the exchequer, reducing the tax loss from self-employment, and would help shift some of the risk from workers back onto employers. Policy should also help people to protect themselves. Asset based welfare needs rebooting. The current approach—a mixture of tax relief on savings accounts, tax-efficient investment vehicles and relief on pension contributions, alongside punishing savings in Universal Credit—is expensive, regressive and does little to encourage low earners to save. Auto-enrolment means that the infrastructure is in place to encourage work-based saving, with opportunities for the state to make matched contributions and protect these savings in the benefit system. Expanding schemes that target those on low incomes, such as 'Help to Save', would help. Crucially, this should be a complement, not a substitute, to traditional forms of welfare support or to the social investment strategies pursued in the 1990s and 2000s.

Technological change and the expansion of AI means that policy makers need to support sustained increases in workforce skills. To date this has been done almost entirely through post-A-level university enrolment, but this expansion has slowed sharply and routes for those who do not attend university remain limited in both quality and scope. There are other options. The development of a technical education route at the end of normal schooling remains an unfulfilled vision. To make it reality requires ensuring that the Apprenticeship Levy and the move to T-levels boosts the technical education system, so that young people are better served by them being offered more quality and choice. This simply has not happened under the current system.

Furthermore, this isn't all about improving labour supply. The (limited) experience of the Apprenticeship Levy to date shows that how *employers* interact with the skills system and utilise the talents of their employees is just as important as what goes on in the education system. The lack of preparation by many firms for a reduction in migrant labour and the fact that three-quarters of senior business decision makers are unaware of T-levels (and the role that businesses will be expected to play in delivering them) shows that the government needs to engage more, and systems need to be designed so that they encourage skills utilisation and not just the hitting of targets.

Finally, we need to get wages moving again. A good (set of) post-Brexit trade deal(s) may lead to a recovery in sterling, lower inflation and a boost to real wages. And unemployment may fall further which should eventually bid up pay. However, minimum wages rates are already set to rise to among the highest in the developed world, and pushing further would be to move into uncharted territory. The NLW is reducing pay differentials at the bottom of the labour market, blunting incentives for workers to seek promotion and take on more seniority. At some point, further falls in pay differentials may become problematic for an efficient labour market.

Trade unions—or other new forms of worker organisation—are an obvious answer. They counteract the imbalance of power between firms and workers when setting wages, and help ensure that workers take a share of any monopolistic rents. In this way, they have similar effects as minimum wage legislation, but are more sensitive to a firm's specific ability to pay and preserve pay differentials. However, halting the decline in membership, especially among the young, would require active support from government. As well as this, other forms of worker empowerment should be considered, for example, occupational licensing (where there are specific concerns about quality or safety), improving the transparency and power of workers in pay negotiations and helping lower-paid workers overcome barriers that may prevent them from moving employer.

The labour market may feel relatively benign right now, but we are probably closer to the next recession than the last one. When it comes, there is no reason to think that the recent mix of small job losses and large wage falls will occur again. More importantly, the large increase in economic risk being borne by workers, especially those in atypical work, is shifting the costs of a downturn onto workers and away from firms. This, along with the pressures that Brexit will place on the UK economy, means that business as usual is not enough. Recent history shows us that policy can help address the weaknesses of the UK labour market and prepare for what lies ahead. We must adapt now rather than in the teeth of the next crisis.

## Notes

1 D. N. F. Bell and D. G. Blanchflower, 'Underemployment and the lack of wage pressure in the UK', *National Institute Economic Review*, vol. 243, no. 1, February 2018, R53–R61.

2 Migration Advisory Committee, *EEA Migration in the UK: Final Report*, 18 September 2018.

3 S. Clarke, *Work in Brexit Britain: Reshaping the Nation's Labour Market*, Resolution Foundation, 7 July 2017.

4 D. H. Autor, F. Levy and R. J. Murnane, 'The skill content of recent technological change: an empirical exploration', *The Quarterly Journal of Economics*, vol. 118, no. 4, 2003, pp. 1279–1333; and M. Goos and A. Manning, 'Lousy and lovely jobs: the rising polarization of work in Britain', *Review of Economics and Statistics*, vol. 89, no. 1, 2007, pp. 118–133.

5 A. Corlett, *Robot Wars: Automation and the UK Labour Market*, Resolution Foundation, 4 July 2016.

6 K. Leary, 'AI can diagnose heart disease and lung cancer more accurately than doctors', *Futurism*, January 2018; and K. Leary, 'The verdict is in: AI outperforms human lawyers in reviewing legal documents', *Futurism*, February 2018.

7 C. B. Frey and M. A. Osborne, 'The future of employment: how susceptible are jobs to computerisation?', *Technological Forecasting and Social Change*, vol. 114, issue C, 2017, pp. 254–280.

8 L. Nedelkoska and G. Quintini, 'Automation, skills use and training', OECD Social, Employment and Migration Working Papers, no. 202, OECD Publishing, 2018.

9 D. Tomlinson and P. Jefferson, Resolution Foundation, forthcoming.

How to cite this article: S. Clarke and P. Gregg, 'The Prospects for the UK Labour Market in the Post-Brexit Era', in G Kelly and N Pearce (eds.), Britain Beyond Brexit, *The Political Quarterly*, Vol 90, Issue S2, 2019, pp. 53–61. https://doi.org/10.1111/1467-923X.12618

# Dual Disruptions: Brexit and Technology

DIANE COYLE

THE UK FACES two significant economic challenges in the years ahead: Brexit, and digital disruption. They are likely to reinforce each other. Although there are largely separate public debates about each, businesses, policymakers and citizens will have to deal with both at the same time. To make matters worse, they are going to interact in challenging ways. It is not obvious that the British state has the capacity to develop a strategic approach to managing the economy in order to respond to the disruptions ahead, although there are signs of a dawning recognition that the existing model will not serve in the context of significant structural economic change and diminished access to the European market.

## Dual disruptions

The economic consequences of Brexit have been hotly debated, but the heat generated by the media and political debate does not reflect the overwhelming balance of opinion among economists that these consequences will be negative. For the forty-five years since the UK first joined the EEC, the trading links between this country and the growing number of other member states have increased in number and in scope. Adam Smith's original insight that mutual gains would come from specialisation and exchange applies across borders as well as within them. The Single Market, signed into being in 1986, accelerated the growth of this network of economic links between the UK and our nearest neighbours. Brexit does not mean 'leaving' as in leaving a club one no longer wants to belong to; it means breaching commercial (and human) relationships dating back decades. It is not possible to 'leave' history without damage. So, Brexit is without question going to disrupt the economy.

Meanwhile, continuing technological change promises to be another source of economic disruption. In one way, a big dose of new technology is exactly what the economy needs, given the Brexit headwinds. The widespread adoption of innovations to use the available resources more effectively in producing better goods and services is precisely the mechanism driving higher living standards, the quality of life, health and longevity over time. Britain's longstanding poor productivity performance compared to other major economies has many contributing factors, but low business investment in new capital equipment—automation, in other words—is one of them.

For example, the 2017 annual report from the International Federation of Robotics showed the UK to have been lagging well behind the other large

Published by John Wiley & Sons Ltd, 9600 Garsington Road, Oxford OX4 2DQ, UK and 350 Main Street, Malden, MA 02148, USA

European countries in the number of multi-purpose industrial robots pur-chased. The UK has the lowest business investment as a proportion of GDP of all the G7 nations. Low quality management in many British firms is part of the story too, Britain having a fewer high productivity firms and a longer 'tail' of low productivity firms than comparable economies.[1]

Given this lacklustre record, it is hard to believe that some of the more sensational predictions of job losses due to automation will be realised. Yet even 10 per cent of existing jobs falling to 'robots' in sectors ranging from law to retail to manufacturing poses a substantial policy challenge. It is a challenge that Britain has failed to address in the previous waves of creative destruction, due to technology, the deindustrialisation of the 1980s and 1990s, when manufacturing was substantially automated. High unemploy-ment, low skills, ill health and the whole cluster of markers of poverty and powerlessness scar the former manufacturing heartlands. Indeed, we are still living with the consequences in many ways, not least in the geography of the Brexit vote itself.[2]

This is not to say we should hope to halt the wave of digital disruption. The official productivity figures may not show it, but access to new tech-nologies has brought consumers amazing services at low cost. We can easily access information, education, entertainment from almost anywhere at low cost. People place great value on the world that digital technology has opened up to them.[3] The consumer benefits are large. Newer technologies on the horizon offer possibly larger benefits, in areas from synthetic biology to new materials to green energy, as well as continuing innovations in digi-tal such as robotics and AI.

However, there are some obvious costs, among them the disruption borne by the businesses who lose out, and their employees. This is the normal churn of a market economy; there is a surprising amount of employment turnover all the time. It becomes a problem if there is too much, too quickly, or in too concentrated an area. The UK has a record high employment rate so to the extent that technology-driven disruption is already affecting jobs, it is happening through conditions of employment, including pay. The avail-able evidence—which is less complete than would be ideal—suggests that patterns such as self-employment, 'gig' work, short term and zero hours con-tracts either offer satisfying flexibility for professionals or badly paid, casu-alised work for people with no labour market power. And average real earnings in the UK were, in late 2017, still lower than at the end of 2008, although the earnings premium for the highly skilled remains high. Income inequality is another troubling result of digital disruption.

Why do these two sets of challenges amplify each other? Digital disrup-tion makes Brexit costlier, because the UK's capacity to respond to the speci-fic challenges it poses will be hampered by the reduction in the scale of the market that British firms, especially in technology, can address; by with-drawal from EU competition and regulatory processes; by the potential loss of British engagement with overseas researchers and the financial harm the loss of overseas students will do to our universities.

Brexit will make the technology-driven creative destruction harder to respond to because the upheaval will probably be occurring when the economy is weak, whereas buoyant growth would help make the labour market adjustment as smooth as possible. And yet without the adjustment, the UK's productivity record will continue to be disappointing.

## The importance of scale in the digital economy

The UK has significant areas of digital expertise and existing important clusters of research and employment. These would not disappear and could continue to grow and produce innovative research, as long as the supply of skilled people from British universities continues (although it should be noted that overseas researchers and students form an important part of this pipeline). However, scale is fundamental to the dynamics of digital markets and—outside the Single Market—the UK would face two sets of limits due to loss of scale: in terms of the capacity to shape digital markets and in financing innovative companies.

Large economies of scale feature in many technology-intensive products and services, since much of the cost is weighted toward upfront elements of investment, including software, research, design, development and prototyping. Some also involve major investments in capital equipment, including parts of the digital sector (think of server farms for cloud computing, or the infrastructure for high frequency trading). When initial costs are so high relative to ongoing costs of selling an extra unit (which are nearly zero for many digital products), the most efficient market structure is to have just a few very large firms. In digital markets, this advantage of large scale on the production side is reinforced by network effects on the user side: the more users there are, the more all of them gain from the service, as in telephone networks, but also booking platforms, online marketplaces or social media networks.

Scale is so fundamental to these kinds of markets, both digital or physical networks, that the UK will have to adhere post-Brexit to European and global technical standards and regulations (whatever the political rhetoric). As an example of the power of a common technical and regulatory framework, consider the rapid spread of mobile phones. Europe's GSM standard, first agreed in the EU in 1987 and now serving more than 80 per cent of global mobile markets, enabled roaming agreements between networks, reduced manufacturers' and operators' research and development costs, and allowed mass production on a consistent technical standard, greatly reducing the prices of handsets and network equipment.

When initial costs are high, the bigger the market that can be addressed, the better; and a common framework makes for a big market. We should never want UK-specific regulation, or technical specifications in any of these markets, if we are to avoid lower quality and more expensive products and services. We certainly want to ensure continued access to the large European market. So, it is hard to think of anything more damaging for the prospects or possibly even viability of the UK's thriving tech sector than Theresa May's assertion that Britain will not stay in the digital Single Market.[4] A balkanised digital world has fewer benefits and higher costs than British voters are used to, at least in markets smaller in scale than China. Outside the Single Market, the UK is unlikely to be anything other than a taker of rules and standards set elsewhere, and at best, riding on the coat-tails of regulation and enforcement action by the EU authorities.

Another aspect of the importance of economies of scale is the need to capture a large enough market quickly enough not to go out of business. Many new tech-based companies fail. The success stories typically need to raise large amounts of investment to cover their loss-making initial phase. This means that access to sufficiently patient investors with deep enough pockets is essential; venture capital fits the bill. A large home market, with consumers inclined toward domestic businesses, is also a huge benefit. There is a reason the digital giants are American and Chinese, and it is because of the characteristic economic structure of these businesses rather than any nefarious favouritism, although that helps too. The European Union is a similarly large market, although barriers of language and the remaining barriers in services are hindrances. British entrants into digital and high-tech markets will be at a disadvantage in terms of potential initial scale, post-Brexit. Nor do we have a good record in financing innovative companies to compensate for it; indeed in 2015 most of the venture capital finance in the UK came from government (including EU) sources, at £286 million out of a total of £321 million (Industrial Strategy Commission, 2017). Brexit will hamper our start-ups even more, given the probability of British businesses having more restricted market access to the EU's 500 million people.

## Competition

Finding the right structure of ownership and regulatory framework for markets featuring large economies of scale is inherently difficult, as demonstrated by the unsettled history of the electricity and rail industries, for instance. The dilemmas are similar in any network markets, digital ones included. These are dominated by the American tech giants, collectively known as GAFA (Google, Amazon, Facebook, Apple; sometimes Microsoft is added; sometimes Uber features). Market concentration in the digital sector has become a recent focus of policy concern, including for the European Commission. The EU's much-admired competition Commissioner, Margrethe Vestager, has taken a robust stance against the GAFA group, among others. The Commission has moved much further than US authorities in regulating data use and privacy, including through the new GDPR rules; a number of

European countries have also announced investigations into the online advertising market, dominated by just Google and Facebook.

Adapting competition policy to the digital era requires rethinking the standard tools used to assess markets. The analyses currently used are not suited to the dynamics of winner-take-all markets, where a handful of large companies are dominant at any given time, in what economists describe as competition 'for' the market, rather than 'in' the market. But this does not mean a suitably tough competition policy is impossible within the current policy framework. If the markets are more or less natural monopolies, delivering large consumer benefits short-term, competition in the long-term depends on the incumbents staying vulnerable to the next wave of Schumpeterian creative destruction. The GAFA group claim this keeps them awake at night. Myspace looked all-conquering until Facebook vanquished it; now Facebook perhaps worries that its user engagement is in decline, or that young people are moving to other platforms.

Some scepticism about this is in order. There is a vigorous debate about how to regulate the digital markets, where one or two very large companies are likely to dominate—and indeed the consumer benefits depend on that scale, thanks to the network effects—but need to remain vulnerable to a newcomer taking over their position. Some lawyers and economists argue for a wholesale retreat from modern competition policy based on economic analysis, and direct government intervention in the form of regulation, or breaking up the dominant businesses, on the grounds that the giants are obviously just too big.[5] The problem with tackling dominance by reducing scale through break-up or regulation is the *inevitable* counter-productive effects, degrading or limiting access to services that consumers love.

The alternative is to update regulatory and competition policy to enable new entrants to get a foothold and grow, and to prevent the incumbents buying up future rivals or innovating in predatory ways designed to keep out future competition. Competition authorities should clearly investigate the online advertising market, which is a duopoly marred by extensive fraud and abuse. Some additional regulation will surely be needed too, concerning transparency of terms and conditions, fair dealing with consumers and other businesses, and inter-operability between platforms—especially in the transferability of personal data. But the outlines of what is needed are emerging. The regulators need to focus on the possibility of entry and the scope for innovation and investment, and also need to rule out more readily than in the past certain kinds of acquisition by digital companies.[6]

Given that the dominant companies are American, the countervailing weight of the EU's competition and regulatory apparatus is probably necessary to bring about changes in their practices and behaviours. When it comes to policing the behaviour of the American giants, the European Commission will be a more effective watchdog than any individual national competition authority. Not even Google can afford to ignore the EU, whereas it may try to politely ignore a post-Brexit Britain that has removed itself from the digital Single Market.

## Innovation

A final area of significant challenge lies in the research-intensive character of new and growing technology businesses. The UK has some long-standing weaknesses here, including in converting research glory into commercially viable applications. The institutions we have for converting academic results into products and services that will both drive the economy and, more importantly, make people's lives better do not function well. Other countries have less of a gap between thinking about the blue skies and tilling the commercial soil, with varying kinds of intermediary institutions, such as Germany's admired Fraunhofer Institutes. Brexit will not make any difference here, but it may do some harm to the basic research the UK excels in.

The UK has an enviable record in basic research, with our universities punching well above their weight internationally. This is under threat in two ways and Brexit is clearly one of them. The anti-immigrant thread in UK politics and Theresa May's stubborn refusal to exclude students from the migration statistics form a backdrop; the financial viability of UK higher education involves a large cross-subsidy from overseas students' fees to domestic students.[7] Brexit is also driving away overseas-born academics, who currently form 28 per cent of the academic workforce in British universities (16 per cent EU and 12 per cent non-EU). What's more, UK researchers' access to European research funding and collaborations is under threat, at least according to ample anecdotal evidence.

## Taking a strategic view?

In short, Brexit is interacting with challenges due to changing economic structure and technology in ways that are mutually reinforcing. This is going to make it harder than ever to overcome longstanding weaknesses in the economy—yet also more urgent than ever that the problems are finally tackled.

Successfully meeting the challenges will involve multiple areas of policy, in some of which the UK government will be at a big disadvantage in being outside the EU structures. The British economy is going to be less linked into international scientific research structures, to funding for new and growing businesses, less well able to achieve the necessary rapid expansion in new high-tech businesses that depends on scaling quickly in a large market, less effective in ensuring there is no abuse of dominant market positions, and either divergent from international standards and regulations or compelled to observe them while having no influence on them.

In addition to the challenges this poses for policy development and implementation in specific areas, above all, it calls for a more strategic approach to the management of the economy than the UK has been able to achieve for well over a generation. The government's Industrial Strategy White Paper, published in November 2017, gave some hope that realisation had dawned that the chimera of 'free' markets and absence of government from any coordinating role in the economy may explain why the level of UK productivity and living standards have been so much lower than comparable economies for so long.

Subsequently, there have been some welcome individual policy initiatives, but not amounting to the joined-up, strategic view that will be needed. The UK, more than ever in the light of Brexit, needs to develop the full range of capabilities needed in some key technology-led domains. This includes basic and advanced skills, a stable regulatory framework, investment in research and its translation into business applications, infrastructure improvements in everything from fixed and mobile broadband, to commuter transport around the country, along with the regulatory wiring that helps any economy function. This includes competition policy and a replacement for the EU's state aid rules—for without that, the old complaint that 'picking winners' means propping up losers is likely to be validated. Achieving this across the whole waterfront of new technologies will not be possible, so selectivity of aims (not sectors, still less, individual companies) is necessary. Using the power of the state as a purchaser via the NHS and social care makes a focus on innovation in these areas an obvious priority, given the rising demands of an ageing population. There is real scope here, too, to export any successful innovations. Other aims could include clean energy or batteries, or life sciences. The UK could build on existing strengths in the creative industries.

## Digital policy innovation

Regardless of Brexit, although perhaps given more urgency by the context of likely economic disruption, alternative approaches to some digital market are desirable. It is not only that they have high fixed, upfront costs. They also feature 'network effects', meaning that the more people use them, the greater the benefit to the people already using them—hence the winner-takes-all dynamic described earlier. They feature other externalities, such as the way personal data becomes valuable when it is combined with other people's data—think of the scope to made medical discoveries from large-scale health data, for example. And they are 'public goods' in the technical sense that one person using them does not prevent other people using them at the same time (hence clean air is a public good, but an apple is a private good). The big digital companies therefore have a lot in common with other sectors which have either often been in public ownership and are highly regulated, even when privately owned and operated. The state, as well as the market, has a role—and yet the digital firms delivering essential services in the modern economy are both private and relatively lightly regulated.

As noted earlier, the UK's withdrawal from the EU and the Single Market will lead to weaker bargaining strength vis-à-vis the digital powers. Yet there is scope for creative policy drawing on lessons from other sectors.

One kind of lesson comes from the UK's success in broadcasting, where the regulatory framework for public service broadcasting in general, and the licence fee funded BBC in particular, have achieved several outcomes: a competitive market where the presence of the licence payer-owned BBC has ensured that competition is about quality and not a lowest common denominator race; a public research and development engine (the BBC again) which has played a big part in setting global technical standards and making audiences in Britain early adopters of innovations such as on-demand services and HD; an important public source of skills and experience for the commercial sector; and—thanks to all of these—a thriving creative sector which successfully exports. The mixed economy approach of having a publicly-owned entity with a public service mission is attractive, because it means there is an alternative business model and culture. It potentially changes the dynamics of the market for the better. What's more, this is a policy approach the UK could try solo, and goes to the heart of some of the gravest concerns about the impact of a small number of giant digital companies.

Ownership is not the key point, though. In general, the features of digital markets mean effective policies need to consider the balance between the state and private sector in their regulation and governance. The zero-marginal cost of digital goods means the economically efficient price is zero too. Users often have a choice between commercial versions funded by advertising—with all the adverse consequences that has for quality and for investment in quality content—and open source alternatives funded by voluntary activity, which will be limited in scale and capacity, even if excellent. Neither the 'free market' nor the 'collective' approach seems ideal. Is the answer just to apply tougher regulation to the private providers, and if so are there any effective lessons from the older regulated utilities? This is a dispiriting prospect, given the present dissatisfaction with water, rail and energy markets. Nor is it clear how the digital companies would react to a post-Brexit UK trying to get tough in regulatory terms. Unfortunately, there has been little thought given to other, more creative ways of achieving the public good through what we must never forget are amazing and highly appreciated technologies. The dual disruptions, Brexit and digital, make this an urgent agenda.

## Conclusion

Is the British state up to the task of implementing a strategic approach to the management of the economy in the face of some daunting challenges? The answer is not clear.

One complication in terms of developing a strategic co-ordinating role for government in managing the economy is the process of devolution, to the nations and the English city regions. This is a highly desirable development in one of the most centralised and regionally unbalanced economies (and polities) in the OECD. There are many aspects of economic policy, from commuter transport planning to further education that, devolved, can potentially deliver better productivity growth and living standards outside of south-east England and London. However, devolution makes it harder to achieve coordination at national scale and in international markets. Developing the political and governance framework to both devolve and coordinate is a significant challenge.

There are several other challenges. The civil service, although depleted and damagingly frequently attacked by ministers, has many capable people. But its age-old weakness of focusing on analysis rather than implementation persists, and Whitehall officials have too little experience of either the country outside London or of business in general. Their naivety can occasionally be breath-taking. Better and more strategic economic policy requires administrators with more experience of other worlds. There is a delicate balance in public life between not enough and too much understanding of the commercial world, but the scale is presently tipped toward the former.

More serious is the absence of a solid political consensus about the economic policy imperatives. Politicians are not thinking about much apart from Brexit, when Brexit makes it more important that they think about all the other challenges. In many policy areas, the political seesaw has been highly disruptive. Think for example of the twenty-eight major reforms of vocational education policy (under forty-eight secretaries of state) in less than forty years, with no delivery institution surviving for longer than a decade.[8] Or the successive upheavals in energy policy, likely to be upended again with Brexit. Another political and governance challenge is finding a balance between political accountability (and thus the possibility of changing policies) and the continuity essential for investment, be that by businesses or by individuals planning their education and training.

Nor has the broader climate of ideas—yet—coalesced around a paradigm for strategic economic management in the context of significant technological innovations driving new productive forces and business models. The intellectual conversation is underway, and there have been some important recent contributions to it;[9] but the UK does not have the luxury of waiting long for a national economic vision—a new British economic model—to get the country through the twin challenges of Brexit and technological disruption.

Consensual political leadership could speed this up; all that is visible is division within and between the major parties.

## Notes

1 Organisation for Economic Co-operation and Development (OECD), *The Future of Productivity*, 2015; http://www.oecd.org/eco/OECD-2015-The-future-of-productivity-

book.pdf (accessed 1 November 2018). A. Haldane, 'Productivity puzzles', speech at the London School of Economics, March 2017; https://www.bankofengland.co.uk/-/med ia/boe/files/speech/2017/productivity-puzzles.pdf?la=en&hash=708C7CFD5E 8417000655BA4AA0E0E873D98A18DE (accessed 1 November 2018).

2 S. Becker, T. Fetzer and D. Novy, 'Who voted for Brexit? A comprehensive district-level analysis', *Economic Policy*, vol. **32**, no. 92, 2017, pp. 601–650. See also VoxEU, 'The fundamental factors behind the Brexit vote', 31 October 2016; http://voxeu.org/(...)s-behind-brexit-vote (accessed 1 November 2018).

3 E. Brynjolfsson and J. H. Oh, 'The attention economy: measuring the value of free digital services on the internet', International Conference on Information Systems (ICIS), 2012.

4 Theresa May speech on our future economic partnership with the European Union; https://www.gov.uk/government/speeches/pm-speech-on-our-future-ec onomic-partnership-with-the-european-union (accessed 1 November 2018).

5 L. Khan, 'Amazon's antitrust paradox', *Yale Law Journal*, vol 126, posted: 6 February 2017; https://papers.ssrn.com/sol3/Papers.cfm?abstract_id=2911742 (accessed 1 November 2018).

6 D. Coyle, 'Practical competition policy tools for digital platforms', *Antitrust Law Journal*, forthcoming. Working paper version, subject to revision: https://www.be nnettinstitute.cam.ac.uk/media/uploads/files/Practical_competition_policy_tools_f or_digital_platforms.pdf (accessed 1 November 2018).

7 S. Machin and R. Murphy, 'Paying out and crowding out? The globalisation of higher education', Centre for Economic Performance Discussion paper, 2014; cep.l-se.ac.uk/pubs/download/dp1299.pdf (accessed 1 November 2018).

8 Industrial Strategy Commission, *Laying The Foundations,* July 2017; http://industrial strategycommission.org.uk/2017/07/10/laying-the-foundations-the-first-major-re port-by-the-industrial-strategy-commission/ (accessed 1 November 2018). E. Norris and R. Adam, 'All change: why Britain is so prone to policy invention and what can be done about it', Institute for Government, 2017; https://www.instituteforgovernme nt.org.uk/publications/all-change (accessed 1 November 2018).

9 See for example: M. Best, *How Growth Really Happens: The Making of Economic Miracles*, Princeton, Princeton University Press, 2018; M. Mazzucato, *The Entrepreneurial State*, London, Anthem Press, 2013; E. O'Sullivan, A. Andreoni, C. López-Gómez, M. Gregory, 'What is new in the new industrial policy? A manufacturing systems perspective', *Oxford Review of Economic Policy*, vol. 29, no. 2, July 2013, pp. 432–462. G. Tassey, 'Competing in advanced manufacturing: the need for improved growth models and policies', *Journal of Economic Perspectives*, vol. 28, no. 1, 2014, pp. 27–48.

How to cite this article: D. Coyle, 'Dual Disruptions: Brexit and Technology', in G Kelly and N Pearce (eds.), Britain Beyond Brexit, *The Political Quarterly*, Vol 90, Issue S2, 2019, pp. 62–71. https://doi.org/10.1111/1467-923X.12613

# Brexit and the Future of the UK's Unbalanced Economic Geography

## ANDREW CARTER AND PAUL SWINNEY

IT IS OFTEN said, but bears repetition, that by international standards, the UK has some of the largest geographical inequalities in the developed world. Significant inequalities between different areas are evident in almost all aspects of the economy, including productivity, incomes, employment status and wealth. Brexit Britain is a nation made up of cities and towns with contrasting economic trajectories (see figure 1 below).

While the traditional economic dominance of London and its hinterland is growing, the economic outcomes of many towns and cities in the Midlands, the north of England, Northern Ireland and Wales have more in common with poorer places in Central and Eastern Europe or the US South.

Most big cities outside London still have productivity and employment rates lower than the national average and their weaker performance also holds back surrounding towns. Many de-industrialised areas, often on the fringes of city-regions, present difficult combinations of social, educational and economic problems, while some of the country's most disadvantaged communities are found on our coasts and in isolated rural places.[1] And even our most successful local economies are often our most unequal.[2]

These economic divides map closely to political ones (as discussed in the chapter by Jennings and Stoker). In the 2016 referendum, smaller cities and towns in the north and Midlands and on the coast tended to poll a greater share of votes for leaving the EU. It's perhaps not surprising, then, that it has become conventional wisdom among commentators to cast the Brexit vote as the 'revenge of the left behind places',[3] a chance for those living in struggling places to stick it to the Westminster 'metropolitan' elite.

If we are to address these spatial inequalities, and close the economic and political divides associated with them, we have first to understand their long history.

## The past century of economic change across the UK

Over the last century, economic change has come to all places in the UK, from the biggest cities to the smallest towns and villages. Globalisation, technology and shifts in transportation have demanded continual adaptation, both to continue to provide jobs and to contribute to national economic growth.[4] But the impacts of these changes have played out unevenly across the country. At the regional level, for every one additional job created in the whole of the north, Midlands and Wales since 1911, 2.3 have been created in

Published by John Wiley & Sons Ltd, 9600 Garsington Road, Oxford OX4 2DQ, UK and 350 Main Street, Malden, MA 02148, USA

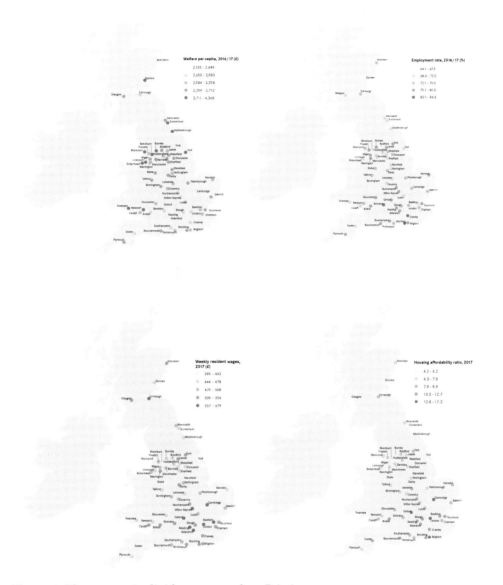

**Figure 1:** The economic divides across urban Britain

Source: ONS, Annual Survey of Hours and Earnings (ASHE); NOMIS, Annual Population Survey; Land Registry, Market Trend, Price Paid data. Simple average used. Scottish neighbourhood statistics, 2016, mean house prices; DWP; HMRC; DCLG; Welsh government; Scottish government; NOMIS, population estimates; ONS, birth summary tables; National Registers of Scotland, births by sex, year and council area.

**Figure 2:** Jobs growth in cities, 1911–2016
Note: Map does not display Crawley and Milton Keynes due to their very small size in 1911 and the subsequent distortive impact this has on their growth figures.

the south. In 1911, the north, Midlands and Wales accounted for 57 per cent of all jobs in England and Wales. By 2016 this had fallen to 47 per cent.

Looking specifically at Britain's largest urban areas, figure 2 shows that the majority have grown over this period. Fifty-five cities had more jobs in 2016 than 1911, and twenty-eight have more than doubled their total, while only seven cities had fewer jobs in 2016 than 1911.

But looking at jobs growth alone is insufficient—understanding the *type* of jobs that have been created is important too. Some places, particularly in the

Greater South-East such as Reading, Aldershot and Brighton, have been particularly successful at reinventing their economies in the face of constant change, seeing strong jobs growth in knowledge-based employment as a result. Crucially, this success has also been beneficial to their surrounding towns and villages, providing work for their residents and making them more attractive places for business investment.[5]

Many places in the North, Midlands and Wales—such as Hull, Doncaster and Swansea—have struggled to adapt to the changes that technological developments and globalisation have brought. Whilst these post-industrial economies have been successful in creating jobs, they replaced coal mines with call centres, and dockyards with distribution centres. In other words, they have replaced one set of relatively low-skilled, lower-paid jobs with another, essentially replicating rather than reinventing their economic structure. Moreover, some places have struggled even on this front. Burnley, for example, had half the total number of jobs in 2016 that it did in 1911.

The pattern of job creation seen in recent decades results from the relative advantages that different places offer to businesses, particularly knowledge-led businesses. Those cities that have reinvented their economies have been able to offer these types of businesses two things—access to a pool of high-skilled workers and access to a network of other knowledge-based businesses and institutions, including universities and research institutes.

The jobs growth seen in replicator cities also shows that they have been able to attract business investment. But this has mainly been based on their offer of providing access to a pool of lower-skilled workers, access to motorways and cheaper land. Relatively speaking, they continue to play the role of places of low-cost production that they played 100 years ago, rather than becoming centres of knowledge production.

History matters in explaining these patterns. Firstly, success begets success. The better-performing places in the twenty-first century typically began the last century with a higher base of knowledge-rich and professional jobs, and responded to the evolving global landscape through innovation and adaptation. Over time, their economies transformed to favour knowledge-intensive industries and workers, enabling them to offset job losses in declining fields and build competitive and dynamic places.

Secondly, the sheer scale of traditional industries in 1911 and their decline over the subsequent century has cast a long shadow over some places. Manchester, for example, lost around 530,000 jobs in manufacturing over the last century, creating a vast employment challenge. The recovery from these losses has been a long and painful process for many places—only in the last couple of years has Manchester surpassed the number of jobs it had in 1911—while in some places like Burnley, Bradford and Liverpool, that recovery is still a work in progress.

## From new towns to city deals—how policy has influenced economic geography

Globalisation and technological advancement have been the two major economic drivers of change over the last 100 years. But policy has also had an influence. There are two policy agendas that, without having an explicit geographical focus, have had a marked influence on the economic geography of job creation across the country.

The first is the postwar new towns agenda which resulted in the creation and expansion of tens of cities and towns across the country. The southern new towns have been noticeably more successful than those established in the Midlands and the north. Crawley has many times the number of jobs today than it did a century ago, while Milton Keynes didn't even exist until the 1960s, but now has over 150,000 jobs within its boundaries, many of them highly skilled and highly paid.

The second strategic policy direction has been the expansion of the state after the Second World War and the subsequent growth of public sector employment. Public sector jobs, particularly in health and education, account for an estimated 1 million of the 1.6 million extra jobs in London today compared to a century ago. In Liverpool, public sector jobs have cushioned the extent of the city's private sector employment decline, adding around 90,000 jobs over the last 100 years, as it has simultaneously lost over 130,000 private sector roles.

Significantly, policies that have more explicitly attempted to reduce the north-south divide have been much less effective. We have had eighty years of policy attempting to boost growth in the regions, but the gap in performance has widened over this time. This is because the majority of interventions have tended to reinforce existing industrial structure—encouraging the replication of local economies by implementing policies designed to support low-knowledge, routine activities—as opposed to supporting reinvention by increasing their attractiveness to more knowledge focussed jobs.

This approach was evident in former Chancellor George Osborne's call for a 'march of the makers' in 2011, and the overt focus of the Regional Growth Fund (launched by the coalition government in 2012) on manufacturers in the north and Midlands. Of the £720 million allocated in the first three rounds of the fund across England, 42 per cent was allocated directly to manufacturers in the north and Midlands. In the north-east, 73 per cent of the £114 million allocation to the local enterprise partnership was given to manufacturing.[6] Enterprise zones have had a similar focus— of the new wave of zones set up in 2012, fifteen of the sixteen located in the north and Midlands explicitly cite manufacturing or engineering as their sector focus.[7]

This approach ignores the prevailing economic trends of the past few decades, during which overall manufacturing employment has been declining across Britain (today, it accounts for just 8 per cent of jobs across the country). Moreover, this approach to the north contrasts quite dramatically with the patterns of the government's innovation-focussed investment which has been heavily concentrated on the south's 'Golden Triangle'. As the government's 2017 Industrial Strategy White Paper notes, 46 per cent of money from the UK's research councils goes to Oxford, Cambridge and London, where about a quarter of the UK's 163 higher education institutions are based.[8]

## What impact will Brexit have on the UK's economic geography?

Several studies have been undertaken on the economic impact that different forms of Brexit will have on different parts of the country.[9] Some suggest that a 'Chequers' style deal might provide some short to medium term shelter to the manufacturing-intensive parts of the country—mainly in the north and Midlands—whilst having more immediate negative economic impacts for those places—mainly in the south-east—that rely on service exports to the EU and have a greater share of EU migrants in their workforce. Others suggest that under any Leave scenario, because of the intricate 'just-in-time' supply chains that many manufacturing companies rely on, it is manufacturing-intensive regions that will be hit the hardest.

What all of these studies agree on is that whichever Brexit deal is struck, even the most advantageous will have a negative impact on future economic growth for all places across the UK in the short to medium term. And they also agree that over the *longer term* its places that are already struggling that are likely to struggle the most, further exacerbating the country's unbalanced economic geography. This is because those places that are more productive and have highly-skilled workforces today will find it easier to adapt tomorrow. Cities such as London, Reading and Edinburgh are home to large highly-skilled workforces, significant numbers of innovative firms and strong business networks, all of which will greatly assist them in reinventing their economies to reflect changed circumstances.

In or out of the EU, these fundamental drivers will remain unchanged. The importance of enabling the creation of, and access to, knowledge that benefits both businesses and workers will continue in the future.[10] While the attractiveness of these successful cities relative to their counterparts on the continent is likely to shift somewhat as a result of Brexit, there is much less likely to be a change in the relative position of more and less successful places *within* the UK. Indeed, the situation for struggling local economies may well deteriorate.

Brexit may not, therefore, change the nature of the challenges associated with the country's unbalanced economic geography. But it certainly should

bring more urgency—political as well as economic—to the imperative to trying to address these long-standing problems.

## Rising to the challenge—what can be done?

Addressing the country's imbalanced economic geography will require concerted efforts across a range of policy areas over the long term. The north-
south divide has been with us for at least a century, so reducing it will obviously not be easy or immediate. Any attempts to address it must be mindful
of this fact.

If the government is to succeed in re-balancing growth, then 'place' should
be the over-arching framework for reducing inequalities—not pan-UK wide,
'one size fits all' policies. Place-based policies can supplement those that are
institutional or place-blind, such as those set out by the Industrial Strategy
Commission in its November 2017 *Final Report* and the 'mission-oriented'
policies of the government's Industrial Strategy White Paper. This will
require additional investment and significant changes to the way that policy
is designed and delivered:

### 1. Focus on cities as the hubs of the modern economy

Economic activity in the UK is not evenly or randomly distributed across the
country—it is clustered in cities. Britain's sixty-two largest urban areas
accounted for 9 per cent of land but were home to 55 per cent of businesses,
60 per cent of jobs and 62 per cent of national output in 2016.

Cities are particularly important for the ability of the national economy to
continue to specialise in ever more knowledge-based economic activity. Over
70 per cent of knowledge-based jobs were based in cities, and the trend is
towards more urban concentration. Cities also provide jobs for people well
beyond their boundaries—around 22 per cent of workers living outside cities
were employed in a city in 2011, accounting for 2.4 million jobs.

Despite all this, the big cities in the north and Midlands all underperform
the national average. Addressing this problem needs to be the organising
mission for addressing the overall under-performance of the north and Midlands. It will be impossible to achieve a more balanced and prosperous
national economy without the improvement of its big urban centres.

### 2. Recognise that growth can't be easily pushed around the country

Policy has been attempting to push private sector activity around the country for at least eighty years, going back to the Special Areas Act of 1934, yet
the persistent differences in economic performance across different places
suggest that this has not been particularly successful. In order to help create
growth across the country, policy needs to look at what influences business
location decisions, and to address the barriers that prevent businesses from
starting up and expanding in some parts of the country, such as low skills
levels, poor transport infrastructure, or unaffordable housing.

## 3. Devolve more powers and responsibilities

In an increasingly economically differentiated country, it is not possible for central government to get to grips with all the diverse economic challenges facing different parts of the country. For too long, the bizarre British response to the increasing economic variation seen across the country has been a top–down, 'one size fits all' approach to policy making. It has not worked and will not deliver the political economic settlement the country needs.

Instead, government needs to instigate a power-sharing initiative which has the strategic aim of empowering places so they can make the strategic economic decisions that affect the prosperity of their places. This will be crucial in enabling places to adapt to Brexit, and to address other big 'future of work' challenges arising from globalisation and automation, which will become increasingly significant in the decades ahead.

In part, this means building on the progress made on city-regional devolution in recent years, which among other things, led to the introduction of metro mayors in seven of England's biggest city regions. These metro-mayors should be given significantly more control of the total public sector funding spent in their areas, including education, skills, transport, health, aspects of welfare, planning, business support and innovation (which, in Greater Manchester's case, would amount to roughly £22 billion of funding) to create an 'area-based block grant'.

But given the scale of economic changes resulting from Brexit, as well as automation and demography, these changes are unlikely to be sufficient to deal with the existing and new challenges that many places face.

So, devolution will need to go much further. The government should consider adopting a more 'federal system' for the UK. In the short term, this would give London and the other big English city-regions powers similar to those currently available to Scotland and Wales, including tax and borrowing powers. The model for this should be the 'reserved powers' approach used for the original Scotland Act which enshrined in legislation only those areas where the Scottish government does not have competence—such as foreign affairs and defence. Over the medium term, we should aspire to a more federal system and learn from the constitutional and fiscal settlements of countries such as Germany, Spain and Canada.

## 4. Raise the demand for, as well as the supply of, knowledge

To support the ability of places to adapt, the long term strategic objective of economic development policy should be to improve the stock, flow and use of knowledge in cities and towns. This is the approach successful reinventor cities in the UK have adopted, as well as their global counterparts such as Seattle, San Diego and Pittsburgh in the US, or Munich, Amsterdam and Stockholm in Europe.

Achieving this objective will mean not just focussing on the supply side. Many of our poorly performing places are trapped in a low skill, low investment and low wages equilibrium. This reflects a lack of demand for more skilled labour which generates wider problems of inequality and in-work poverty, and associated social and health problems.

Demand-side policies will also be required to support struggling places to shift away from a low skills equilibrium position through the growth and attraction of more knowledge-intensive and higher-skilled exporting firms. This means a combination of top–down 'mission-orientated' strategies like those set out in the Industrial Strategy White Paper and bottom–up strategies that encourage and support entrepreneurship, export promotion, management capacity, and local living wages as well as encouraging greater worker organisation and participation in firm decision making.

### 5. Prioritise skills and education

More than anything else, we need to focus on raising skills levels in places outside the greater south-east. Belfast, for example, has the highest share of residents with no formal qualifications of any UK city (16 per cent), and Birmingham and Bradford fare little better (14 per cent and 13 per cent respectively). That means improving school standards across the north and Midlands, and reforming the education system to give young people in these places the cognitive and interpersonal skills they will need to thrive in the changing world of work.

We also need a much bigger focus on (and a significant increase in funding for) lifelong learning and technical education, to help adults adapt to the changing labour market, and to retrain those who lose their jobs. Sadly, current skills and education policy largely ignores these big issues. For example, the government's plan to raise the earnings threshold for repaying student loans—expected to cost £2.3 billion each year—will help middle class students, but will do nothing for people who have few or no qualifications or no prospect of going to university.

A better use of that money would be to invest it in the severely under-resourced further education (FE) sector. That would help more people in places outside the greater south-east gain the skills they need to go into work—a crucial point raised by the Sainsbury Review into improving technical education.[11]

### 6. Extend and integrate public transport within city-regions

Transport policy needs better to reflect the economic and structural changes that are shaping the UK's economic geography. Given that high-skilled jobs are likely to continue to concentrate in cities, and city centres in particular, public transport will need to play a greater role in supporting the economic success of cities and their hinterlands in the north and Midlands.

Debates on transport policy in recent years have been dominated by a focus on the better linking of cities, through the *grands projects* of HS2 and Northern Powerhouse rail (which proposes to improve rail links between northern cities). But to improve the performance of our largest northern and Midlands cities, policy must prioritise improving transport links within these cities and to their surrounding towns. This means improving and expanding city-region metro systems: introducing Crossrail for Greater Manchester, the Leeds City Region, and for Greater Birmingham, rather than Crossrail for the north or the Midlands as a whole.

Better metropolitan transport requires better governance. London, and to some extent Manchester and Birmingham, have benefitted from having a mandate to transform its transport systems. Other places, large and small, need to be able to take the same approach. For example, the powers that London has to regulate and integrate its bus system with other forms of public transport should be rolled out to the rest of the country.

*7. Create dense, vibrant city centres as a means to boost innovation*
Growing, attracting and retaining innovative businesses will be key to the future performance of local economies across the country. We know that high-skilled businesses have increasingly clustered in cities in recent years (and city centres in particular), and that the concentration of these businesses in one place allows them to share ideas and information which in turn spurs innovation and productivity.[12]

Policy should specifically encourage this density and interaction of businesses, by supporting the further expansion of successful city centres and addressing the barriers that make less successful city centres less attractive places to do business. Specifically, city centres should be viewed as part of the UK's strategic infrastructure, and part of the £30 billion National Productivity Infrastructure Fund should be allocated to creating dense and diverse city centres that are attractive to innovative businesses.

# Conclusion

The geography of the Leave vote in the EU referendum symbolises the varied outcomes of many decades of economic and political change in the UK. In or out of the EU, the fundamental reasons why some places have struggled to adapt will remain unchanged. To make sure that the coming decades do not bring a re-run of what we have seen in decades past, there will need to be a concerted push to help places adapt to ongoing change, rather than attempting to fight against it.

If Brexit leads to central government further centralising power in Whitehall, the already difficult issue of adapting national policies to meet the economic and political needs of increasingly diverse places will only get worse. On the other hand, if it triggers the wholesale devolution of policies, powers and resources, allowing local politicians to exercise much more control over the issues that affect the daily lives of the people they represent, then bridging the stark political and economic divides within the country might be possible.

Geographical inequality and over-centralisation blighted the UK long before the 2016 referendum gave a reluctant Westminster elite a new problem to solve. Good deal, bad deal or no deal, Brexit should mark the moment they conclude they have the power, but not the answers—and that handing real power to places across the country will be crucial in finding the right political and economic solutions.

## Notes

1 Industrial Strategy Commission, *The Final Report of the Industrial Strategy Commission*, Manchester, University of Manchester, 2017; http://industrialstrategyc ommission.org.uk/wp-content/uploads/2017/10/The-Final-Report-of-the-Industria l-Strategy-Commission.pdf (accessed 16 January 2019).

2 Centre for Cities, *Cities Outlook 2018*; https://www.centreforcities.org/wp-conte nt/uploads/2018/01/18-01-12-Final-Full-Cities-Outlook-2018.pdf (accessed 16 January 2019).

3 A. Rodriguez-Pose, 'The revenge of the places that don't matter (and what to do about it)', *Cambridge Journal of Regions, Economy and Society*, vol. 11, no. 1, pp. 189–209; http://eprints.lse.ac.uk/85888/ (accessed 16 January 2019).

4 P. Swinney and E. Thomas, *A Century of Cities: Urban Economic Change since 1911*, London, Centre for Cities, 2015; https://www.centreforcities.org/wp-content/ uploads/2015/03/15-03-04-A-Century-of-Cities.pdf (accessed 16 January 2019).

5 P. Swinney, R. McDonald and L. Ramuni, *Talk of the Town: The Economic Links between Cities and Towns*, London, Centre for Cities, 2018; https://www.centreforc ities.org/wp-content/uploads/2018/09/18-10-04-Talk-of-the-Town.pdf (accessed 16 January 2019).

6 Source: Regional Growth Fund Secretariat; https://www.gov.uk/guidance/unde rstanding-the-regional-growth-fund (accessed 16 January 2019).

7 Department for Communities and Local Government, *Looking for a Place to Grow your Business?*, London, DCLG, 2015; http://enterprisezones.communities.gov. uk/enterprise-zone-finder/ (accessed 14th January 2015).

8 HM Government, *Industrial Strategy: Building a Britain Fit for the Future*, London, HMSO, 2017; https://assets.publishing.service.gov.uk/government/uploads/sys tem/uploads/attachment_data/file/664563/industrial-strategy-white-paper-web-ready-version.pdf (accessed 16 January 2019).

9 N. Clayton and H. Overman, *Brexit, Trade and the Economic Impacts on UK Cities*, London, Centre for Cities, 2017; https://www.centreforcities.org/wp-content/ uploads/2017/07/17-07-26-Brexit-trade-and-the-economic-impacts-on-UK-cities. pdf (accessed 16 January 2019). W. Chen, B. Los, P. McCann, R. Ortega-Argiles, M. Thissen, F. van Oort, 'The continental divide? Economic exposure to Brexit in regions and countries on both sides of the Channel', *Papers in Regional Science*, vol. 97, no. 1, 2018, pp. 25–54; HM Government, Treasury analysis, *The Long-Term Economic Impact of EU Membership and the Alternatives*, April 2016; https://www.gov.uk/government/publications/hm-treasury-analysis-the-long-term-economic-impact-of-eu-membership-and-the-alternatives (accessed 16 January 2019).

10 J. Haskel and S. Westlake, *Capitalism with Capital: The Rise of the Intangible Economy*, Woodstock, Princeton University Press, 2018.

11 The Sainsbury Review, *Report of the Independent Panel on Technical Education*, April 2016; https://assets.publishing.service.gov.uk/government/uploads/system/upload

s/attachment_data/file/536046/Report_of_the_Independent_Panel_on_Technical_
Education.pdf (accessed 16 January 2019). Full disclosure: Lord Sainsbury is the
main funder of Centre for Cities through the Gatsby Foundation.

12 See for example, G. Carlino and W. Kerr, 'Agglomeration and innovation', Harvard Business School working paper 15-007, 2014; and Haskel and Westlake, *Capitalism without Capital*.

How to cite this article: A. Carter and P. Swinney, 'Brexit and the Future of
the UK's Unbalanced Economic Geography', in G Kelly and N Pearce (eds.),
Britain Beyond Brexit, *The Political Quarterly*, Vol 90, Issue S2, 2019, pp. 72–83.
https://doi.org/10.1111/1467-923X.12649

# Can a Post-Brexit UK Grow a Knowledge-Based Economy that Works for Everyone?

## GEOFF MULGAN

WILL THE UK use its new freedoms post-Brexit to become a dynamo of the Fourth Industrial Revolution? Or will its pockets of global excellence stall while the rest of the economy sees productivity stagnate even further? In this chapter, I try to provide an answer, focussing on two big tasks the UK faces post-Brexit. The first is to maintain, and grow, the position of its advanced, knowledge-based industries: from artificial intelligence (AI) to life sciences, to design and fashion. The other is to make that economy radically more inclusive, giving many more people, firms and places the chance to take advantage of its potential, and to address some of the underlying pressures that fuelled public support for Brexit.

I argue that three clusters of problems—stagnant productivity, inequality, and political alienation—have some common causes, and potentially some common solutions that are essentially about the depth and breadth of engagement in the knowledge economy.[1] The problems reflect the confinement of the advanced knowledge economy[2] to particular sectors, firms and places—a phenomenon which can be seen in the wide gaps between frontier firms and the average; the highest paid individuals and the average; and the leading places and the rest. This strategic challenge faces many countries, but it will be particularly acute for a UK that is pulling away from its main trading partners, that faces new difficulties in selling the services and creative products that have become particularly important to its economy into the EU, and that will have to decide how to use greater autonomy in regulation.

To address these interconnected problems, I argue for a shift of policy in several dimensions:

- In industrial policy, combining more investment in research and development (R&D) and the frontiers with a proportionately bigger expansion of action to promote diffusion and adoption of new technologies, particularly to small and medium-sized enterprises (SMEs).
- In innovation policy itself, a shift towards services and the creative economy rather than a primary focus on manufacturing, spreading and deepening the ability to create new value.
- In education, a greater emphasis not just on attainment, which has dominated policy for a generation, but on such things as problem solving, collaboration and creativity, which are key to an inclusive knowledge economy, and growing the pool of innovators.

Published by John Wiley & Sons Ltd, 9600 Garsington Road, Oxford OX4 2DQ, UK and 350 Main Street, Malden, MA 02148, USA

- In adult education, reversing the 40+ per cent cuts in funding in the 2010s to rebuild institutions with entitlements and navigation, so that many more people can adapt to potentially far-reaching changes in jobs demand.
- In markets, more aggressive competition policy to ensure new monopolies don't consolidate, and more use of tools like open data and 'anticipatory regulation' to shape markets in key new sectors, ranging from AI to drones, autonomous vehicles to networked energy.
- In government itself, reinforcing an experimental open approach that staves off the threats of stagnation and productivity decay that may become even more serious as a huge amount of state brainpower is absorbed in negotiations over trade during the long aftermath of Brexit.

These are some of the elements of a post-Brexit strategy. Some would be necessary whether or not Brexit happened, but they become more urgent in the context of a series of micro and macro shocks that may accompany leaving the EU.

## Interlinked problems

Three sets of problem overshadow the UK and other developed countries. The first is stagnant productivity, with a wide gap between the frontier firms and the average, and a long tail of low productivity firms in every region and every sector. Economic theory predicts that market forces will naturally solve this problem. But reality is proving different.[3]

The second problem is inequality, and the gap between the rich and the middle and the poor. The exact shape of this inequality varies. In some countries, it is only the very rich who have pulled ahead. But in many countries, median wages have stagnated while both income and wealth at the very top have grown rapidly. Some of the explanation lies in tax policies, heavily influenced by wealthy donors becoming more powerful in political parties. But some of this reflects the nature of the knowledge economy which has concentrated gains in elite groups and places.

The third dimension is politics, and growing evidence that voting behaviour increasingly correlates with levels of education, and perhaps perceived participation in the gains of a knowledge-based economy.

## Political and policy strategies

How to respond? One, still common, response is the 'trickle-down' theory of the knowledge economy: the claim that the gains from dynamic innovation in places like London or San Francisco, and dynamic firms like Google, will naturally spread out to the rest of the economy. That was a plausible hypothesis a generation ago. It has dominated policy in practice, though often disguised by a more inclusive rhetoric. But it is now clear that the trickle down doesn't generally happen. Many may benefit as consumers from cheaper products and services, but only a small minority benefit as workers. This imbalance can be seen in the dramatic declines of the work-force of the highly valued firms of now, compared to a few decades ago (for example, 70,000 in Apple and 75,000 in Alphabet compared to many hun-dreds of thousands in firms like General Electric and General Motors in their heyday).

Another response is the 'strategy of nostalgia'—the attempt to return to a previous economic model based on mass manufacturing jobs and protected markets. This is clearly attractive in many countries but very hard to achieve, given the dramatic changes that have occurred in manufacturing technology and supply chains.

A third alternative strategy is also beginning to be discussed, though it hasn't yet been adopted. This is the strategy of extreme distributionism: encourage the maximum deployment of AI and automation; accept mass job destruction; and then reward the rest of the population with benefits such as a Universal Basic Income (UBI) as compensatory distribution. This position has been supported by some groups in Silicon Valley, on the libertarian right and the egalitarian left across Europe, and UBI has recently been proposed for piloting by the Labour party.

In place of these strategies, I argue that we need to create a more inclusive knowledge economy that involves more people upstream and addresses inequalities through production as well as distribution. For the UK, this means growing its advanced industries while also enabling many more peo-ple to play a part in the economy and in the innovation that increasingly drives it.

## The frontiers

The UK starts with considerable strengths at the frontiers of the current and next generation of key technologies, whether in financial technology (Fin-Tech) or AI, biomedical or the wider creative economy. There are many mea-sures of this strength: the UK's research base is strong in terms of citations, PhD involvement in industry, and global connections. Financial services make up 6.5 per cent of GDP, and have remained very innovative, turning London into one of the world's most successful FinTech centres. The creative industries are equally strong, making up 5.3 per cent of the whole economy, including important new strengths like the 1,000 companies using immersive or virtual reality technologies in the UK, employing around 4,500 people (more than coal) and generating £660 million in sales, potentially represent-ing as much as 9 per cent of the global market share.[4] These strengths are deep; they are embedded in particular places, firms and relationships; they involve synergies with each other and with tangible assets as well as spil-lovers.

But there are some long-standing concerns. Too many growing firms in leading technologies are bought up from overseas once they reach scale—from ARM Holdings (bought by Softbank) to Autonomy (bought by HP). The UK still does relatively better upstream than downstream. The growing industries are highly concentrated in the south-east, reflecting imbalances in public R&D that are much greater than imbalances in private R&D. Moreover, retaining these strengths will be harder post-Brexit. Brexit threatens participation in EU funding, which has already declined markedly since the referendum (though the UK can negotiate to remain in the big programmes); the UK will lose the European Medicines Agency; Brexit may diminish the attractiveness of UK universities to both students and academics; and it may limit high-skilled migration, though this will depend more on how future governments choose to use their freedoms post-Brexit than on the Brexit deal itself, and the government has already widened its use of 'exceptional talent visas'.

There are also big risks associated with exclusion from the European Digital Single Market, which aims to achieve economies of scale through things like common data protection laws. The threat is not just loss of market access, but also loss of influence in opening up individual EU member markets. The government commitment to raise R&D from 1.7 per cent to 2.4 per cent of GDP aims to mitigate some of these risks. Globally, public investment in R&D broadly correlates with intangible spending by the private sector.[5] But it remains unclear how the 2.4 per cent target will be reached and, in particular, how the private sector contribution will be achieved.

There are also obvious questions about the allocation of resources which will have to be made by the newly created UK Research and Innovation (UKRI). For example, recent years have seen a growing dominance of the biomedical sector, which has taken a rising share of public support even as its results have deteriorated, with steady declines in the flow of new drugs per £ billion of investment.[6] This slow-burn crisis in the business model of pharmaceuticals represents a big challenge for the UK given the strategic importance of firms like GlaxoSmithKline. It will also fuel doubts about the traditional skew of public R&D spending towards hardware and manufacturing relative to services or the creative economy, which is more a reflection of history and assumption than of evidence or strategy. In principle, the creation of UKRI, responsible for over £6 billion of public spending, should allow for a more strategic, and cross-disciplinary approach, which will be all the more vital post-Brexit, especially if it can align with policies on tax (to favour intangible investment—for example, extending R&D tax credits to design), and on clusters.

## Spread and adoption throughout the economy

Even if the frontiers look relatively healthy, any examination of the averages and distributions shows a much less rosy picture. It shows uneven productivity, the slow spread of new business methods, as well as weaknesses in skills. The UK isn't alone in this. Many nations and cities have learned how to cultivate dynamic vanguards, creative quarters, knowledge industries, universities buzzing with spinoffs, technology hubs and incubators. But far fewer have spread the benefits widely.

Within markets, information and knowledge encourage economies of scale—since the marginal costs of products and services tend to zero—hence the new dynamics of monopoly. The same applies to places—where agglomeration of talent and knowledge creation creates a dynamic that widens the gap with the left behind. There are also powerful new economies of scope, particularly for the dominant platforms that can diversify rapidly, extending their power from one industry to another—as Google has done from search to cars and as Amazon has done, moving into every field of retailing and then cloud services. So, while the vanguards on the frontier need to be sustained—the cutting edge in life sciences, AI, materials and so on—as much effort needs to be devoted to spread, adoption and diffusion of new ideas and new technologies, contributing to strength in depth.

This has been a missing part of policy in recent decades, but is beginning to be addressed. A small example of a step in the right direction was the recent announcement by the Department for Business, Energy and Industrial Strategy (BEIS) of the Business Basics Fund—promoting more attention to adoption of new methods, and using an experimental method to do so with control groups (the model used by Nesta's Innovation Growth Lab). This is not an entirely new task: it was key to German industrial policy in the late nineteenth century; to US industrial policy in various phases of the late nineteenth and twentieth centuries; and more recently, to policy in places like Bavaria and South Korea. Some of the tools are familiar. They involve business networks, intermediary organisations, subsidies for coaches and mentors, more aggressive competition policy, more deliberate industrial policies to spread adoption of new tools, like data analytics or AI. But others are newer, like more encouragement of open source technologies, or tougher requirements on big firms to open up their data.

## Regulation to accelerate and spread the knowledge economy

The question of how much the UK aligns with the EU on regulation has been central to many of the negotiations over Brexit. It matters crucially—not just to export oriented manufacturing sectors like cars, but also to services, many of which are equally dependent on trade. The creative industries, for example, export nearly £40 billion, of which 45 per cent go to the EU, so maintaining reciprocal market access for sectors like TV matters.

The negotiations are aiming to stay in the single market for goods but not services, which simultaneously poses a big threat to these export oriented sectors, but also some opportunities. The threats are obvious and already visible in a clutch of issues up for negotiation around such areas as design (like the unregistered community designs much used in fashion), EU trademarks and patents. The current draft agreements aim to ensure smooth transitions and to protect rights, and the UK has some bargaining power of its own, like the threat not to recognise GIs—the geographical indications that strongly protect names such as Champagne, Roquefort and Parmesan cheese. But there remains considerable uncertainty about whether the UK will retain easy market access—particularly, for example, if the EU introduces new rules on content on the big platforms like Amazon and Netflix.

This takes us to another set of dilemmas the UK will face: how far to collaborate with the EU in dealing with the newer oligopolies—Amazon, Facebook, Google in particular, and their Chinese counterparts, Tencent and Alibaba, which are increasingly active in Europe. These have reaped the vast economies of scale and scope of a data-driven economy. Traditional approaches—vertical and horizontal separation—are less effective in these cases, because they risk destroying more of the network value these firms create. The EU is likely to be taking a more aggressive stance in the years ahead (whether on fake news, data or tax), and the UK will have to decide what positions to take in relation to firms which extract significant value from the UK and pay little tax.

Regulation will also become increasingly central to the UK's attempts to improve productivity and competitiveness post-Brexit. It can play a central role in advancing the frontiers through what I've called 'anticipatory regulation',[7] providing spaces for experiment and innovation, as financial regulators have shown with sandboxes; or cities with zones for the Internet of Things. In principle, the UK could aim to use new freedoms to move faster in creating favourable regulatory frameworks for fourth industrial revolution technologies, such as blockchain or advanced genomics, and in influencing standards from outside the EU.

Regulation will also be relevant to the challenge of diffusing technologies and techniques. A good example is the open data rules in banking that require banks to give customers control over their own data. Combined with funding for innovative firms to make the most of these rules, regulators are helping the UK to remain at the forefront of innovation, while also increasing competition and helping smaller firms adopt new tools, such as AI-driven tools for managing cash flow, treasury or assets. Similar approaches—opening up both data and algorithms and allowing data portability—may in time be applied to the platform giants, and could greatly help strategies to drive up SME productivity.

The recent 'Regulators' Pioneer Fund', run by BEIS, is a recognition of the importance of innovation in regulation to maintaining competitive position—extending the new tools to fields like energy, transport or law. How, for example, can legal services for SMEs be transformed to make the most of AI, cutting costs and raising efficiency? Or how can driverless cars be encouraged, with smart rules to govern everything from payments to liability? If the UK can achieve faster collaboration between the pioneers of new technology and the makers of rules, then in principle, it may be able to support both faster growth at the frontiers and faster diffusion to the rest of the economy.

Drones throw up similar challenges: this is a potentially very large industry which requires alignment of law, regulation, experiment and public acceptance. There are already 650 firms involved in the UK industry, and forecasts of big impacts on many sectors (PricewaterhouseCoopers estimate a £42 billion increase in UK GDP by 2030, £16 billion in annual cost savings to the UK economy and over 600,000 jobs in the drone economy).[8] But to become part of the mainstream of city life, they need new rules: on noise; where they can fly; how they land; as well as business models for retail delivery or human transport; and protocols for sharing data in real time. This is a new challenge for policy, requiring approaches that link national policy and regulators to city authorities and industry, and are tested through experiment. The simplistic view that the UK can simply refashion itself as a deregulated offshore entrepot falls apart in relation to these emergent industries.

## Education that grows makers and shapers

A more strategic approach to the UK economy post-Brexit cannot ignore education, and its role in both advancing the frontiers of the economy and spreading engagement in the knowledge economy. In recent decades, education policy has been dominated by the goal of raising attainment, and with good reasons given the uneven and often poor levels of attainment in maths, English and science. But this looks increasingly inadequate in preparing children for the likely labour market conditions of ten to twenty years' time. Every survey of current and future skills needs in the workforce confirms that education has to be about more than the transmission of knowledge, important as this is. It needs also to cultivate the ability to solve problems, to work in teams, to create and invent. This was also the conclusion of a detailed study[9] combining expert panels and machine learning to make forecasts on likely skills demand in 2030.

The implication is that the UK needs schooling models that give young people experience of agency, making the world around them rather than just observing it. Programmes to teach coding are not just of direct value, but also matter because of the indirect value of learning how to be a maker not just a consumer. Project-based learning and entrepreneurship embedded into schooling—the sort of models promoted by HighTechHigh in the US, Lumiar in Brazil or Studio Schools in England—are another response both to economic imperatives and to feelings of disempowerment. They are also aligned with what we know labour markets will be demanding in the future—more ability to work in teams, solve problems, and create. Unfortunately, education policy in England sometimes appears to be running in an opposite direction.

A recent study in the US showed just how crucial education policy could become to industrial policy in the future. It argued for a big shift in spending away from downstream activity in firms and upstream into schools. The study, *Lost Einsteins*[10] analysed 1.2 million inventors in the US over a twenty-year period and showed the very strong correlation between parental influence, direct experience of invention and quality of schooling and the likelihood of a child ending up as an inventor. Children born into wealthy families where the parents had direct involvement in science and technology were far more likely to become inventors themselves. The implication was that the majority of bright children's potential was going to waste, which led the researchers to argue that shifting public resources from tax incentives towards subsidising more opportunities for invention in early childhood would amplify the creative and economic potential of the US and deliver bigger long-term returns. Very similar considerations are likely to apply in the UK.

## Adult skills taken seriously

Few doubt that millions of jobs will either disappear or change as a result of automation and other pressures in the decades after Brexit. As that reality dawns, attention will turn to adult education and retraining to help the millions at risk of losing their job adapt to growing industries. The UK's problem is that the systems for supporting lifelong learning are largely broken. Despite great traditions—from the Workers' Education Association to the Open University—the current system is demoralised and suffering from neglect, not to mention a 40 per cent cut in funding since 2010. Governments will need to do three things. One is to provide funding and new entitlements. Singapore and France show one way forward, offering adults personal accounts with which they can buy training (through Skillsfuture in Singapore and France's Compte Personnel de Formation). The scales are modest—150 hours in France and $500 in Singapore—but the numbers are set to rise. Tax changes are also needed. Some countries (again, including Singapore) use the tax system to encourage firms to invest more in their lower paid workers. Public finance is also likely to be needed to help people on low incomes take time out of work to upgrade their skills.

To reinforce these, a post-Brexit state will need to be much more active in providing navigation tools (and not relying on a market that has provided many services, but which are confusing, rely on poor data and aren't well suited to use). Where there are gaps, it will also need to get involved in provision (of the kind originally provided by Learndirect before its ill-fated privatisation and more recently by FutureLearn).

## Government experimentation and adaptation

The public sector still represents a fifth of the economy, and obviously plays a big role in productivity. It faces very similar challenges to those described above—how to sustain a presence at the leading edge of services, while also ensuring that the average doesn't fall behind. After several years of severe austerity, Brexit has already had a remarkable negative effect on the cognitive capacity of government. While thousands more have been recruited to cope with complex new tasks, the capacity for other tasks has shrunk. Many fear that this pattern could last for a decade or more. The risk is a serious stagnation of government capacity at the time when it will be needed more than ever, and when there are many new opportunities, helped by technology, for redesigning services—from tax collection to social security, health to planning.

Many of these are essentially about using digital tools to redesign services. There are important lessons—both good and bad—to be learned from the digital teams within governments that have attempted to create cross-cutting tools for such things as payments and identity to reduce the huge duplication of current methods. Faster adaptation can also be helped by the use of experimental approaches to spread new methods—as governments of countries including Canada, Finland and United Arab Emirates are doing—including attention to evidence about what works. The more ambitious governments are starting to think about how they can act as an orchestrator of collective intelligence—curating the combination of data, analysis, memory and innovation in fields like labour markets, cancer care or transport, and so creating value for both society and the economy. None of these issues are currently prominent in the thinking of the main UK parties. The risk is that they will mirror the economy's productivity stagnation in a comparable stagnation of public sector productivity.

Post-Brexit governments will also need to look more seriously at their role in creating fundamental infrastructures that make life easier for their citizens and allow smaller businesses to thrive. In recent years, infrastructures have been privatised, broken up and regulated—sometimes successfully and sometimes at a high cost. But there are many infrastructural roles that only government can perform. A good recent example is India's creation of a universal ID card, with biometric identity. Now in use by well over a billion people, it has massively opened up financial services for the very poor, doubling the number with bank accounts in four years. It also appears to be cutting corruption of all kinds and is experienced as empowering. Countries such as Singapore and Denmark have created personal accounts for citizens, making possible much more creative ways of providing welfare. Another example is opening up central banking to offer cheaper mortgages and other financial products to the public.[11] Both the Unique Identification Number (UID) and these ideas offer a potential future in which governments can offer much more flexible kinds of welfare—lending money for a first home, new skills, a university degree, with repayments through the tax system spread over a full working life. Done properly, these can greatly enhance freedom, economic security and feelings of power.

If we are entering a Fourth Industrial Revolution, then one implication is that there will need to be a far reaching remaking of institutions, as happened after each past industrial revolution, in order to reap the rewards of productivity enhancements and then ensure those rewards are shared. This is the central task for post-Brexit Britain, one that is shared with many other countries, but applies with particular force to a country facing profound uncertainties about its future place in the world.

## Notes

1 I use the term knowledge economy as shorthand for those parts of the economy that are predominantly dependent on knowledge, creativity and intangibles of all kinds.
2 This concept draws on work underway with Professor Roberto Mangabeira Unger, Nesta and the OECD.
3 Some more recent research shows that the top-end firms are improving more slowly than before the crash, with explanations including declining competition—a perhaps not surprising result of strengthening oligopoly, particularly in the knowledge intensive sectors. So, the gap may not have widened in recent years, but it remains a crucial fact about the UK economy.
4 J. Mateos-Garcia et al., *The Immersive Economy in the UK*, Nesta and Innovate UK, 1 June 2018; https://www.nesta.org.uk/report/immersive-economy-uk/ (accessed 27 December 2018).
5 J. Haskel and S. Westlake, *Capitalism without Capital*, Princeton, Princeton University Press, 2017.
6 J. Wilsdon and R. Jones, *The Biomedical Bubble*, London, Nesta, 12 July 2018; https://www.nesta.org.uk/report/biomedical-bubble/ (accessed 27 December 2018).
7 G. Mulgan, *Anticipatory Regulation*, London, Nesta, 15 May 2017; https://www.nesta.org.uk/blog/anticipatory-regulation-10-ways-governments-can-better-keep-up-with-fast-changing-industries/ (accessed 27 December 2018).
8 *Flying High: the Future of Drone Technology in UK Cities*, London, Nesta, 23 July 2018; https://www.nesta.org.uk/report/flying-high-challenge-future-of-drone-technology-in-uk-cities/ (accessed 27 December 2018).
9 H. Bakhshi, M. Osborne and P. Schneider, *The Future of Skills: Employment in 2030,* London, Nesta/Pearson, 2017; https://media.nesta.org.uk/documents/the_future_of_skills_employment_in_2030_0.pdf (accessed 27 December 2018).
10 A. Bell, R. Chetty, X. Jaravel, N. Petkova and J. Van Reenen, *Lost Einsteins: Who Becomes an Inventor in America? The Importance of Exposure to Innovation*, CEP Discussion Paper No. 1519, spring 2018; http://cep.lse.ac.uk/pubs/download/cp522.pdf (accessed 27 December 2018).
11 N. Gruen, *Central Banking for All: a Modest Case for Radical Reform,* London, Nesta, 17 March 2014; https://www.nesta.org.uk/report/central-banking-for-all-a-modest-case-for-radical-reform/ (accessed 27 December 2018).

How to cite this article: G. Mulgan, 'Can Post-Brexit UK Grow a Knowledge-Based Economy that Works for Everyone?', in G Kelly and N Pearce (eds.), Britain Beyond Brexit, *The Political Quarterly*, Vol 90, Issue S2, 2019, pp. 84–93. https://doi.org/10.1111/1467-923X.12642

# Tax and Spending in the 2020s

GEMMA TETLOW

## Introduction

THE UK STANDS at a potentially critical juncture in the evolution of the shape and size of the state. Eight years of spending restraint—and, in many areas, cuts—mean many public services are finding it difficult to continue to meet demand without compromising the quality of the service they offer. Continued cuts to welfare benefits are squeezing the living standards of those on the lowest incomes and are predicted to lead to rising rates of child poverty. At the same time, the ageing population is putting growing pressure on health and social care spending and on state spending on pensioner benefits, while economic changes are straining the tax system's ability to raise revenue.

These trends would have had to be addressed at some stage, but Brexit adds new challenges and arguably some opportunities too, and could be a catalyst for a more fundamental review of the role of the state in the UK (as suggested, for example, by Christopher Bickerton).[1] Indeed, the Brexit challenge has arisen just as, for the first time in many years, the two main parties offered markedly different visions for the UK state at the 2017 general election. But Brexit is occupying a huge amount of ministers', officials' and parliamentary time, leaving little scope to think about and address other looming challenges.

This chapter examines recent and predicted economic and fiscal trends in order to assess the choices facing the current and future UK governments about what levels and scope of tax and spending the UK should have after Brexit. Section 2 describes the changes to tax and spending that have occurred over the past eight years, setting the scene for the decisions to come. Section 3 examines the longer-term pressures facing the UK's public finances from an ageing population and other economic changes. These have been known about for some time—and long predate the vote for Brexit—but previous governments have not fully got to grips with them. Section 4 outlines the additional problems and opportunities posed by Brexit before section 5 considers how the current and future UK governments might react. Section 6 concludes. The focus throughout this chapter is on the fiscal constraints and trade-offs that will face any UK government and shape their decisions about tax and spending.

Published by John Wiley & Sons Ltd, 9600 Garsington Road, Oxford OX4 2DQ, UK and 350 Main Street, Malden, MA 02148, USA

# Recent changes in tax and spending

Following the financial crisis, it was clear that there was a large hole in the UK's public finances. At the depth of the crisis in 2009–10, UK public borrowing reached 9.9 per cent of national income, a level unprecedented in the postwar era. New economic forecasts showed the UK economy was expected to be smaller and grow less quickly than had been expected before the financial crisis. Successive forecasts have suggested an increasingly weak outlook as productivity growth in the UK has failed to recover. The composition of economic growth is also expected to be less tax-rich, particularly because the financial sector—which had generated a disproportionately large share of tax revenues pre-crisis—was especially hard hit.

This was the background against which the Conservative-Liberal Democrat coalition government, David Cameron's majority Conservative government and then Theresa May's minority Conservative administration embarked on and then ramped up a programme of tax increases and spending cuts to reduce public borrowing. The initial objective was to eliminate the current budget deficit—in other words, to ensure that the government borrowed only to invest. This was similar to the objective that the Labour government had set itself before the financial crisis. But the target for reducing public borrowing was extended after the 2015 election, with then Chancellor George Osborne committing to eliminate public borrowing altogether. This is a target that Philip Hammond has remained committed to, although he has extended the timescale for achieving this objective to the 'mid-2020s'.

The package of measures implemented since 2009 to help reduce public borrowing has been weighted towards spending cuts, with tax rises playing a smaller part. Since 2009–10, spending on public services has been cut by about 10 per cent in real terms.[2] But population growth means spending per person has been cut by about 15 per cent in real terms. These cuts have been particularly concentrated on some specific areas of public services, with other areas having been protected. As a result, the shape of the state has changed. Spending on the justice system—from prisons to the courts—and on local authority provided services has been cut relatively sharply. Meanwhile, spending on the NHS and overseas aid has been increased and spending on schools has been protected. The share of total departmental spending devoted to health rose from 27 per cent in 2010–11 to 34 per cent in 2017–18 and the plans set out in the October 2018 Budget imply that this will rise further—to 38 per cent—by 2023–24. This protection of the NHS relative to other areas of public spending continues a long-running trend in the UK, driven both by the growing health needs of the ageing population and rising expectations of what the NHS should provide. The share of national income spent on health increased by 4.1 percentage points between 1953–54 and 2015–16, while total public spending fell by 0.7 per cent of national income.[3] Cuts have also been made to benefits paid to working age people, while benefits for pensioners have been protected and—in some areas—made more generous. These choices made about how to allocate scarce spending have reshaped what the state provides, with UK public spending increasingly focussed on health and social care services and transfers to pensioners.

Some taxes have been increased since the financial crisis. The coalition government announced tax increases worth £64 billion a year for the Exchequer.[4] This included, for example, raising the main rate of value added tax from 17.5 per cent to 20 per cent. But these were offset to a large degree by tax cuts elsewhere. In particular, the annual level of income that is exempt from income tax (known as the personal allowance) has been increased significantly, the headline rate of corporation tax has been cut from 28 per cent in 2010 to 19 per cent (and is due to be cut further to 17 per cent in April 2020) and fuel duty has been frozen, rather than rising with inflation.

The latest official forecasts suggest that the UK tax system will generate tax revenues this year totalling 34.6 per cent of national income. Other sources of revenue are expected to generate a further 2.4 per cent of national income,[5] leaving the public sector needing to borrow 1.2 per cent of national income (or £25.5 billion) to bridge the gap between receipts and spending. But the government faces difficulty—and thus important choices—in eliminating this remaining borrowing. Eight years of spending cuts have left some public services struggling to cope with the demands they face. For example, levels of violence in prisons have risen markedly, ultimately prompting Mr Hammond to allocate additional funding to recruit more prison officers. Local authorities are having to devote a growing share of their budgets to fund adult and children's social care, at the expense of other services. Tax revenues have also become increasingly reliant on the income and behaviour of a relatively small group of high-income individuals. Projected socioeconomic trends are also likely to compound, rather than ease, the problems, as the next section discusses.

## Long-term pressures on tax and spending

The latest official long-term projections for UK tax and spending suggest that—rather than falling—public borrowing is likely to rise over the next decade unless changes are made to public policy.[6] This will pose a problem not only for a government—like the current one—which is committed to eliminating borrowing, but to any UK government that hopes to keep the UK's public finances on a sustainable course. Like many other ageing advanced economies, the pressures of an ageing population on public services and welfare spending will ramp up sharply in the 2020s and 2030s, as Figure 1 shows.

The Office for Budget Responsibility (OBR)—the UK's independent fiscal watchdog—has estimated that public spending, excluding debt interest spending, is likely to rise from 36.4 per cent of national income this year to 37.7 per cent by 2030–31, as Figure 2 shows. This increase is mainly driven by projected increases in spending on health (+1.7 percentage point), state

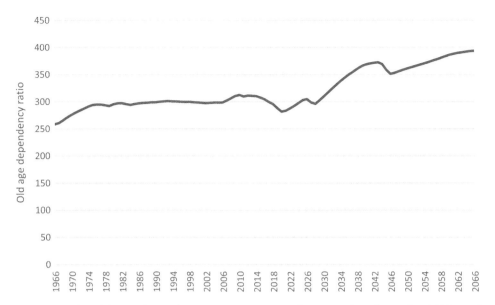

**Figure 1:** The old age dependency ratio is projected to rise sharply in the 2020s and 2030s
Note: The old age dependency ratio is defined here as the number of people aged over the state pension age per 1,000 people of working age.

Source: Office for National Statistics (2018), Figure 11.

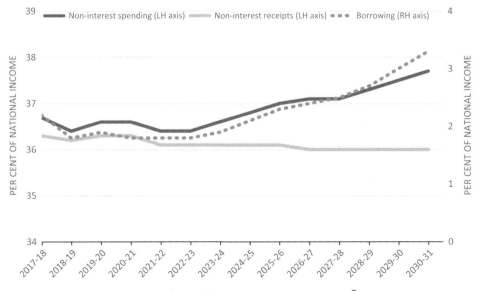

**Figure 2:** Long-run forecasts for public spending and revenues[7]

pensions and pensioner benefits (+0.3 percentage point) and long-term care (+0.2 percentage point). These upward pressures are expected to be only partially offset by a fall in spending on education (as the share of the population of school age falls) and a fall in spending on working age benefits.

Other economic trends are depressing tax receipts.[8] The depletion of North Sea oil, declining rates of smoking and the increasing fuel efficiency of vehicles are expected to lead to declining revenues of off-shore corporation tax, tobacco duties and fuel duties, respectively. Changes to working patterns—in particular, the growing prevalence of self-employment—are also reducing the average effective tax rate on earned income. The latest long-term projection from the OBR suggests government receipts, excluding debt interest, are likely to fall slightly from 36.2 per cent of national income in 2018–19 to 36.0 per cent by 2030–31. Without changes to policy, these trends in spending and revenues would imply public borrowing rising to 3.3 per cent by 2030–31 and continuing to rise thereafter. These projections factor in the recent announcement of an additional £20 billion a year of funding for the NHS. But they do not make allowance for other objectives that the government has mentioned, such as reforming the funding of social care or addressing what Theresa May has described as the UK's 'broken housing market'.

Previous governments have known about these pressures but not fully addressed them. But ignoring the issue and leaving public services and the tax and welfare systems unchanged will become increasingly untenable. The OBR's latest projection for public borrowing is clearly not in line with the current government's objective of eliminating public borrowing. It is also likely to be an unsustainable path even for a government that was happier to maintain a somewhat higher level of public borrowing and debt. While it is difficult to know exactly what the maximum sustainable level of borrowing and debt for the UK is,[9] annual borrowing in excess of 10 per cent of national income probably would not be. This leaves the current and future governments with three options: to pare back the scope of public services and benefits, to raise taxes, or to accept a higher level of public borrowing.

## How does Brexit change the picture?

It is difficult to predict exactly how Brexit will affect the UK economy and public finances, not least because—at the time of writing—it remains unclear what sort of deal can be agreed both by officials in Brussels and the UK Parliament. However, the vast majority of economists predict that Brexit—in whatever form it occurs—will raise additional barriers to trade between the UK and the EU and so harm economic growth over the long-term. On the basis of these sorts of forecasts, it has been estimated that public borrowing could be up to £49 billion a year higher as a result of Brexit than it would be if the UK remained in the EU.[10] This includes the budget boost that would come from no longer having to contribute to the EU budget.

In the short-term the UK government may also face additional costs in setting up new systems and institutions to replace those currently shared with the EU. Whitehall departments are estimated to have spent over £300 million on Brexit preparations in 2017–18[11] and Philip Hammond set aside more than £3 billion for this purpose, but the eventual costs could be much larger. Adjusting to a new relationship with the EU will require not just money but also a considerable amount of time from public sector employees. For example, creating a new customs system would require coordination across thirty government departments and over 100 local authorities.[12]

In principle, Brexit also provides opportunities to change aspects of the UK's tax policies which were not possible as a member of the EU. For example, outside the EU the UK would be able to change value added tax (VAT) and potentially sign new free trade agreements to reduce tariffs on imports from some non-EU countries. But in practice, these would be unlikely to help address the fiscal challenge that the UK already faces and could weaken the public finances further. For example, most of the restrictions imposed by the EU on VAT policies limit the government's ability to cut VAT or introduce new exemptions. Consequently, the main result of Brexit is likely to be greater pressure on government to reduce VAT or to complicate the system further by introducing new lower rates for certain goods or services. The Vote Leave campaign, for example, advocated the benefits of being able to cut VAT on fuel. Such reforms might be politically popular but would do nothing to help address the looming fiscal pressures and would be economically inefficient.

Brexit also offers the opportunity to amend certain EU-set rules and regulations to better suit the needs and preferences of the UK. The eurosceptic thinktank Open Europe suggests that deregulation could reduce costs to businesses and boost UK economic output by up to 0.7 per cent (or £12.8 billion a year).[13] However, that saving could be on the high side of what is politically feasible, as such deregulation would come at the cost of reduced protection for workers and the environment. The figure assumes, for example, that a post-Brexit government would scrap the agency workers' directive, which guarantees the same pay and conditions for agency workers as for permanent employees doing the same job in the same organisation.

Future UK governments may also—for the first time in decades—be able to negotiate new free trade agreements directly with other non-EU countries. As a smaller entity with fewer conflicting priorities, the UK may be able to strike free trade agreements that would not be possible for the EU as a whole. However, the UK may have less bargaining power acting alone than it would in concert with the twenty-seven other EU member states. Whether or not such trade deals are likely to be quickly concluded, most economic analysis suggests the benefits to the UK economy would be relatively modest. For example, concluding a 'broad and deep' trade agreement with the US has been predicted to boost economic output by around 0.2 per cent.[14]

In addition to these opportunities that are newly opened up by Brexit, some have argued that Brexit provides new impetus for other reforms to UK domestic policies that could tackle the UK's low rate of productivity growth, which has made the fiscal arithmetic more difficult. For example, Brexit could be a necessary catalyst to reforming employers' attitudes to training their workers—and thus addressing the UK's long-running skills shortage. It is important to note, as Swati Dhingra does in her chapter on Brexit and the future of trade elsewhere in this issue, that since the referendum exactly the opposite has happened: training has been cut. But this is not really a guide as to what will happen over the long-term, once new migration rules have been finalised and the ready supply of European migrants restricted. Others argue that the 'decade of disruption' expected in the 2020s provides an opportunity for major changes to produce a fairer and stronger economy.[15] However, while such reforms could boost productivity in the long-term, which would ultimately increase tax revenues, they would be likely to cost money in the short-term.

The House of Commons Defence Select Committee has suggested that the UK needs to increase its military capabilities to secure its place on the world stage and Theresa May has said that spending on research and development needs to be increased to ensure the UK remains a world leader. The government has already announced it will spend an extra £2.3 billion on research and development by 2021–22. Meeting the Defence Select Committee's recent suggestion that the UK should spend an additional 1 per cent of national income on defence would mean raising defence spending by around £20 billion a year. To raise this amount of money from taxation would require—for example—a 4 percentage point rise in the basic rate of income tax.

But any plan to increase (or even maintain) the size of the state would be in conflict with the proposal that some have put forward, whereby the UK should seek to compete aggressively with the EU by cutting taxes and relaxing regulations. This vision for the post-Brexit UK economy has been dubbed 'Singapore on Thames', alluding to the economic model adopted by the south-east Asian city state that helped transform it from a relatively poor tropical port into one of the world's richest countries. Implementing such a proposal would require the size and scope of the UK state to be radically scaled back. But there is no clear public support for such an idea: indeed, the proportion of people in the UK saying they would be happy to pay more tax to fund public services has been growing and now exceeds the numbers who say they are happy with the status quo.

Taken together, the most optimistic assessments by mainstream economists suggest that the new opportunities opened up by Brexit will do little or nothing to tackle the fiscal difficulties that face the government, described above. Most economic analyses suggest that Brexit will result in lower economic growth, which would exacerbate, rather than mitigate, the pressures.

Brexit could prove a watershed moment for re-examining important domestic economic policies—such as on training and infrastructure investment. Such reforms could provide a welcome boost to productivity growth and ease some of the fiscal problems of the ageing population. But such policies would likely require upfront investment at a time when implementing Brexit is likely to take up a significant amount of civil servants' and politicians' time, and place additional demands on the public purse.

## How could the government address these challenges?

Previous governments have regularly used two tactics to help cut borrowing by raising tax revenues in a way that is little noticed by the electorate. First, they have tended to raise tax thresholds less quickly than incomes have grown, dragging an ever larger share of people's incomes into tax. But this effect—known as 'fiscal drag'—raises less revenue the slower is economic growth. The OBR has estimated that fiscal drag raises revenues by around 0.17 per cent of GDP (or £3.6 billion in today's terms) each year. Second, governments have been fond of announcing anti-avoidance measures aimed at closing tax loopholes to raise revenue. Between 2010 and 2017, governments announced over a hundred anti-avoidance measures, which together were expected to raise revenues by around £10 billion (or roughly 0.5 per cent of GDP) this year. However, the OBR has found that these measures sometimes have not raised as much as originally expected, not least because these measures target taxpayers who are already actively changing their behaviour to lower their tax liability.

Past governments have also managed to free up extra resources for health spending by cutting the share of national income devoted to other services. The clearest example of this is the decline in defence spending that has occurred since the 1950s. The latest increase in health spending—confirmed in the October 2018 Budget—was paid for by an unexpected upgrade to the OBR's economic forecasts. However, future forecast revisions could go in the opposite direction. Extra money has also been freed up over the past thirty years by declining spending on debt interest costs. Public sector debt interest spending fell from 5 per cent of national income in 1980 to just over 2 per cent today (a difference of 3 per cent of national income, or over £60 billion a year, in today's terms). This decline was aided in recent years by the Bank of England's very loose monetary policy, which has reduced the interest rates charged on government debt. But it is highly unlikely that future governments will benefit from any similar further reduction—in fact, the reverse is more likely.

More significant active choices are likely to be required over the coming years. The OBR estimates that future governments would need to announce measures that would increase taxes or reduce spending by 1.7 per cent of national income (or £36 billion a year in today's terms) every decade for the next half century if they want debt to stabilise at around 60 per cent of national income. That equates to, for example, a 6-percentage point rise in the main rate of VAT or wiping out almost the entire defence budget. Dealing with such a large fiscal hole is highly unlikely to come from one tax or spending change—it will take a whole raft of new thinking and policy on tax and spend.

## Conclusion

Tax and public spending after Brexit will be heavily shaped by economic and demographic trends that have long been anticipated in the UK. The ageing population is placing increasing demands on public services and pension spending. Trends towards greater self-employment, increased energy efficiency and declining oil reserves are threatening the ability of the current tax system to raise sufficient revenues. A decade of low productivity growth has made these issues more difficult.

Dealing with these fiscal pressures is made harder by the fact that the UK has already undergone nearly a decade of fiscal restraint, involving significant cuts to spending on some public services and cuts to benefit entitlements for those of working age. As a result, there appear to be few areas where spending could easily be cut without affecting the scope or quality of what the state provides or requiring new ways of working to achieve more with less.

Negotiations and preparations for Brexit have diverted government and civil service time away from addressing these problems. The Conservative government's lack of majority since June 2017 has also made it more difficult to pass legislation. As some have argued, Brexit could provide the political impetus to more radical reform of the UK tax system, public services and welfare than has been achieved in the past. But it is also expected to reduce UK economic growth and creates new short-term spending needs, which will limit the resources available to—for example—invest in education and training.

To ensure longer-term fiscal sustainability, the OBR estimates that significant tax increases or cuts to the scale and scope of public services and welfare will be needed. This is likely to require more than simply relying on fiscal drag, clamping down on tax avoidance and incremental cuts to some public services. In the face of these fiscal challenges, the current government and those that follow face important choices about how to balance the books: how much to scale back the quality and scope of public services and welfare benefits, how much to raise taxes or accept higher levels of borrowing, and what role there is for active state intervention to try to boost UK productivity growth to reshape the economic outlook. Demographic trends mean these choices would always have had to be made, but Brexit adds to the challenges, provides some new opportunities and possibly also new impetus to consider more radical changes.

# Acknowledgement

I am grateful to Gavin Kelly, Nick Pearce and attendees at a conference hosted by the Resolution Foundation in May 2018 for comments on an earlier draft of this paper. The views expressed are those of the author and do not necessarily represent the views of the Institute for Government.

# Notes

1 C. Bickerton, 'Brexit and the British growth model', Policy Exchange, 2018; https://policyexchange.org.uk/publication/brexit-and-the-british-growth-model/ (accessed 24 September 2018).
2 C. Emmerson, 'Two parliaments of pain: the UK public finances, 2010 to 2017', IFS Briefing Note BN199, 2017; https://www.ifs.org.uk/uploads/publications/bns/BN199.pdf (accessed 24 September 2018).
3 R. Crawford and C. Emmerson, 'Inevitable trade-offs ahead: long-run public spending pressures', IFS Briefing Note BN207, 2017; https://www.ifs.org.uk/uploads/publications/bns/BN207.pdf (accessed 24 September 2018).
4 S. Adam and B. Roantree, 'The coalition government's record on tax', IFS Election Briefing Note 9, 2014; https://www.ifs.org.uk/uploads/publications/bns/BN167170315.pdf?_ga=2.260103685.92102283.1536313461-1395306327.1524674590 (accessed 24 September 2018).
5 These include, for example, the gross operating profits of public sector companies and interest payments.
6 Office for Budget Responsibility, *Fiscal Sustainability Report—July 2018*; http://obr.uk/fsr/fiscal-sustainability-report-july-2018/ (accessed 24 September 2018).
7 Ibid.
8 Office for Budget Responsibility, *Fiscal Risks Report—July 2017*; http://obr.uk/frr/fiscal-risk-report-july-2017/ (accessed 24 September 2018).
9 T. Herndon, M. Ash and R. Pollin, 'Does high public debt consistently stifle economic growth? A critique of Reinhart and Rogoff', *Cambridge Journal of Economics*, vol. 38, no. 2, March 2014, pp. 257–279; https://academic.oup.com/cje/article/38/2/257/1714018 (accessed 24 September 2018).
10 C. Emmerson, P. Johnson, I. Mitchell and D. Phillips, 'Brexit and the UK's public finances', IFS Report 116, May 2016; https://www.ifs.org.uk/uploads/publications/comms/r116.pdf (accessed 24 September 2018).
11 J. Owen and L. Lloyd, 'Costing Brexit: what is Whitehall spending on exiting the EU?', 2018; https://www.instituteforgovernment.org.uk/publications/costing-brexit-what-whitehall-spending-exiting-eu (accessed 24 September 2018).
12 J. Owen, M. Shepheard and A. Stojanovic, 'Implementing Brexit: customs', 2017; https://www.instituteforgovernment.org.uk/publications/implementing-brexit-customs-september-2017 (accessed 24 September 2018).
13 Open Europe, *What if. . .? The Consequences, Challenges and Opportunities Facing Britain Outside the EU*, 2015; https://openeurope.org.uk/intelligence/britain-and-the-eu/what-if-there-were-a-brexit/ (accessed 24 September 2018).
14 HM Government, 'EU exit analysis: cross Whitehall briefing', 2018; https://www.parliament.uk/documents/commons-committees/Exiting-the-European-

Union/17-19/Cross-Whitehall-briefing/EU-Exit-Analysis-Cross-Whitehall-Briefing. pdf (accessed 24 September 2018).

15 Institute for Public Policy Research, *Prosperity and Justice: a Plan for the New Economy*, 2018; https://www.ippr.org/research/publications/prosperity-and-justice (accessed 24 September 2018).

How to cite this article: G. Tetlow, 'Tax and Spending in the 2020s', in G Kelly and N Pearce (eds.), Britain Beyond Brexit, *The Political Quarterly*, Vol 90, Issue S2, 2019, pp. 94–104. https://doi.org/10.1111/1467-923X.12622

# Brexit and the Politics of Housing in Britain

BEN ANSELL AND DAVID ADLER

## Introduction

POLITICAL earthquakes—both real and perceived—are trembling through Britain. In the 2015 general election, the Scottish National party and the UK Independence party mounted successful challenges from the periphery. In the 2016 referendum on EU membership, the Vote Leave campaign captured a surprising number of votes from both sides of the traditional political divide. And in the 2017 general election, an unlikely Labour leader turned metropolitan areas red, while the incumbent Conservative Prime Minister turned post-industrial towns blue—bringing the whole party system back into a familiar bipolarity. At this breakneck pace of political change, scholars have struggled to make sense of what is driving British politics, and how.

In this paper, we argue that the answer to this question might lie right under our feet. Over the last three decades, the British housing market has undergone a rapid transformation. In the postwar era, British housing featured high levels of social housing and low levels of housing wealth inequality. Today—following a mass social housing sell-off and a historic boom in asset prices—it features the inverse. We argue that this transformation has had a profound impact on British politics by dividing regions, tenures, and generations in a new housing cleavage.

To make this case, we examine the recent history of British housing and its relationship to political changes both past and future. We begin by arguing that the performance of the British housing market—both the cause and the effect of local economic fortunes—shaped attitudes toward Britain's relationship to the European Union by structuring voters' sense of inclusion in the project of international integration. We argue that house prices, even at a highly disaggregated local level, strongly predicted the vote for Leave or Remain. We then turn to the post-Brexit period. Our analysis suggests that housing played a similarly crucial role in the 2017 general election, with parties divided over their representation of different tenures. We conclude with a discussion of the prospects for housing policy reform in the context of new tenure coalitions.

## The Brexit vote and housing

Real estate has come centre stage in the story of advanced capitalism. While advanced industrial economies relied on manufacturing to drive economic

© The Authors 2019. The Political Quarterly © The Political Quarterly Publishing Co. Ltd. 2019
Published by John Wiley & Sons Ltd, 9600 Garsington Road, Oxford OX4 2DQ, UK and 350 Main Street, Malden, MA 02148, USA

growth in the postwar period, today they rely in large part on the performance of assets like real estate.[1] Citizens who once relied on wages for
income and pensions for retirement now rely on credit and real estate.[2]

But Britain presents an extreme case. Since 1971, the stock value of British
real estate has risen from roughly $60 billion to over $6 trillion—a 100-fold
increase, adjusted for inflation. Housing now accounts for more than 44 per
cent of all household wealth.[3] The figures are equally striking in terms of real
estate's flow contribution to the British economy. Real estate accounts for
more than 12 per cent of Britain's gross domestic product—larger than the
entire manufacturing sector[4]—the majority of which comes from house prices
through 'imputed rent': hypothetical rental income from owner-occupied
homes. The performance of the British economy has long been closely linked
with its housing market and, as we shall see, so too is its politics.

## Brexit and the politics of housing in Britain

Figure 1 uses data on (nominal) mean house prices at the ward level
(around 5,000 people) between 1996 and 2016. For each year, we order the
wards by their mean house price and show the overall distribution across
wards, with the circle reflecting the median ward. Two things jump out.
First, average nominal prices rose dramatically across the period—from

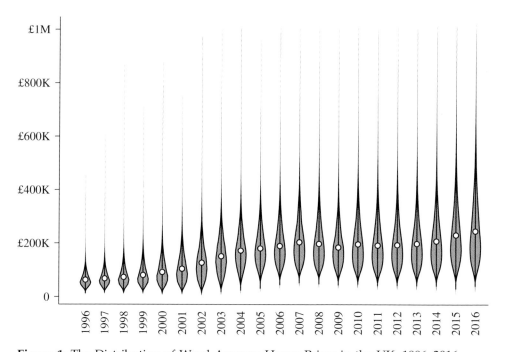

**Figure 1:** The Distribution of Ward Average House Prices in the UK, 1996–2016

**Table 1: Ward voting for remain and median house price levels and changes**

|  | Model 1 | Model 2 | Model 3 |
|---|---|---|---|
| Log Median House Price (Ward) | 10.53 | 10.36 | 8.88 |
|  | (1.84) | (1.62) | (1.73) |
| Change in Ward Prices 1996-2014 |  | 4.85 | 4.55 |
|  |  | (0.77) | (0.86) |
| Log Median House Price (LAD) | 8.08 |  | 2.46 |
|  | (2.80) |  | (2.85) |
| Observations | 1109 | 1109 | 1109 |

*Note.* Numbers represent effect of a unit increase in the relevant variable on ward level support for Remain. The figures in parentheses are the standard errors of those estimates.

£60,000 in 1996 to £250,000 in 2016, a quadrupling of nominal prices during a period where UK inflation rose just 76 per cent. Second, the distribution of average prices across wards also rose dramatically. The gap in prices between the wards at the 75th and 25th percentile rose from around £35,000 in 1996 to around £185,000 in 2016. Property in Britain has become not only more expensive relative to other goods, but also much more unequally distributed across the country.

The broader economic effects of this transition have also been highly unequal. For those who own property in areas like the south of England, rising house prices have heralded greater prosperity. According to Andy Haldane, the chief economist of the Bank of England, property today is a 'better bet' for retirement than a pension.[5] For those who rent property, however, rising house prices have heralded greater exclusion. In 2015, the average private renter in Britain paid more than 28 per cent of her income on rent. In London, that figure rose to 40 per cent.[6]

Housing markets also engender inequality in the daily lives of owners and renters. While homeowners enjoy security of tenure, renters in Britain have very few protections compared to their European neighbours. Section 21 of the 1988 Rent Act permits landlords to evict tenants with two months' notice without citing a grievance. Section 21 evictions have spiked alongside rising property values, as many landlords pursue new tenants to pay higher levels of rent. The result is increasing inequalities of space. While homeowners have enjoyed an increasing ratio of rooms per person, renters have been pushed into smaller units because that is what they can afford.[7]

The transformation of the British housing market is both product and producer of a new geography of fortune. Regions like the south of England have been well served by the service sector transition of the British economy, while the traditional manufacturing powerhouses in the north of England have suffered. The former have enjoyed higher levels of investment and the inflow of workers that accompany it, driving up demand for housing. The latter have lost out, and the housing market reflects this dearth of demand. The geography of house prices tells the story of the British wealth and well-being.

The enormous disparities seen above reflect, in part, the longstanding differences between Britain's regional economies since industrialisation. It is no surprise that homeownership has historically correlated well with Conservative party support:[8] richer, more Conservative-supporting areas, tended to have higher house prices on average.

The housing boom and bust of the past two decades has to some extent accentuated these divisions. Yet they have also unearthed new political divisions that cross the traditional geographic patterns of voting. In particular, the recent 'triumph of the city'—wherein inner cities moved from apparently crime-ridden and destitute areas to become highly desirable, well-positioned neighborhoods[9] —has created an unfamiliar political geography in Britain.

The Brexit referendum of 2016 exposed these new cleavages. The Leave/Remain patterning of vote across local authorities in England and Wales did not match standard Labour/Conservative patterns. In particular, a large number of wealthy cities, towns and nearby rural areas in the south-east and south-west voted Remain, despite a long history of voting Conservative. Similarly, many poorer towns in the Midlands and north-east, traditional Labour strongholds, voted to leave the European Union. Split in this way, both parties remain fundamentally divided on how to approach Brexit.

What does explain the geographical pattern of voting in the EU referendum? Ansell argues that house price levels and changes at the local authority level are strong predictors of support for remaining in the European Union.[10] In particular, he shows that local authorities with houses twice as expensive had support levels for Remain around 15 percentage points higher, even controlling for their region in the country and local demographics such as age profile, migration rates, unemployment, and local wages.

Although data were only officially collected at the local authority level, the BBC was able to acquire ward voting rates for some 1,100 wards. We analyse this data to see if the pattern of high house prices and Remain voting holds at a very local level. Table 1 shows results from statistical regressions at the ward level.

Model 1 includes indicators for (logged) median house prices at the ward level and at the local authority (LAD) level. To interpret these results, if we move from a ward where median house prices were £85,000 in 2014 to one where they were £230,000, support for Remain jumps by 10.5 percentage points. A similar shift at the local authority level results in an 8.1 per cent point increase in support for Remain.

Models 2 and 3 repeat the exercise adding between 1996 and 2014 in ward median house prices. Moving from a ward with a 'mere' tripling of nominal house prices to one with a quadrupling is associated with a 5 per cent increase in support for Remain. The implication is that both long-run levels of house prices and relative growth over the past two decades shaped the Brexit vote. Places that had always done, or were recently doing, 'better' were happier with the status quo of remaining in the European Union.

Figure 2 provides a striking example of this relationship, splitting out the voting pattern for wards in pro-Leave Wakefield, marginal Stockport, and pro-Remain Cambridge. In each district, there is a very strong relationship between wards with higher house prices having greater support for Remain, even though the three districts had very different average house prices (and indeed support for the EU). House prices both proxy for local economic fortunes and directly drive (dis)satisfaction with the status quo (since those in cheaper houses may resent their exclusion from the housing boom and those with highly appreciated houses have benefitted substantially). In both cases, these mixed fortunes appear to have filtered over into broader (dis-)satisfaction with contemporary British life.

## Housing politics after Brexit

The obvious question to ask, given the relationship between housing and the Brexit vote, is whether it transferred over to voter preferences in 2017. The answer appears to be—only partially. That is, many richer Remain voting areas did back the nominally harder Brexit Conservative party in 2017—for example, in David Cameron's old constituency of Witney. Similarly, while

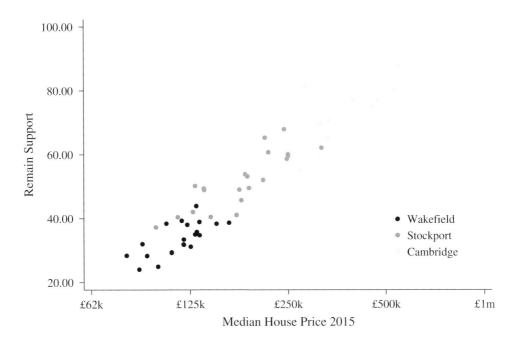

**Figure 2:** Brexit support at the ward level and 2015 house prices in three cities

the Conservatives had hoped to win many Leave voting Labour constituencies in the Midlands and the north, in reality only a handful of these seats switched sides.

Figure 3 gives a sense of the degree to which the Brexit vote scrambled existing voting patterns and their relationship to the housing market. It plots, using the British Election Study of 2017, the probability of an individual voting for the Conservative party by two factors related to where they live—house prices in their local authority and support for Remain in their local authority (controlling for age, gender, education, income, and region). The three unbroken lines represent predicted probabilities of voting Conservative for individuals in areas where house prices average £750,000, £270,000 and £100,000, with the 'whiskers' on the plot showing the confidence interval around those predictions. The standard pattern where richer areas vote Conservative and poorer areas vote Labour broadly held up in 2017: voters in local authorities with more expensive housing tended to vote Conservative. However, it is notable that the 'Remainness' of areas was negatively connected to Conservative support and that was particularly the case in areas with expensive houses. The support for Conservatives in areas with cheap houses and high support for Leave failed to make up this gap. Graphically, we see a 'narrowing' in the effect of house prices on Conservative support as we move from pro-Leave to pro-Remain districts.

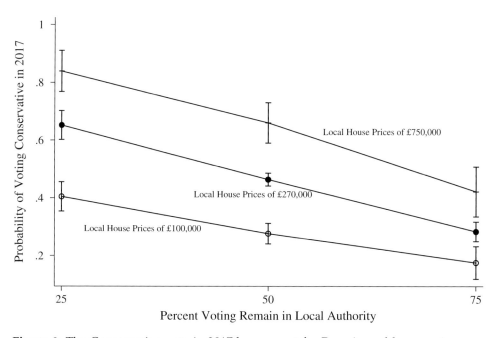

**Figure 3:** The Conservative vote in 2017 by support for Remain and house prices

Since more expensive areas were also more likely to vote Remain (and cheaper places for Leave) on aggregate the sharp drop-off in Conservative support in expensive pro-Remain areas, accompanied by a failure to pick up enough support in pro-Leave poorer areas, arguably lost the Conservatives their majority. In other words, the connection between housing and support for Remain, which cut across traditional class geographies, likely shaped the final outcome of the 2017 general election.

Geographically then, house prices cut across traditional lines of political support. What about at the individual level? How did homeowners feel about the Conservatives and was there really a 'rentquake'? The answer is mixed—it might be better, though awkwardly, described as a 'rent plus mortgage-quake'. Returning to the British Election Study of 2017, we abstract away from geographical setting and look at individual level characteristics alone in explaining support for the Conservatives.

In Figure 4, we examine the effect of housing tenure—conditional on age—on voting Conservative in 2017 (controlling for education, income, gender, Brexit vote, immigration attitudes, and employment status). The figure plots the predicted probability of an individual voting Conservative, with the grey line denoting renters and the black line denoting homeowners (with the confidence intervals around these predictions denoted by the dashed lines). Perhaps the most striking result to consider is that whereas among renters (in private and social housing) age is essentially unrelated to vote choice, among

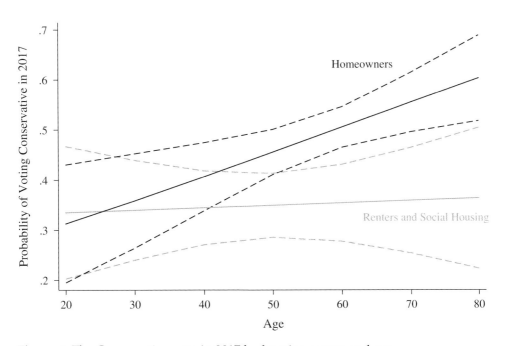

**Figure 4:** The Conservative vote in 2017 by housing tenure and age

homeowners, there is a striking difference of around 30 per cent as we move from people in their twenties to people in their eighties. Put differently, young people behave very similarly regardless of housing status, whereas among the old, homeowners are much more pro-Conservative than private renters and social housing tenants.

The relationship between age and partisanship among homeowners is a function of the variable conditions of their property ownership. For an older cohort, homes were bought cheap and held dear: they reaped the largest gains from the asset boom of the late 1990s and early 2000s, and have since transitioned into outright ownership. For a younger cohort, by contrast, homes were purchased at exorbitant price levels—and only by signing onto decades-long mortgages, which expose them to continuous risk of negative equity. Between 2005 and 2016, the percentage of mortgages issued that last thirty-five years or over rose from just 2 per cent to over 15 per cent. In other words, two mechanisms separate young and old homeowners: wealth and risk. Together, they constrained support for Conservatives among younger homeowners in the 2017 election—many of whom voted for a Labour manifesto with strong social protections—while driving it among older homeowners.

As is well known, relatively few people own homes in their twenties at present. Still, the longstanding gap in preferences between owners and renters—around which Margaret Thatcher based her political strategy of Right to Buy—only emerges among the middle-aged. Homeowners under the age of around forty behave very similarly to renters politically. Since almost all of these younger homeowners will still have mortgage payments to make, we see here a new 'coalition' of renters and mortgagees, against those who fully own their property. Another way of viewing this is that those who benefitted most greatly from rising house prices, by virtue of having bought their house over a decade ago, were the core Conservative support base.

One final regional dimension of the 2017 general election is worth noting. House price differences have dynamic effects on political behaviour in that they can 'lock' people out of expensive housing markets, forcing them to look for cheaper property elsewhere. There is some evidence that this pattern had political implications in 2017. London house prices rose much more dramatically in the post-2013 housing boom than did prices elsewhere. Accordingly, many younger workers and families moved into the wider south-east and east regions to seek cheaper property, often while continuing to work in London. As Ian Warren argued in a post-election analysis in *The Guardian*, many of these people carried their previous voting habits and social attitudes with them.[11] Analysis of the British Election Study of 2017 shows that, controlling for age, education, gender, and income, individuals were most likely to switch towards Labour from 2015 to 2017 if they lived in the south-east and east regions, as opposed to London. Should this pattern continue, it will further scramble the longstanding political geography of Britain, again driven by the housing market.

## Housing policies and their political economy

We have seen that housing is increasingly shaping the geography of British politics in novel ways. What about the possibility of reforms to the housing market itself? We see three key general areas for reform, each with striking political difficulties. The first is to lower prices by reducing the demand for housing relative to other goods. The second is to lower prices by increasing the supply of dwellings, both private construction and social housing. The third is a broader regional recalibration of the British economy that serves to reduce geographical inequalities in house prices.

Reducing demand for housing essentially means reducing the growth of mortgage credit both for owners and landlords. This is probably the most advanced area of policy generation given the tighter restrictions on mortgage lending brought in by the Financial Conduct Authority in 2014, which required much more stringent accounting of borrowers' income and expenditure and capped loan to income ratios. On the tax side, fiscal reforms have made buy-to-let substantially less attractive by increasing stamp duty and reducing tax deductibility.

However, such policies lack an obvious political support coalition—landlords and would-be borrowers are directly negatively affected, owners in general may see lower prices, and the only obvious beneficiaries are future buyers—typically young and politically inactive.

In terms of increasing housing supply, there may be some more obvious winners, but our analysis suggests that overall policy preferences are deeply divided along the tenure cleavage. Homeowners, eager to protect the value of their nest egg, tend to oppose new housing construction—especially when they expect house prices to rise in the coming years. Renters, by contrast, become increasingly supportive of social housing construction as their expectations of house price inflation rise. The divergent interests of these two groups, in other words, produce direct conflict over policy preferences.

Some indicative results appear in Figure 5, which uses the British Social Attitudes Survey of 2010, asking people what their expectations are of future growth in the housing market and their attitudes towards the construction of social housing. The line with hollow circles represents the average predicted probability of supporting construction of social housing among homeowners, whereas the line with filled circles represents average support among renters (the whiskers represent the 95 per cent confidence intervals for these predictions). While attitudes of renters and homeowners are similar in declining or stable housing markets, in rising markets, the two diverge, with homeowners substantially less supportive, and renters more supportive, of social housing. Hence, building a cross-group coalition has been difficult during the secular rise of house prices over the past two decades.

The support for social housing construction among renters reflects a significant change in ideal tenure. When house prices were low and stable, renters

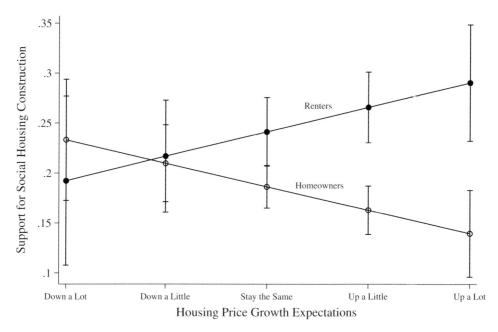

**Figure 5:** House price expectations and social housing attitudes, BSAS 2010

could expect to rise up the property ladder and move comfortably into homeownership. As house prices rise, however, renters are driven away from the desire to purchase an exorbitantly expensive home and toward a 'social' alternative that can protect them from the inflation of the private market. We find a strong and significantly positive relationship between renters' sense of house price inflation and their desire to live in social housing. Such a shift is reflected in the changing position of the Labour party, which now advocates large-scale investment in social housing over the commitment to first-time buyers that was so central to the New Labour platform.

There is some evidence that homeowners are becoming more sympathetic to government attempts at housing reform. Recent data from YouGov suggest that over 40 per cent of homeowners support efforts to 'bring down house prices' and 'build large numbers of new homes'. From the demand side, this shift is likely driven by the intergenerational sympathies: home-owning parents concerned for struggling children in the rental sector. From the supply side, this shift is likely driven by the Conservative party's recognition of renters as a rapidly growing proportion of the electorate, leading Theresa May to proclaim it her 'personal mission' to fix the housing market.

Yet the prospects for reform, on the whole, appear partisan. The 'rentquake' of 2017 has given the Labour party a strong mandate to deliver housing policies that reflect renters' interests: tenant protections, landlord regulation, and social housing construction. The Conservatives, while showing real movement toward issues like land reform, are likely to back away from policies that undermine the interests of their core constituency of homeowning voters.

These sharp differences between renters and owners are further amplified when we consider the possibility of a regional shift in the economy that might 'recalibrate' the British housing market, through a systematic attempt to move production, jobs, and investment away from the south-east. The difficulty with doing so is fairly obvious for the Conservative party: by and large this means a relative decline of house prices in core Conservative home counties constituencies. The inability of the Northern Powerhouse agenda to outlive the political fortunes of its creator, George Osborne, testifies to the unlikeliness of a successful Conservative regional agenda. Yet, as we saw in earlier sections, a Labour party that is growing in Remain supporting, high house price areas, will also find itself potentially undermining part of its support base in the metropolitan south-east.

Finally, the future of housing policy hinges crucially on the performance of the housing market itself—which, in the context of Brexit, remains highly uncertain. High and rising levels of house prices are likely to lock in partisan sympathies and drive an even deeper tenure divide, allowing for the Labour party to champion even more radical rental sector reform, while increasing the cross-pressure on the Conservatives to strike a balance between their renting and homeowning constituencies. Falling prices—or price gain 'disappointment,' which seems more likely—may create a new opportunity for political parties to take the lead in initiating fundamental reforms to the land and housing markets. Such a shift does not imply a radical change in the preferences of British homeowners. While rising house prices tend to reduce support for spending on social housing among homeowners, falling house prices do not necessarily imply the inverse: as we saw in 2008, falling house prices can trigger panic among homeowners who fear slipping into negative equity, pushing political parties to introduce measures like mortgage guarantees that prop up prices and entrench homeowner privileges. Such is the curse of Britain's asset-price addiction: with so much wealth stored in the property market, political parties struggle to navigate a price downturn.

In the context of falling prices, then, the prospects for reform depend largely on the priorities of the party in government and the simple chronology of Britain's electoral politics. A Conservative government, dependent on happy homeowners, may well let a crisis of price deflation go to waste—pulling out every trick in the book to keep house prices afloat. A Labour opposition may be able to harness the widespread discontent of the downturn to introduce a new housing regime—but only if it can win a general election on that basis. As Britain enters the greatest period of uncertainty in recent history, the politics of housing hang in this balance.

# Notes

1 H. Schwartz, *Subprime Nation: American Power, Global Capital, and the Housing Bubble*, Ithaca, Cornell University Press, 2009; R. Shiller, *Irrational Exuberance*, Princeton, Princeton University Press, 2007.

2 J. S. Ahlquist and B. W. Ansell, 'Taking credit: redistribution and borrowing in an age of economic polarization', *World Politics*, vol. 69, no. 4, 2017, pp. 640–675.

3 Office of National Statistics, *Statistical Bulletin: Wealth in Great Britain Wave 5: 2014 to 2016*, 2018.

4 Office of National Statistics, *United Kingdom National Accounts, The Blue Book*, 2013.

5 'Property is a better bet than pensions, says Bank of England Economist', *The Guardian*, 28 August 2016; https://www.theguardian.com/money/2016/aug/28/property-is-better-bet-than-a-pension-says-bank-of-england-economist (accessed 22 November 2018).

6 Department of Work and Pensions, *Family Resources Survey: United Kingdom, 2015/16*, 2017.

7 D. Dorling, *All That is Solid: How the Great Housing Disaster Defines Our Times, and What We Can Do About It*, London, Penguin, 2014.

8 D. T. Studlar, I. McAllister and A. Alvaro, 'Privatization and the British electorate: microeconomic policies, macroeconomic evaluations, and party support', *American Journal of Political Science*, vol. 34, no. 4, 1990, pp. 1077–1101.

9 E. L. Glaeser, *Triumph of the City: How our Greatest Invention Makes us Richer, Smarter, Greener, Healthier, and Happier*, London, Penguin, 2012.

10 B. Ansell, 'Housing, credit, and Brexit', paper presented at Conference on Europe and the Credit Crisis, Madison, WI, 2017.

11 I. Warren, 'How the Conservatives lost their home counties heartland', *The Guardian*, 12 October 2017; https://www.theguardian.com/commentisfree/2017/oct/12/conservatives-lost-home-counties-influx-young-people-london-south-east (accessed 22 November 2018).

How to cite this article: B. Ansell and D. Adler, 'Brexit and the Politics of Housing in Britain', in G Kelly and N Pearce (eds.), Britain Beyond Brexit, *The Political Quarterly*, Vol 90, Issue S2, 2019, pp. 105–116. https://doi.org/10.1111/1467-923X.12621

# Energy Supply and Decarbonisation Beyond Brexit: Politics and Policy

MATTHEW LOCKWOOD AND ANTONY FROGGATT

## Introduction

THERE will be no long-term sustainable future for capitalism in the twenty-first century unless climate change can be limited. For a country like Britain, this means completely decarbonising the economy by the second half of the century, if not before. Britain's path towards a low-carbon economy has been significantly shaped by membership of the EU, especially through legislation and regulations affecting the energy sector, so Brexit raises important questions about whether and how that path will continue in the future.

At the same time, Brexit poses some immediate and direct challenges for the security and costs of energy supply. This is because over the last twenty-five years the UK energy system itself has become intertwined with that of EU member states, through the development of the Internal Energy Market and the associated infrastructure. The UK is increasingly dependent on energy imports, many of which come from or pass through the EU. The EU has sought to increase its energy security, both through solidarity mechanisms between member states, and by forging better relationships with suppliers and transit countries. Leaving the EU therefore raises serious questions about the security and costs of Britain's future energy supplies.

Moreover, Brexit is happening at a time of significant flux in energy systems around the world. After thirty years of free markets (at least in theory), state intervention and even re-nationalisation are increasingly back on the agenda. Even more fundamentally, new technology in electricity, coupled with developments in ICT and data handling, is leading to a rapid decentralisation of energy systems, disrupting established industry players and giving new roles to consumers.

In what follows, we outline the key issues for energy and climate policy in a post-Brexit Britain. The next section looks at the potential impacts of different Brexit scenarios on energy supply, with a focus on costs and security. In the third section we consider how domestic political support for decarbonising energy may be affected by Brexit, and some of the low-carbon policy issues raised by separating from the EU. The fourth section looks at post-Brexit Britain in the light of long term technological and ownership trends in the energy sector. Our energy future could end up looking a lot more isolationist than it does now, or we could remain fairly integrated with

Published by John Wiley & Sons Ltd, 9600 Garsington Road, Oxford OX4 2DQ, UK and 350 Main Street, Malden, MA 02148, USA

the EU. Both futures are feasible, but differ significantly in the challenges they pose and opportunities they offer.

## Energy supply after Brexit

The UK's energy policy and system have become increasingly integrated with the EU in recent decades, through regulatory harmonisation, common policy frameworks and infrastructure. But there has been little discussion of energy supply or its environmental impact within Brexit debates, except in the broadest terms. The July 2018 White Paper did not clarify the UK government's ambitions for the future relationship in this area.

Effects of Brexit on energy supply will come via two routes: direct and indirect. Indirect effects work through routes outside energy policy and regulation. One of these is the impact of currency shocks or depreciation, leading to increases in the costs of fuels and imported inputs to supply chains. Another is potential disruption to supply chains as the UK leaves the Customs Union or the Single Market or both. There is also the possible effect of loss of access to skilled labour; for example, Oil and Gas UK estimate that around 5 per cent of the workforce in the North Sea is from EU countries.[1] More generally, uncertainty linked to Brexit has cast a pall over investment decisions in the whole sector.[2]

The direct effects will come as a result of whether or not the UK stays in the Internal Energy Market (IEM). The IEM has developed over a number of decades through increasing European oversight and in areas such as market rules and environmental protection, legislative control of policy and regulation in the energy sectors of Member States. Thus, the IEM is not about tariffs but rather about a set of shared policies and rules and, more recently, participation in a linked automated network of trading platforms.

The issues involved in leaving the IEM differ across gas, electricity and oil. Oil is globally traded, so the effects of Brexit can be expected to be fairly minor. By contrast, trade in gas and electricity, being largely or entirely networked through pipes and wires, is much more regional in nature. In the short term, the implications for gas security of supply are more important, but in the medium term it will be electricity that matters more, as we are likely to switch over to using electricity for cars and at least partially for heat as well, in order to decarbonise the economy.

Gas trade with European countries from outside the IEM is entirely possible (as the example of Russia shows). The UK is well connected physically to the Continent, and with both North Sea fields and the largest liquefied natural gas (LNG) infrastructure in Europe, it is a useful trading partner. The main concerns are therefore less about trade per se and more about security of supply and price stability at times of peak demand, when we become more dependent on imported gas.

When the UK joined the then European Economic Community in 1973, it was poised to enter the North Sea oil and gas boom period (Figure 1). By

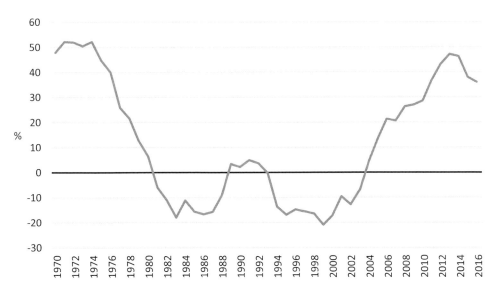

**Figure 1:** UK net energy import dependency, 1970-2016

contrast, it leaves as its energy import dependency has re-emerged, with domestic production of gas and oil expected to continue to decline. The UK is highly dependent on Norway for winter imports, which might become a problem if there were a situation in which the UK had to compete for Norwegian gas with the remaining EU Member States, since Norway, being a member of the European Economic Area, is more closely aligned with the latter. This situation, and resulting price volatility, may make a post-Brexit Britain seek other options, including more LNG and strategic gas storage which could cost in the order of a £100 million a year.[3]

For electricity, the present trade (which tends to run from the Continent to Britain) could, in principle, continue. But experience from Switzerland suggests that the EU increasingly sees electricity in terms of participation in a system with common rules and interlinked trading platforms. The latter have developed in the last two years into a 'market coupling' system that has reduced transaction costs and led to more efficient allocation of interconnector capacity. Exiting this system as part of the IEM would mean a loss of economic benefits, as prices are likely to rise. Estimates of what is potentially at stake are of the order of €100 million a year. However, the market coupling system is expected to evolve to allow shared electricity system balancing services (that is, matching supply and demand in real-time), access to which would be worth a lot more, potentially of the order of several billion pounds a year.[4] The balancing service offered by interconnectors will be of increased value as the share of wind and solar and other variable renewables increases. Any resulting rise in final energy prices is likely to sharpen the politics of energy affordability and the costs of decarbonisation.

There are, therefore, good security and economic reasons for remaining within the IEM. However, doing so whilst leaving the EU would also come with some 'sovereignty costs'. These would include having to accept future EU energy legislation and regulation without having a formal say in their development, and the jurisdiction of, if not the European Court of Justice, some other arbitration mechanism acceptable to the EU-27. This loss of influence would be considerable, as the UK has historically been a strong voice in the development of an integrated European energy system.

Before leaving energy supply issues, it is worth briefly considering two other special problems. One is the Single Electricity Market (SEM), a common integrated electricity market and system across Northern Ireland and the Republic of Ireland which has been in place since 2007. The SEM involves shared regulation and major investments going into increased interconnection between the two. There are a number of possible post-Brexit arrangements, somewhat mirroring those arising from the wider Irish border problem. Maintaining the SEM has been recognised as a priority by all negotiating parties, and the UK government has reaffirmed its commitment to maintaining the SEM in the July 2018 White Paper, but finding a solution will be politically delicate.

The other special problem is 'Brexatom' (British withdrawal from the Euratom Treaty). For more than sixty years, the Treaty has shaped the UK's domestic nuclear legislation, including standards and rules on nuclear safety and non-proliferation, health and safety and nuclear waste management. Of greatest concern is the non-proliferation of nuclear material. Currently, this is overseen by Euratom safeguards inspectors on behalf of the international community. Outside of Euratom, inspections will need to be carried out by the UK's Office for Nuclear Regulation (ONR), directly reporting to the International Atomic Energy Agency. The ONR accepts that it will not be possible to have capacity in place by March 2019 to inspect the same number of facilities as under Euratom, although it says that it will meet international standards. In addition, the UK will need to negotiate and ratify new bilateral agreements for supply of nuclear material and equipment, in particular with Australia, Canada, Japan, and the United States before the UK leaves the EU, or if there is one, at the end of the transition period. All of this is possible, but will take additional resources for the ONR and time is pressing.

## Decarbonisation after Brexit

Post-Brexit, concerns about energy security, affordability and competitiveness are likely to rise up the agenda, which raises the question of whether the low carbon agenda survives. A common view is that it will, because the two key frameworks setting the UK's ambition on climate policy—the 2008 Climate Change Act (CCA) and the 2016 United Nations Framework Convention on Climate Change (UNFCCC) Paris Agreement—are not dependent on the EU.

Brexit is likely to require the UK to adopt its own Nationally Defined Contribution under the Paris Agreement, but this is a relatively minor technical change. More important is the argument that the UK will lose influence because it will no longer be part of the EU bloc, but rather just one country with around 1 per cent of global carbon emissions.[5] Moreover, with the loss of UK advocacy internally, there is a risk that the EU will be a weaker ally in the international arena. However, at present both the UK and the EU have signalled a desire to continue working closely together at the international level.

At the same time, the 2008 CCA commits the UK to emissions reductions targets that are more ambitious than those of the EU. However, a significant part of expected UK emissions reduction to 2030—the Committee on Climate Change (CCC) puts it at 50 per cent—is through areas covered by EU legislation and regulation, such as energy efficiency and vehicle emissions standards. These frameworks should be incorporated into UK law through the Great Repeal Act, but they have been flagged as delivery risks by the CCC[6] and there are concerns that without the EU to enforce them there will be a governance gap.

In practice, both the UK's efforts in international climate leadership and the future efficacy of the CCA depend in large part on the domestic politics of climate change policy. There is broad support for action on climate change in the UK, but the issue is of low salience to most voters, so that support is not deep. The CCA does benefit from strong support from business, both in the energy sector and more generally; for example, in April 2018, twenty-one major energy firms and other businesses called on the UK government and the EU to continue to work closely towards meeting the goals of the Paris Agreement.[7] Nevertheless, two fears remain.

One is that if there is a deep economic shock on leaving the EU, public support for climate policy will be overwhelmed by concerns about costs. It is already the case that policy costs associated with carbon reduction, especially on electricity bills, are set to grow to 2020.[8] A second fear is of hostile attacks on climate change policy and science from a resurgent right-wing populism. Surveys show that Leave voters tend to be more sceptical of climate science than the general population, and while UKIP as an organised force has dissipated, its supporters and voters are still around. One would expect their presence to be felt especially within the Conservative party. Yet it is far from clear that the current party leadership is tacking to the right on climate change. While there has been significant dismantling of policy, for example on support for solar photovoltaic (PV) and onshore wind, and scrapping the zero-carbon homes standard, there have also been some proactive steps, such as a suggested phase-out of conventional diesel and petrol cars by 2040 and an instruction to the Committee on Climate Change to look at the implications of increasing ambition on the UK's 2050 target. It is hard to think this approach is not at least in part a political strategy from a

Conservative government aimed at appealing to younger voters, who are both more concerned about climate change and more likely to vote Labour. While the Conservatives need to appeal more to such voters, the party is in a brittle and unstable state, and a stronger shift towards right-wing populism is a significant possibility, as is some successor to, or resurgence of, UKIP. Such developments would be a major threat to the decarbonisation agenda, and could see the weakening, if not the repeal of the 2008 CCA.

If commitment on climate change action remains strong, what are the post-Brexit policy issues? One is how to price carbon emissions. The EU's Emissions Trading System (ETS) has been a centrepiece of Europe-wide climate policy since 2005. The UK government wants to stay in the scheme until 2020, but it is not clear what the desired relationship will be beyond this. The ETS has been largely ineffective because of lobbying, and a domestic emissions trading scheme might be an opportunity for a better design, but it would have a smaller trading pool, and the practicalities of setting up a new scheme could take several years. The simplest option would be to build on the current UK carbon floor price policy by bringing in a carbon tax. However, the effectiveness of a tax will depend on the level at which it is set, and this in turn will be determined by the political considerations discussed above.

A second issue is support given to low carbon technologies, at present mainly in electricity generation. Renewables are most vulnerable, as historically, UK governments have been lukewarm towards such technologies, and policy has really been driven from the EU via the Renewables Directives. The exception here is offshore wind, which has now reached a critical mass where it is producing such employment, investment and potential export benefits that it has won government backing. Looking beyond 2020, a post-Brexit Britain would have to be extremely isolationist to resist the global trend towards cheaper renewables. Investment will depend on market design, which needs reform, and planning rules. Recent UK governments have been keen on new nuclear power, but here there are potential headwinds post-Brexit. Nuclear remains less popular with the public than renewable energy and it currently looks expensive, as noted in the 2018 National Infrastructure Assessment.[9]

A third issue is the loss of low-carbon investment support. The UK has received around £2.5 billion a year in energy loans and grants from the EU, including infrastructure finance, regional development funding and grants for research and development. The most significant loss would be reduced or even loss of funding from the European Investment Bank (EIB), as nearly 30 per cent of loans to the UK have supported energy infrastructure, amounting to over £8 billion in the past five years, levering in investment from others. Ninety per cent of EIB investment goes to Member States, so outside of the EU it will be more difficult for the UK to access loans and a replacement will be needed.

# Brexit and longer-term trends in the energy system

In addition to decarbonisation, the UK energy system is evolving in a number of other ways. One relates to ownership and markets. When the UK joined the EEC in 1973, energy industries were state-owned monopolies. This situation was transformed by the liberalisation revolution of the 1980s and 1990s. However, this Thatcherite project was barely complete when a slow drift back towards state intervention began from the early 2000s onwards. The retreat from free markets was initially linked to decarbonisation goals, but as energy prices rose sharply in the latter part of the decade, scepticism about the true extent of competition in retail markets also came to the fore, leading to price controls. Labour under Jeremy Corbyn has gone further, calling for a return to public ownership in the energy sector in the 2017 election manifesto.

Public ownership is allowed within the current rules of the IEM as long as networks, generation and supply are not owned within the same part of the state. Indeed, ironically, many of the companies active in British markets have parents in other EU Member States that are state owned; not just four of the 'Big Six' energy utilities, but also major players in offshore wind and new nuclear developments. In a post-Brexit Britain, that foreign ownership might come under scrutiny. However, it is worth noting that the parts of the energy sector specifically targeted by Labour for renationalisation are gas and electricity networks owned mainly by companies and banks in Asia, Australia and North America.[10] Public ownership in energy is a post-Brexit approach to 'taking back control' that offers an alternative to sovereignty and ethno-nationalist narratives. But a return to the statism of the 1970s is not feasible; the challenge will be how to make public ownership work for a twenty-first century energy system that is undergoing major technological and institutional change.

A second trend is in the devolution of policy making. Historically, British energy policy has been set centrally, and markets and networks have operated within GB-wide regulatory frameworks. This unitary approach changed with devolution in the late 1990s. Energy policy is somewhat of a grey area in devolution: Whitehall has retained control of the key legal frameworks and financial resources, but there are important differences between the nations and regions. Energy policy, regulation and markets in Northern Ireland are now largely run separately from the rest of the UK, except for nuclear power. At the other end of the spectrum, Wales has only a few devolved powers, in areas such as energy efficiency and fuel poverty. Scotland is in an intermediate position, having a degree of control over policy which it has used to mark out a somewhat distinctive position.

Some have argued that Brexit, through the transfer of powers directly from Brussels to devolved administrations, might provide an opportunity for a 'race to the top', for example on climate ambition.[11] However, it is not clear that Brexit is needed for this to happen. For example, the Scottish government is currently consulting on a Climate Change Bill that would have a greater emissions reduction target than the 2008 CCA. It has opposed hydraulic fracturing ('fracking') for shale oil and gas, ruled out any new nuclear plants in Scotland and is actively promoting district heating, all policies that set it apart from the UK's central government. Scotland also has some control over renewables policy, and greater political support for wind power has led more extensive deployment there, as well as greater community wind farm ownership. Barring a power grab from Whitehall, what would change with a hard Brexit would be the removal of the common EU framework for energy and climate policy, and the possibility that existing divergence between England, Wales and Scotland would intensify—mostly likely with Scotland pursuing more renewable energy, and England going for more nuclear (possibly taking Wales along with it). Ultimately, given the technical incompatibilities between these two approaches, we could see the development of two largely separate energy systems, reinforcing Scotland's wider distinctiveness.

The third important trend is about the decentralisation of the electricity system itself. An architecture based solely on big power stations and one-way distribution networks is fast giving way to one with a large number of small-scale technologies, including wind and solar PV, increasingly interconnected locally through smart communication and control systems. The distinctions between producers and consumers of electricity are breaking down, with a number of experiments in local electricity markets and peer-to-peer trading already underway in parts of Britain. Whereas the flexibility needed to keep the electricity system stable has historically been provided by coal and gas-fired power stations, it will increasingly come from the demand side in homes and businesses and through battery storage, the costs of which are falling rapidly. With growing uptake of electric cars and the trialling of 'vehicle-to-grid' technologies, the role of battery storage will grow.

These changes present a number of opportunities. One is that major investments in the upgrading of infrastructure across the country will be needed. Another is that, since energy decentralisation is an emerging global phenomenon, there are huge potential export markets with high-skilled jobs for those companies able to take a lead. However, the ability of the UK to access the EU part of that market will be influenced by the post-Brexit settlement, including trade in services. There are also potential regional development opportunities in the strategic deployment of research and development funding, which could offset some of the anticipated uneven impacts of Brexit. For example, under its industrial strategy, the government has invested £80 million in electric vehicle battery research in the West Midlands. However, far more will need to be done, not least because the UK may lose access to a large share of EU low carbon R&D funding and will be no longer eligible for EU Structural and Regional funds.

There is also a possibility that Brexit might actually accelerate the pace of change. This is partly because under any scenario in which the UK is no longer in the IEM, there will be less electricity interconnection, and as a result, domestic low-carbon decentralised sources of flexibility will be at a greater premium. It may also be that leaving the IEM gives Britain more freedom to pursue policy and regulatory changes that might facilitate the use of decentralised energy resources, especially in types of local experimentation that is currently difficult under EU rules.[12]

The decentralised energy revolution is proving disruptive for large energy utilities and network companies. It holds out the promise that communities and households could become far more engaged in the production and consumption of energy, more aware of the implications for climate change and able to 'take back control' from large utilities, which suffer low public trust. The agendas of 'energy citizenship' or 'energy democracy' are exciting, if sometimes vague. However, there are other competing visions for a decentralised system in which consumers delegate control to incumbent utilities seeking to carve out new roles for themselves in the emerging landscape, perhaps acting in partnership with online platform giants such as Amazon or Google, who will use algorithms to optimise the use of consumer resources around existing lifestyles, thereby eradicating the need to engage in any active sense. Which vision comes to dominate is clearly bound up with deeper questions of control and trust in digital capitalism.

## Conclusions

Because gas and electricity are networked industries, a Brexit involving leaving the IEM will mean a more isolated and costly energy future for Britain (and Northern Ireland if the Irish SEM is broken up). We could potentially lose access to the efficient trading mechanisms of market coupling and plans for expanded electricity interconnection with continental Europe are likely to slow or even contract. Immediate price rises for consumers would be relatively small, but the longer-term opportunity costs of access to shared balancing services will be higher. Britain may have to build more LNG and gas storage facilities to offset greater price volatility, adding to costs. Loss of access to billions of pounds worth of EIB funding annually would also make investment costs higher, unless an equivalent domestic public investment bank is created.

Economic shocks and lower growth are very real prospects following a hard Brexit which, along with the possibility of an accompanying resurgence of right-wing populism, would represent a serious challenge to the current political consensus on decarbonisation. Alternatively, a swing to the left might possibly see a return to public ownership in energy. Further tensions may arise from different parts of the UK, especially Scotland as against England and Wales, developing their energy systems in divergent ways.

However, there are also major long-term transformations going on in energy that are global in nature, and so profound that even a more inward-looking post-Brexit Britain is likely to be affected by them. Key trends include the falling costs of renewable electricity and electricity storage technologies, and the digitisation of energy systems. As a result, regardless of domestic climate policy, in the longer term Britain's energy system is likely to continue to decarbonise, decentralise and digitalise.

A heavier reliance on electricity and more variable-output power from wind and solar PV means that balancing the system will become more difficult but also more important. Expanded interconnection with Britain's neighbours would play an important role, but in an isolationist post-Brexit future, we would need to fall back more heavily on domestic forms of flexibility. This constraint could potentially be turned into an opportunity, but only if access to global markets can be retained and expanded.

Finally, what Britain's energy future will look like in terms of ownership and consumer engagement depends on which visions of society win out in post-Brexit politics. At the moment, different visions—a return to statism, maintaining the current corporate-owned approach, or a distributed community and citizen-led model—can to some degree be found across the major political parties. But the real debate about them remains lost amidst the all-consuming noise of Brexit.

## Acknowledgement

The authors gratefully acknowledge funding from the UK Energy Research Centre, supported by the Research Councils UK under the Engineering and Physical Sciences Research Council award EP/L024756/1, for the research on which much of this chapter is based.

## Notes

1 Communications team, Oil and Gas UK, 'Brexit and the UK oil and gas industry', 3 May 2017; https://oilandgasuk.co.uk/brexit-and-the-uk-oil-and-gas-industry/ (accessed 7 July 2018).

2 Energy Barometer 2017, 'Views from UK energy professionals', London, Energy Institute, 2017; https://knowledge.energyinst.org/__data/assets/pdf_file/0017/304451/Energy-Barometer-2017.pdf (accessed 27 May 2018).

3 Redpoint, *The Impact of Gas Market Interventions on Energy Security*, report for DECC, 2013; https://assets.publishing.service.gov.uk/government/uploads/system/uploads/attachment_data/file/236757/DECC_FI_Final_report_09072013.pdf (accessed 1 June 2018).

4 A. Froggatt, M. Lockwood and G. Wright, 'Staying connected: key elements for UK-EU27 energy cooperation after Brexit', London, Chatham House/University of Exeter/UKERC research paper, 2017, https://www.chathamhouse.org/sites/default/files/publications/research/2017-05-10-staying-connected-energy-cooperation-brexit-froggatt-wright-lockwood.pdf (accessed 25 May 2018).

5 C. Hepburn and A. Teytelboym, 'Climate change policy after Brexit', *Oxford Review of Economic Policy*, vol. 33, no. S1, 2017, pp. S144–S154.

6 Committee on Climate Change, *Progress Report to Parliament*, London, Committee on Climate Change, 2018; https://www.theccc.org.uk/wp-content/uploads/2018/06/CCC-2018-Progress-Report-to-Parliament.pdf (accessed 20 July 2018).

7 Letter from the Prince of Wales' Corporate Leaders Group to Michel Barnier and David Davis, 20 April 2018; https://www.corporateleadersgroup.com/reports-evidence-and-insights/pdfs/brexit-coalition-letter.pdf (accessed 28 September 2018).

8 Citizens Advice, 'Rise in forced prepayment meter installations "troubling" says Citizens Advice', press release, 18 June 2018; https://www.citizensadvice.org.uk/about-us/how-citizens-advice-works/media/press-releases/rise-in-forced-prepayment-meter-installations-troubling-says-citizens-advice/?utm_source=Citizens+Advice+Press+Release&utm_campaign=6dc312cd15-Citizens_Advice_Press_release4_30_2015&utm_medium=email&utm_term=0_108f914b6f-6dc312cd15-284142905&mc_cid=6dc312cd15&mc_eid=180ec832e7 (accessed 24 June 2018).

9 National Infrastructure Commission, *National Infrastructure Assessment*, London, National Infrastructure Commission, 2018, https://www.nic.org.uk/wp-content/uploads/CCS001_CCS0618917350-001_NIC-NIA_Accessible.pdf (accessed 10 June 2018).

10 R. Lowes, 'Who owns the UK's energy distribution networks?', University of Exeter Energy Policy Group blog, 25 May 2017; http://blogs.exeter.ac.uk/energy/2017/05/25/who-owns-the-uks-energy-distribution-networks/ (accessed 20 July 2018).

11 F. Farstad, N. Carter and C. Burns, 'What does Brexit mean for the UK's Climate Change Act?', *Political Quarterly*, vol. 89, no. 2, 2018, pp. 291–297.

12 M. Pollitt, 'The economic consequences of Brexit: energy', Working Paper 1702, Energy Policy Research Group, University of Cambridge, 2017; https://www.eprg.group.cam.ac.uk/wp-content/uploads/2017/01/1702-Text.pdf (accessed 17 June 2018).

How to cite this article: M. Lockwood and A. Froggatt, 'Energy Supply and Decarbonisation Beyond Brexit: Politics and Policy', in G Kelly and N Pearce (eds.), Britain Beyond Brexit, *The Political Quarterly*, Vol 90, Issue S2, 2019, pp. 117–127. https://doi.org/10.1111/1467-923X.12617

# My Generation, Baby: The Politics of Age in Brexit Britain

## TORSTEN BELL AND LAURA GARDINER

GENERATIONAL politics is nothing new, but the extent of the profound generational cleavage that has emerged in British electoral politics is novel. The Brexit vote and the 2017 general election put generational politics centre-stage, eclipsing in some ways the traditionally dominant role of class. Our two main parties now rely on age-based coalitions of support—on the votes of the young in the case of Labour and the old in the case of the Conservatives. Both are severely constrained in their ability to spread their support to other age groups and, partly as a result, to form a government with a significant majority. This matters for understanding the cut and thrust of British politics today, but its importance only grows when we look ahead.

Both sides may be tempted to view this as an equilibrium they can live with, as Labour believes it has the voters of the future and the Conservatives rely on the age groups most likely to actually vote. But the risk is that this 'generational lock' on our politics blocks a much-needed progressive governing shift for post-Brexit Britain—a shift to address two crucial, but generationally charged, economic challenges. First, the need to support young people's living standards, because the expectation of each generation doing significantly better than their predecessors is not being met for younger cohorts today. And second, delivering and, crucially, paying for the health and care that a growing older population will need as the large baby boomer generation retires. Such a governing agenda will involve trade-offs that a generationally polarised politics hinders at best, and blocks at worst.

These generational political divides and economic challenges are not simplistically causally linked—there is more going on than angry young voters choosing the party that opposes what they see as a broken economic system. Culture matters as much as economics in the age-based voting patterns we see today,[1] meaning the age of places matters too, as Will Jennings and Gerry Stoker's discussion of geographical polarisation in this issue sets out. But whatever their related but separate causes, generational rifts in our politics and our economy currently sit centre-stage. This paper first examines their contours, before turning to what they might mean for the shape of Britain's post-Brexit political economy.

## Political divides

The difference in political preferences between young and old is a defining feature of today's politics, shaping coalitions of support for our main political parties to an unprecedented extent. Crucially, this age divide is neither the sudden event many interpreted it as in the aftermath of the 2017 general election, nor something that is likely to fade soon. Initially, Labour's success in exceeding (low) expectations in 2017 was credited to a sea-change in engagement among twenty-somethings. The assumption was that activity by young activists on social media and at rallies had produced something broader and more important: they and their peers voting. The collapse of Theresa May's majority was explained by a so-called 'youthquake' of surging turnout among the youngest electors benefitting Labour. Labour partisans interpreted this youthquake as a vindication of a strategy of targetting 'unlikely' voters, while some Conservatives responded with existential angst about a landmark change in turnout patterns.[2] While some early evidence pointed in this direction,[3] this youth turnout-focussed interpretation didn't age well. Exit poll-based estimates demonstrated not a sea change in turnout, but a general continuation of the post-1992 pattern of higher voting likelihood among older groups.[4] In this respect, far from 2017 marking a watershed in turnout by age differences, it actually looked remarkably similar to 2015. The exception was a small relative turnout increase among thirty-somethings, a more established group of voters than the younger cohorts that drew the initial attention. Insofar as turnout rates shape political parties' approaches, they continue to encourage prioritisation of older voters.

So, if there was no youthquake,[5] should the talk of generational political divides be put to bed? Far from it—the age-related shifts underway are staggering. However, they are not about turnout but about party choice. And far from being just about the 2017 election, they have been building throughout the twenty-first century. The scale of this shift is brought out by a comparison of the 2017 election with the last time Labour and the Conservatives both commanded around a 40 per cent vote share without either winning a landslide victory—October 1974 (shown in Figure 1). Back then, the likelihood of voters aged between thirty and seventy supporting Labour was very similar, with only a slightly stronger age gradient in Conservative support. But by 2017, age had become a key driver of preferences. A thirty-year-old was almost twice as likely to vote Labour as a seventy-year-old, with an opposing shift in Conservative support: a seventy-year-old was 2.2 times more likely to vote for the party than a thirty-year-old in 2017, compared to just 1.4 times as likely in October 1974.[6]

These stark age divisions in partisan preferences were not new in 2017, but rather have been growing from the start of this century (shown in Figure 2 for Labour and in Figure 3 for the Conservatives), so predating the focus on older voters in the electoral strategy of George Osborne and David Cameron. This suggests that these divides are about wider differences in social, political, and (to some degree) policy attitudes of age groups—meaning they have happened to, as much as being created by, political parties. Age divides were also visible in both the Scottish and Brexit referendums, with older voters proving decisive in the No and Yes votes respectively. In

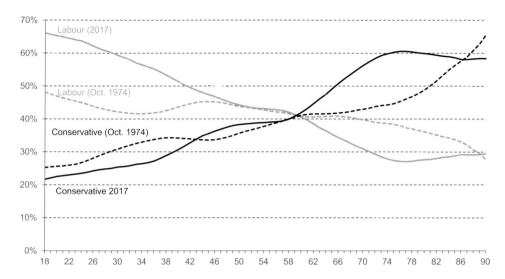

**Figure 1:** Proportion of voters voting Conservative or Labour by age, October 1974 and 2017 general elections.

Source: RF Analysis of British Election Study.

the case of the Brexit vote, the stark age divide in preferences for the single biggest political shift in half a century is shaping the politics of what form of Brexit is delivered, but also risks exacerbating generational political divides long afterwards, a subject we return to below.

The emergence of age-based divisions has eroded, and partially replaced, the division that dominated twentieth century British politics: class. For consistency, we can again compare the divide in voting preferences in October 1974 and 2017 (Figure 4). The change over the past four decades is, if anything, starker, but in the opposite direction, with huge divides in party preference by class in 1974 but only marginal gaps in 2017.

The decline in class-based divides in partisan preferences does not mean that class does not retain a major role in politics—just that it does not play the same or as dominant a role as it once did. Its ongoing role is visible, for example, in the fact that turnout declines since the 1990s have been driven by the working class.[7] This in turn interacts with age, with lower turnout particularly marked among younger parts of lower socio-economic groups.[8]

## Economic challenges

Big divides in party preferences are far from new and may not be overly concerning. But in some circumstances, they can hinder desirable governing agendas—for example when a package of trade-offs across the very groups supporting different parties is required. Therefore, the combination of these

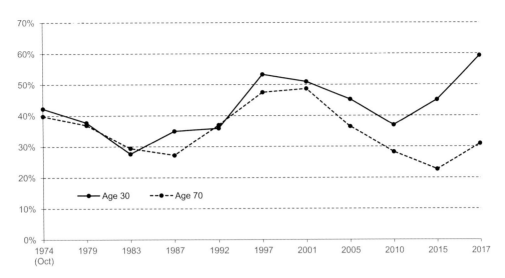

**Figure 2:** Proportion of thirty- and seventy-year-old voters voting Labour at general elections since October 1974.

Source: RF analysis of British Election Study.

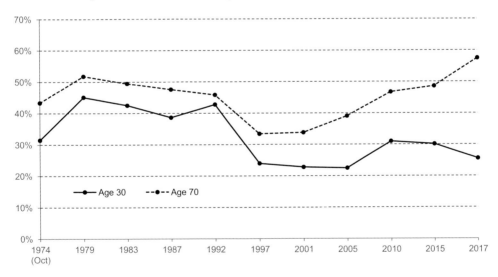

**Figure 3:** Proportion of thirty- and seventy-year-old voters voting Conservative at general elections since October 1974.

Source: RF analysis of British Election Study.

partisan divides with Britain's generational economic challenges is far from straightforward. It is to the nature of these economic challenges we now turn.

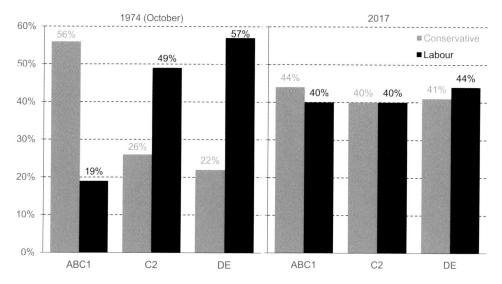

**Figure 4:** Share of vote by party and social class.

Source: Ipsos MORI.

Younger generations today have access to more information, entertainment, travel and educational opportunities than ever, yet pessimism about their prospects is widespread. Behind this is the fact that the significant increase in living standards from each generation to the next that we came to expect in the twentieth century has slowed or actively gone into reverse, owing to a number of related but distinct trends. We touch on three in this paper: weak asset accumulation, a slowdown in earnings progress, and a too-often ignored pattern of risk transfer from firms and the state onto individuals. The single biggest driver of public concern for the prospects of younger generations today is the marked slowdown in home ownership (Figure 5), with millennials (born 1981 to 2000) half as likely to own their home at thirty as the baby boomers (born 1946 to 1965) were. Along with a major decline in access to social housing, this means that at the age of thirty, millennials are four times more likely to be renting privately than baby boomers were.

Bolstering the idea that young people are experiencing capitalism without much capital, they are also less likely to have access to generous defined benefit pension schemes that form a substantial proportion of wealth in older generations. While an increasing number of young adults are saving something into a pension,[9] the decline of defined benefit schemes is now all but complete outside the public sector. Private sector membership around age thirty-five more than halved for those born in the early 1980s compared to those born around 1970.

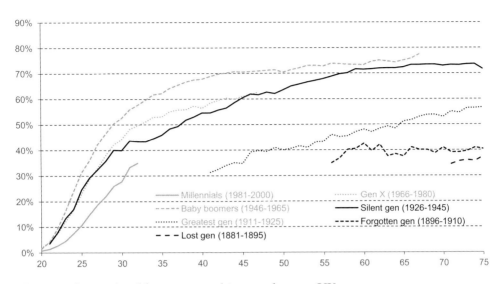

**Figure 5:** Generational home ownership rates by age: UK.

Source: RF analysis of Family Expenditure Survey 1961–1983; Labour Force Survey 1984–2017.

While wealth accumulation challenges have been building for decades, more recent shifts have deepened generational concerns, not least the fallout from the financial crisis. Smaller than expected rises in unemployment meant that young adults have not had to deal with worklessness on the scale that previous generations or their counterparts in southern Europe faced. But unemployment increases were more skewed towards younger people than in the recessions of the 1980s and 1990s, and young workers were hardest hit by the earnings squeeze that has characterised the decade since (Figure 6). In the immediate aftermath of the crisis, pay fell by 11 per cent for those in their twenties compared to just 2 per cent for employees in their sixties. The subsequent pay recovery has been weakest for today's thirty-somethings.

Weak earnings have also undermined common myths that millennials are spending a fortune on avocado toast or city breaks: while young adults were spending the same as fifty-five to sixty-four-year-olds back in 2000, they are now spending 15 per cent less. Yes, they have more access to low marginal cost technology than previous generations had at their age, but most would be happy to swap that for a house and a pay rise. The pay experience of the young is one half of a profound twenty-first century shift, with pensioner living standards overtaking those of the working-age population (Figure 7). The introduction of more generous means-tested benefits in the mid-2000s and, more recently, higher employment and private savings levels, mean pensioner incomes have performed strongly and pensioner poverty has fallen by a third. These welcome improvements require us to change how we think about need today. While many (particularly older, female) pensioners

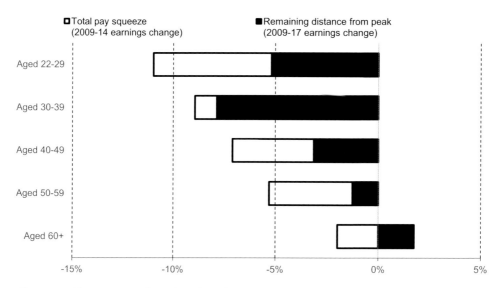

**Figure 6:** Change in real median hourly earnings (CPIH-adjusted) by age.

Source: RF analysis of ONS, Annual Survey of Hours and Earnings.

remain poor, working-age and working poverty have grown just as pensioner poverty has fallen.

The nature, not just the pay, of the work that younger generations are doing raises wider questions of where risk lies in our society. Market forces and policy decisions have together left younger adults bearing significant risks that their predecessors were less exposed to. Young people are disproportionately likely to work on a zero-hours contract or find themselves in lower-qualified self-employment.[10] When it comes to housing, the number of children being brought up in the insecure private rented sector has trebled in the past fifteen years. And the decline of defined benefit pensions means individuals increasingly shoulder the risk of varying investment returns while saving, as well as the uncertainty around how long they may live.[11] The first of these is suboptimal, while the second is indefensible. Importantly, these insecurities may undermine the appetite of young people to take on more desirable discretionary risks, exemplified by millennials having been 20–25 per cent less likely to voluntarily move jobs in their twenties than was the previous generation. This has implications for their pay progression and also for the economy as a whole, as the quality of matching of individuals to jobs is reduced.

It is not just challenges facing young adults that should be central to a governing agenda for post-Brexit Britain. Another long-looming challenge with big generational implications is now coming home to roost—the cost of maintaining our welfare state and, in particular, providing the health and care that older generations rightly expect to receive. The retirement of the

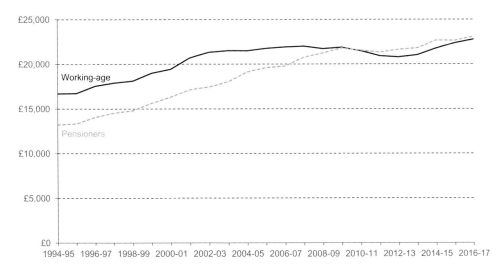

**Figure 7:** Median UK household incomes after housing costs, working age and pensioner households, 2016–17 prices.

Source: ONS, Family Resources Survey.

large baby boomer generation means growth in the older population, even before factoring in increased life expectancy. Combined with other pressures on health costs, this means spending on health, care and social security would need to rise by £36 billion by 2030 and by £83 billion by 2040 simply to maintain existing service levels.

While these funding pressures are in the future, the implications of a system under strain are visible today. Healthcare is the most pressing area of worry for British adults: 42 per cent place it in their top three concerns, significantly above international norms. Increasingly underfunded social care provision in England means the number of older people who do not get the care they need has doubled since 2010. The status quo proves forcibly that policy failures can let down older generations too. However, addressing cost pressures carries generational challenges: the usual approaches of higher borrowing or taxes on working age income would bear down on the same younger generations at the sharp end of recent living standards pressures. So, today's challenge is to give older generations the health and care they need, deserve and expect in a generationally fair way. That is easier said than done technically, and significantly harder politically.

## A bad equilibrium

Ways of addressing these two economic challenges should be central (although far from exclusive) components of the governing agenda into the 2020s. But we can't be certain that they will be, or that the right answers will be found. The political divide we started with could impose what we term 'generational locks' on both parties' attempts to rise to these challenges. One well-established lock is higher turnout at older ages, discouraging parties from focussing on younger adults' needs. But in future, generational locks may operate more broadly, with parties highly reliant on one age group for support finding it hard to ask that group to engage in necessary trade-offs— after all, the point of winning is that you win. So, the best strategy for voters at the other end of the age spectrum is to wait for their team to return to power.

Generational locks can also operate in more complex ways. The inability or unwillingness of a party to address a generational issue can engender a lack of creativity or radicalism in their opponents, even when addressing that issue is core to their voters' needs. And any attempt by parties to ask their own voters to make sacrifices can be easily lampooned by other parties as an abandonment of their base—an obstacle to attempts at lock-breaking.

It's easy to see such generational locks operating in practice. Youth home ownership started falling from 1989, but continuing ownership increases for older families and their higher turnout at elections meant that it wasn't until the financial crisis two decades later that housing moved centre-stage. This is part of a wider trend of older wealth insiders benefitting from policy shifts when they happen, but also benefitting from the status quo. For example, there has been no growth in wealth taxation since the 1980s despite huge wealth increases over that period (Figure 8). Perhaps unsurprisingly, the Conservative party has chosen not to address this challenge and even actively to cut some wealth taxes, including inheritance tax. With no engagement from the Conservatives on the tricky issue of taxing assets, Labour has shied away from thinking creatively about significant reforms to wealth taxation.

More recently, two clear examples of generational locks leading to bad outcomes stand out. First is the burden of welfare cuts since 2010. Reliant on older generations' votes, the Conservatives majored on the protection or enhancement of pensioner benefits, meaning the focus of benefit cuts is on the thirty-somethings who were worst affected by the financial crisis in their twenties (Figure 9). That is not to say that young people were particularly opposed to welfare cuts, even when bearing the brunt of their impact, but that the Conservative party's reliance on older voters undermined the promise that 'we are all in this together' from a generational perspective.

The second example is social care. All parties accept that the status quo is awful, and yet both have played a role in ensuring that no change takes place. George Osborne labelled Labour's 2010 proposals for collective insurance drawing on the wealth in older people's estates a 'death tax'. Similar criticisms were then thrown in the other direction by Labour following the 2017 Conservative manifesto proposal that better-off individuals contribute more towards their care costs from their assets. This was a case of the Conservatives asking an age group it relies on for support to engage in

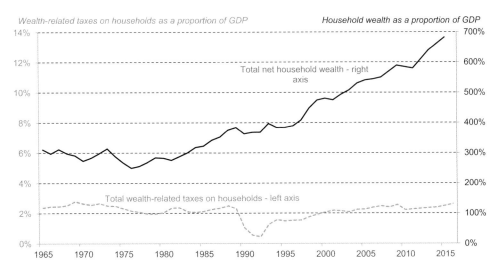

**Figure 8:** Aggregate wealth and wealth-related taxes as proportions of GDP: GB/UK.
Notes: See notes to Figure 11.1 in Resolution Foundation, A New Generational Contract.

Source: RF analysis of ONS, Wealth in Great Britain; ONS, UK National Accounts; D. Blake and J. Orszag, 'Annual estimates of personal wealth holdings in the United Kingdom since 1948', Applied Financial Economics, vol. 9, no. 4, 1999, pp. 397–421.

generational trade-offs (admittedly, with flaws), leaving the party open to criticism from an opposition able to 'hit them where it hurts'. In both cases politicians were (rightly) not prepared to ask younger voters to pay to resolve the situation. So, the social care crisis has dragged on.

Failure in future to address these generational challenges—all the more likely if generational locks are tightened by an ongoing politics of blame or credit for the Brexit decision—would deliver similarly unattractive results. For example, the health funding challenge may echo the social care deadlock. However, widespread support for the NHS could mean that rather than nothing happening we settle for some, but insufficient, additional funding paid for in generationally unfair ways (such as national insurance on the working-age population). The government's announcement in June 2018 of £20 billion extra for the NHS, with no detail on the source of funds, raises this possibility. The result would be older generations let down on the quality of their healthcare, and young generations' living standards squeezed again.

On the needs of younger generations, their support for Labour been matched by a focus on some issues, such as tuition fees, but caution remains in other areas. On housing, the party went into the 2017 election with a more conservative council tax policy than in 2015, while Sadiq Khan explicitly ruled out action on green belt constraints during his London mayoral election campaign. Feeling little threat to their youth support from the Conservatives, Labour may feel worryingly comfortable in this position.

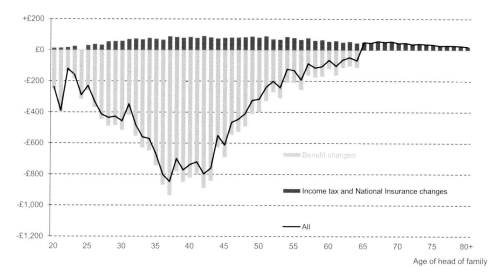

**Figure 9:** Mean change in annual net family income from tax and benefit policy changes implemented during the current Parliament, by age: UK, 2022–23.
Notes: Income is measured before housing costs, and expressed in cash terms.

Source: RF analysis using the IPPR tax-benefit model.

Finally, it's worth considering who will be hit hardest if generational economic challenges continue to be sidestepped. The least well-off older people suffer most in our broken social care system, and those in younger generations without parental assets face the bleakest housing prospects. The irony might be that a partial shift in political divides from class to age puts locks on policy that mean that class-based challenges are deepened, as well as generational ones enduring.

## Better outcomes

While this bad equilibrium is clearly possible, it is far from certain. Luck, supply-side responses in the form of more ambitious party strategies, or demand-side pressure for change, could all precipitate better outcomes. Luck (or an unprecedentedly successful economic strategy) could trigger the return of meaningful productivity growth. This would directly support income progress for younger adults, help to maintain the existing welfare state without tax rises, and ease the political economy of generational trade-offs by reducing the zero-sum nature of choices. It is also possible that age-based cultural cleavages will ease over time, opening up political choices. This could happen structurally as current younger cohorts age or, more optimistically, it could be because individual issues diminish in salience. On the latter, see Rob Ford and Maria Sobolewska's discussion elsewhere in this issue of a range of such scenarios on migration.

But such shifts would not be a panacea, and there may be pressures in the other direction. For example, productivity growth, while crucial in supporting young adults' living standards, is unlikely to address a lack of asset accumulation. And while Brexit may reduce the political salience of divides on migration, it has to-date reduced earnings growth and may entail significant new pressures on resources, exemplified, for example, by recent public commitments to a UK-only satellite programme to replace the Galileo project.

If luck does not solve these challenges then a supply-side response from parties might, with political strategies beyond current superficial attempts such as the Conservatives' offer of a millennial rail card and Labour's promise to keep free pensioner bus passes. This would involve breaking out of current age coalitions to form a majority that allows the internalisation of trade-offs in the combination of a generationally fair health and care funding solution and a wider package of reforms to make Britain work for the young.

That is easier said than done. Labour may believe it has the best chance of such a breakthrough: after all, if this Parliament lasts, it will be running against a twelve-year incumbent. However, much more sensitivity on issues of values and culture that appear to have reduced Labour's support among older voters will likely be required. For the Conservatives, a sensible focus would be on those in their thirties and forties, rather than students who are unlikely to provide high volumes of support. Such a Conservative breakthrough hinges on youthful Labour support proving to be a life-stage—rather than cohort—effect, with more optimistic scenarios for home ownership potentially underpinning middle-age switching of party allegiance. Importantly, to achieve such a breakthrough, either party would need to establish a post-Brexit political narrative that avoids all future outcomes and choices being refracted through the age cleavage that defined the Brexit decision itself.

The parties could also tap into strong wells of generational harmony and support—we do not see the country as divided between generations, even if our politics is. There is already evidence of generational coalitions building for change, even where the beneficiaries are refined to a particular age group. On housing, since 2010 old-age support for house building in the local area has doubled, while younger adults continue to back decent pensions and healthcare for the old. If nothing else, this reminds us that we live not as individuals or representatives of generations, but as parts of families. There are also many areas of policy that are far from zero-sum, not least when the issue is not about tax and spend. For example, action to address the risks young people face in the labour market or in their pension regime needn't have significant implications for older voters.

Wider constraints, such as Labour's loss of Scottish seats, mean we can't necessarily rely on a government with a big majority in the years ahead. An alternative route for escaping generational locks might involve demand-side pressures from voters encouraging a more creative politics. First, while we again have two-party politics of a form not seen since the 1970s, a return to the longer-term trend of political fragmentation is possible. Such a shift would add more volatility and possibly enable cross-party and generational coalition building.

Demand-side pressure for change could also manifest itself if two-party politics continues, by building to such an extent on specific issues that parties are forced to innovate, without owning the solutions themselves. Devices like the Turner Pensions Commission might be more frequently turned to in future.

## Conclusion

British politics may enter the post-Brexit era stuck in a bad generational equilibrium, with different generational blocs gripping our two main parties. That would pose impediments to delivering the changes Britain badly needs.

However, now more than ever, future trajectories are uncertain. These challenges are not going away, but politics is more unstable than it seemed even a few years ago. Sometimes it feels as though our parties are just hoping something will turn up to break the deadlock. But providing a proactive response to these challenges—with honesty about the give-and-take required —may be how a post-crisis, post-Brexit political offer with a broader appeal emerges. That will entail good leadership as well as good luck. That does seem a lot to ask, but then again big change always does.

## Notes

1 An extensive literature examines the cultural drivers behind recent political shifts. For a discussion of how post-industrial, and more highly educated, societies moving in a progressive direction can foster populist reactions among older generations, see R. Inglehart and P. Norris, 'Trump, Brexit, and the rise of populism: economic have-nots and cultural backlash', Harvard Kennedy School Faculty Research Working Paper Series RWP16-026, August 2016; https://www.hks.ha rvard.edu/publications/trump-brexit-and-rise-populism-economic-have-nots-and-cultural-backlash (accessed 30 November 2018).

2 See S. Whale, 'Sam Gyimah: at the election, Jeremy Corbyn was the only game on campus', *The House*, 12 March 2018; https://www.politicshome.com/news/uk/political-parties/conservative-party/house/house-magazine/93438/sam-gyimah-%E2%80%9C-election-jeremy (accessed 30 November 2018).

3 C. Prosser et al., 'Tremors but no youthquake: measuring changes in the age and turnout gradients at the 2015 and 2017 British general elections', Social Science Research Network (SSRN) paper, 6 February 2018; https://papers.ssrn.com/sol3/papers.cfm?abstract_id=3111839 (accessed 30 November 2018). The paper identifies three main survey-based claims, using data from *NME Magazine*, Ipsos MORI and the Essex Continuous Monitoring Survey: see: L. Morgan Britton, 'Here's the NME exit poll of how young people voted in 2017 general election', *NME*

*Magazine*, June 2017; https://www.nme.com/news/nme-exit-poll-young-voters-2017-general-election-2086012 (accessed 30 November 2018); Ipsos MORI, 'How Britain voted in the 2017 election', 20 June 2017; https://www.ipsos.com/ipsos-mori/en-uk/how-britain-voted-2017-election (accessed 30 November 2018); P. Whiteley, 'Underpaid, overworked and drowning in debt: you wonder why young people are voting again?', *The Conversation*, 6 October 2017; https://thecon versation. com/underpaid-overworked-and-drowning-in-debt-you-wonder-why-young-peo ple-are-voting-again-85298 (accessed 30 November 2018).

4 Prosser et al., 'Tremors but no youthquake'.

5 While there was no significant 'youthquake', there was something of a younger places quake as those areas saw bigger turnout growth which benefitted Labour. See O. Heath and M. Goodwin, 'The 2017 general election, Brexit and the return to two-party politics: an aggregate-level analysis of the result', *Political Quarterly*, vol. 88, no. 3, 2017, pp. 345–358.

6 Our thanks to George Bangham at the Resolution Foundation for providing this analysis of voting patterns.

7 See J. Tilley and G. Evans, 'The new politics of class after the 2017 general election', *Political Quarterly*, vol. 88, no. 4, pp. 710-715. Tilley and Evans argue that this class bias in turnout decline reflects all parties (Labour in particular) having a more middle class identity from the 1990s onwards.

8 In 2017, those aged forty and over describing themselves as 'middle class' were 50 per cent more likely to vote than those aged under forty identifying as 'working class', with older working class and younger middle class voters 27 per cent and 39 per cent more likely to vote than younger working class voters, respectively. Source: RF analysis of British Election Study.

9 Firms are now required automatically to enrol employees earning above a (relatively low) threshold into a pension unless they explicitly opt out.

10 See S. Clarke and C. D'Arcy, 'The kids aren't alright: a new approach to tackle the challenges faced by young people in the UK labour market', Resolution Foundation, February 2018; https://www.resolutionfoundation.org/publications/the-kids-arent-alright-a-new-approach-to-tackle-the-challenges-faced-by-young-people-in-the-uk-labour-market/ (accessed 30 November 2018).

11 The former risk derives from the move from defined benefit to defined contribution schemes, while the latter has been compounded by the introduction of pension freedoms.

How to cite this article: T. Bell and L. Gardiner, 'My Generation, Baby: The Politics of Age in Brexit Britain', in G Kelly and N Pearce (eds.), Britain Beyond Brexit, *The Political Quarterly*, Vol 90, Issue S2, 2019, pp. 128–141. https://doi.org/10.1111/1467-923X.12623

# British Culture Wars? Brexit and the Future Politics of Immigration and Ethnic Diversity

MARIA SOBOLEWSKA AND ROBERT FORD

## Introduction

THE ROLE of 'culture wars' driven by divisions over identity and values in American politics have been a source of intense debate since the 1960s. When we borrow this controversial title for our chapter, we risk provoking a strong reaction. Is British society truly divided enough to warrant the claim of a 'culture war', and if so, what are the differences that divide us so deeply? Pragmatic 'Mondeo Man' and 'Worcester Woman' voters of the 1990s and early 2000s have not disappeared, but new divides in the electorate have in recent decades grown in salience owing to demographic change. Issues which mobilise and polarise voters over their identity attachments have come to the fore—in particular those of immigration and ethnic diversity. Both are inherently about groups, boundaries and belonging. They are unavoidably issues—related to basic aspects of psychology and the tendency to divide the world into 'in' and 'out' groups—that invoke questions of 'us' and 'them'. Here, we offer a glimpse of how they have affected and are likely to continue to affect politics and policy making in post-Brexit Britain.

These two issues have become politically potent because the British electorate is changing. A generation ago, a large majority of voters were white and had few qualifications, and all parties had to accommodate their views. But over the past decades, educational expansion and rising diversity have eroded this group's dominance. When Tony Blair was elected in 1997, over six out of every ten English residents were white and left school with GCSEs or less. When Theresa May lost her majority twenty years later, less than four out of ten were in this category. Over the same period the share of the English population who were university graduates, members of an ethnic minority group, or both, more than doubled from 17 per cent to around 40 per cent.[1]

This shift in the electoral balance of power matters, because these groups have profoundly different views on identity issues. Graduates and ethnic minorities are generally open and liberal on immigration and ethnic diversity, while white voters with low qualifications tend to be closed and sceptical. There is also an overlapping generational divide: younger people who

Published by John Wiley & Sons Ltd, 9600 Garsington Road, Oxford OX4 2DQ, UK and 350 Main Street, Malden, MA 02148, USA

grew up in a more open and diverse Britain are more liberal than older voters socialised into a more homogenous society.[2] In aggregate, these changes have moved British society in a liberal direction. For example, expressions of racial prejudice and discriminatory attitudes in surveys have declined sharply over the past few decades. Brexit will not reverse these structural shifts, which have powerful demographic momentum behind them: the voters who come of age in the next decade will continue to be more university educated, ethnically diverse and socially liberal than their parents and grandparents.

But demographic change is slow, and large sections of the electorate are uncomfortable with identity change and rising diversity, ranging from anxiety about high migration to outright hostility to ethnic minorities. While large majorities of both Leave and Remain voters express tolerant views towards minorities on all measures, the divide between the two Brexit groups is substantial, with opposition to immigration and racial conservatism concentrated on the Leave side. The strong links between identity attachments and EU referendum choices mean the Brexit debate could further politicise and polarise these identity politics divisions, even as Britain continues its slow transformation into a more inclusive multicultural society. This is the 'culture war' Britain risks in the wake of Brexit—a heated and divisive argument over immigration and diversity, with substantial electorates holding entrenched views on both sides.

We will discuss in turn the divides over immigration and over ethnic diversity, and how they may develop in post-Brexit Britain. We foresee that both will play a role, but while immigration has long been recognised as politically potent, the less often acknowledged conflicts over diversity loom just as large in the electorate and may come to take centre stage in future. Here, the parallel with the American 'culture wars', with their deep roots in racial divides, is clearer. The election of a first black President, which many saw as chance to move beyond racial division, instead inflamed it, as it intensified the sense of threat felt by ethnocentric white voters. There is a risk of similar dynamics playing out in Britain: while Brexit may help resolve some conflicts over immigration, the conflicts over it may also mobilise other polarising identity divisions.

## Immigration: an opportunity for a fresh start?

Britain's immigration system will change after Brexit. Immigration played a prominent part in the EU referendum debate, and the desire for greater immigration control was strongly associated with support for leaving the EU.[3] This was not primarily the result of Leave campaigners' focus on the refugee crisis and Turkey's potential EU membership, but the product of long run trends. Public concern about immigration had been high since the early 2000s, and the Conservatives' failure to deliver on an election pledge drastically to reduce immigration collapsed public trust in the party. Voters increasingly saw the free movement of labour from the newer members of the European Union as a primary reason why governments could not deliver migration control. By the time of the EU referendum campaign, views about immigration and about the EU were already closely linked,[4] with many anti-migration voters already convinced, and not without reason, that leaving the EU was necessary to achieving national control over migration. The referendum Leave campaign mobilised such beliefs, but did not create them. However, the shock referendum result has changed the script on migration politics in several ways.

The politics of immigration for the past fifteen years has been characterised by three elements: historically high migration inflows; high levels of public attention and concern; and persistent failure by governments from both parties to deliver effective reforms which either brought down migration numbers or assuaged public concerns. Brexit has already changed two of these three elements and could change the third. Views about immigration have become markedly more positive since the Brexit vote, net migration has already fallen (particularly from Eastern Europe) and could fall further, and Brexit could weaken or remove one of the major external constraints on migration policy—European Union freedom of movement rules. However, the legacy of polarised debate over migration will complicate efforts to seize this opportunity, as politicians looking to build a sustainable and pragmatic new immigration system will need to reckon with low voter trust and deep public divides, with roots in different value systems and world-views.

Multiple pollsters have shown a sharp drop since the EU referendum in the share of voters rating immigration as one of the nation's most pressing problems (see figure 1a). While some of this is due to migration now being packaged up with Brexit in the public mind, the drop is nonetheless substantial and the salience of immigration is lower now than at any time since the

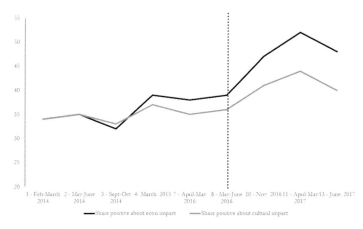

**Figure 1a:** Views of migrants' economic and cultural impact, British Election Study 2017

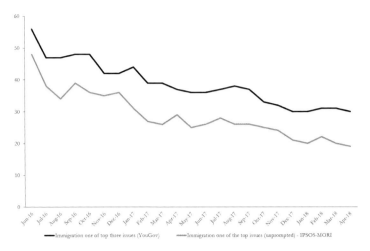

**Figure 1b:** Share naming immigration as one of the country's most important problems since the EU referendum

early 2000s. At the same time, data from several sources document a positive shift in public views about the economic and cultural impact of migration, continuing a longer running trend (see figure 1b). These trends have a complex range of drivers, including a marked shift in the terms of debate about immigration, with greater focus on the need for migrants in sectors such as agriculture and the NHS; greater awareness of the negative consequences of migration control policies due to stories such as the Windrush scandal; a belief among migration sceptics that Brexit will produce greater control; and longer run growth of demographic groups with more open outlooks. However, whatever the precise mix of causes, concern about immigration has declined, and sentiment on the issue has shifted markedly in a positive direction. The public mood on immigration is more benign than it has been for many years.

Brexit obliges a major round of migration reform because some kind of framework for dealing with EU/EEA migration is needed to replace current EU free movement rules. But Brexit is also an opportunity to think more broadly, building a new set of migration rules from first principles, to apply to all potential migrants, without the distortions introduced by EU constraints. The overall logic which must govern any migration policy is clear: governments must decide who can come to Britain and on what terms. If migration is not unconditionally accepted or rejected, then some principles of selection must operate. Once such criteria are decided, governments can then decide whether to accept all migrants who meet them, or impose numerical quotas. Once migrants have arrived, governments then must decide what rights and benefits are accorded to them, and on what terms.

A close reading of public opinion on migration gives cause for optimism in many of these areas, as British citizens are more flexible and pragmatic on the specifics of migration than they are in the abstract. The selection criteria voters prefer are clear, with a strong focus on characteristics which predict economic contribution and social integration: knowledge of English, professional and technical skills, educational qualifications, and labour market demand.[5] A system which integrated such factors into the selection process, as parts of the 'points-based system' applied to non-EU migrants already does, would most likely enjoy strong public support. Indeed, such principles are a central part of both the Migration Advisory Council report published in September 2018 and the government's own proposals announced in early October. Conversely, voters are more negative about the migration of workers with few or no skills, and more limited economic prospects.[6] There are already strict controls on such migrants entering Britain from outside the EU. Extending some or all of these restrictions to EU migrants would likely be a popular move. It is unclear whether numerical quotas would need to form part of the migration rules in order to secure public support. The migration debate in Britain has focussed heavily on numbers, but it is not clear how pivotal overall numbers are to voters rather than perceptions of a lack of control. In addition, specific numerical targets bring their own problems, including measurement, accusations of failure if they are not met, and costs from inflexibility.

Regarding the rights of migrants, there is broad public support for a system of 'earned access'—with full political, economic and social rights extended to migrants after a qualifying period of three to five years.[7] The current system has no consistent rules on this, reflecting the conflicting legacies of different policy regimes. Some, such as Commonwealth and Irish migrants, have immediate access to full political and social rights. Others face formidable barriers to accessing such rights—long qualification periods, and high financial and administrative costs to acquiring status once qualified. Others, such as the British born children of many non-EU migrants, believe they have rights but do not, and face difficult legal and financial challenges when they become aware of this problem. A clear set of rules for the acquisition of long-term residence, social and political rights, with low administrative and financial barriers to acquisition, would remove a lot of the potential for confusion and injustice in the current system, and would be consistent with public preferences on how settled migrants should be treated.

Nonetheless, political polarisation on migration is likely to continue to produce tensions between internal party politics and broader electoral politics. Labour faces a trade-off between demands to enforce rules and controls from parts of its traditional working class base and opposing demands from its increasingly liberal, diverse and university educated core vote and activist base, focussing on migrants' rights. For the Conservatives, the tension is between a socially conservative but demographically declining core electorate that favours strict controls, and the growing socially liberal groups they need to attract by signalling comfort with a more open, diverse society.

These tensions suggest that while a more sustainable immigration policy is possible, deep divides on the issue will endure, and political controversy over immigration is likely to recur. At its root, immigration is an issue about who belongs to a group and who gets to join it. It unavoidably divides an electorate between so-called 'identity liberals' and 'identity conservatives' who have very different views about national citizenship and boundaries. Yet, even if the recent decline in attention to immigration is sustained following the negotiation of a more politically workable migration policy, other political conflicts between identity conservatives and identity liberals are likely to replace it. We turn now to a fundamental one, which has received far less attention than immigration: attitudes towards racial and ethnic diversity.

## Racial and ethnic diversity: towards British culture wars?

Britain's rapidly rising racial and ethnic diversity is the cumulative result of the earlier postwar wave of migration and the more recent one, along with the growth in the British born ethnic minority population, including an explosive growth in the mixed ethnicity population. Yet, public reactions to rising diversity have been relatively under-researched, and the divisions it generates have mostly been ignored as a political issue. Few surveys include measures of attitudes towards diversity, and even fewer are asked frequently enough to discern long-term trends. What we do have, however, suggests that disputes over diversity are rising up the agenda, both in terms of increasing polarisation of views about the equal opportunities agenda, and how such divides predict political behaviour.

Racial attitudes are distinct from attitudes towards immigration and have distinct political effects. For example, only half of those who told the British Election Study at the time of the EU referendum that immigration undermines British culture also agreed that efforts to promote equal opportunities for ethnic minorities had gone too far. These attitudes do tend to correlate better on the positive side—migration scepticism does not line up consistently with diversity scepticism, but voters who are pro migration tend to be pro diversity too. As such, 'identity liberals' include openness to both diversity and immigration within their system of values and beliefs, while 'identity conservatives' include distinct strands of migration scepticism and diversity scepticism.

Moreover, each of these views had a separate and significant impact on votes in the EU referendum. Figure 2 shows that voters who felt that immigration poses a threat to British culture, but thought that equal opportunities for ethnic minorities have *not* gone far enough, were considerably less likely to vote Leave, than those who also believed that minorities' rights have gone too far. In fact, for those anti-immigrant voters who felt very strongly that

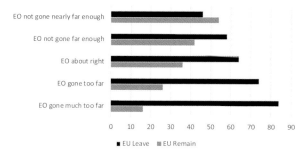

**Figure 2:** Percentage of Leave and Remain voters who felt threatened by immigration, by attitudes to equal opportunity for ethnic minorities have gone too far/not far enough

Source: British Election Study 2016, differences statistically significant.

equal opportunities for minorities required further action, this was enough to make them more likely to vote Remain than Leave, despite their negative position on immigration. On the other side of the coin, those who felt strongly that equal opportunities had gone too far *and* saw immigration as a threat to British culture, voted Leave by an overwhelming 85–15 margin.

Such effects are unlikely to be limited to Brexit. A rather neglected aspect of the oft-made Brexit-Trump comparison helps to explain why. The core of many Brexit-Trump stories is the parallel between the revolt of working class white American voters with low education levels and that of the British 'left behind'.[8] Both Brexit and Trump drew their strongest support from less educated, older white voters resident outside the large globalised cities that increasingly form the focus of economic growth, cultural activity and political influence in both countries. But analysts in the UK have tended to focus on these voters' socio-economic woes and opposition to immigration, while neglecting another important parallel between Brexit and Trump: the importance of negative attitudes about diversity and minorities.[9] We contend that Britain is now—like the US—a racially divided society. White voters, like ethnic minority voters, have an ethnic identity which can be politically mobilised, and hold complex and politically consequential racial attitudes driven by these identity attachments. We need to learn from the US, where this phenomenon has been more widely discussed, how best to measure, analyse and interpret white identity politics, which will play a growing role in British voters' choices.

Parallels between British racial divisions and those in the US are stronger than one would expect given the profound differences in their recent histories on race. Britain has no equivalent to twentieth century America's system of formalised racial segregation and political marginalisation, or to the civil rights movement which fought to overcome these. In contrast, Britain granted full political and social rights to the majority of non-white immigrants upon arrival, on the basis of their earlier colonial linkages to Britain. As a result, despite enduring racial disadvantages, Britain has some positive stories to tell about the political and social integration of ethnic minorities, with non-white representation in Westminster rising sharply, London boasting Europe's first minority-Muslim mayor of a capital city, and a generational shift towards more inclusive and racially tolerant attitudes.

Yet, it is often forgotten that the same is true of the US. President Obama is only one symbol of a non-white American overcoming racial disadvantage. The proportion of people opposing inter-racial marriage, a classic measure of prejudice, has fallen sharply in the US, as well as in the UK, particularly among younger generations. In fact, only a couple of years ago in both countries, centre-right Republicans and Conservatives worried that their parties would struggle to win future elections without improving their appeal to ethnic and racial minorities.[10] However, the sustained shift towards more diverse societies and more positive views of diversity is seen as threatening by the declining but still substantial segment of the white electorate that holds racially conservative views. The emergence of UKIP and its success in pushing Britain towards leaving the EU, and the Trump victory in the US are both, in part, examples of this kind of defensive mobilisation by racially conservative voters. It is the common trends of rising diversity, rising identity liberalism, and growing feelings of threat and marginalisation among racially conservative whites that make the politics of white backlash similar in the UK and the US, despite the large differences in their political and social histories on race.

So what are the potential fault lines that could mobilise racial conservatives behind either mainstream right parties such as the Conservatives, or any successor parties to the radical right UKIP? We want to make two observations here: first, that the substantial segment of the white British public with conservative attitudes on race and diversity makes playing the 'race card' a continuing electoral temptation; and second, that how this card is played in politics risks deepening existing identity politics divides and may introduce them into new policy areas, most notably welfare and redistribution. Thus, the first part of this argument deals with racial attitudes, and whether these can be made politically salient, and the second with how these attitudes can also alter social support for policies that traditionally rely on a sense of social solidarity and fairness.

Firstly, looking into attitudes, it is important to underline some important differences between the two countries. While we believe the broad concept of white racial conservatism makes sense in Britain as in the US, its nature is different in the two contexts. The first measure is one widely used in America: 'racial resentment'.[11] This measures pervasive negative stereotypes of African Americans, and is a product of the United States political context, in particular the polarising process of desegregation and partisan realignment

**Table 1: Racial attitudes in the UK: percentage of British public agreeing with racial resentment and colour-blindness statements**

| % | Racial resentment | | Ideological colour-blindness | |
|---|---|---|---|---|
| | If only black and Asian people tried harder* | Nearest US comparable figure | Black and Asian people do not face discrimination ** | Nearest US comparable figure |
| Strongly agree | 4.3 | 16 | 4 | 6 |
| Agree | 12 | 19 | 12 | 15 |
| Disagree | 18.5 | 14 | 44 | 30 |
| Strongly disagree | 23.5 | 22 | 14.5 | 31 |
| Undecided | 34.5 | 28 | 18 | 17 |

*UK: 'If black and Asian people would only try harder, they could be just as well off as white people'; US: 'It's really a matter of some people not trying hard enough; if blacks would only try harder, they could be just as well off as whites.'

**UK: Item reversed as original wording was in a positive direction: 'In Britain today, black and Asian people still face plenty of discrimination because of their race.'; US: 'racial problems are rare, isolated situations.'

Source: UK: authors' data collected by YouGov, March 2018; US: YouGov USA (resentment), April 2018 and the Cooperative Congressional Election Study, 2016

in the American South. As table 1 illustrates, the most widely used measures of racial resentment do not attract much public support in Britain, although it is present in a minority.

Another measure of racial conservatism travels somewhat better from the US to Britain: ideological colour-blindness.[12] Those who are 'ideologically colour-blind' do not express explicitly negative views of minorities, or use racial caricatures to explain their disadvantage. They instead reject the argument that racial discrimination exists as a significant social problem which shapes lives unequally, and argue that all individuals regardless of race have equal chances to succeed. People who reject the notion of discrimination as a structural disadvantage in this way tend also to reject targeted policies designed to offer redress for racial disadvantage. In the US it has been shown that people holding such views are less likely to self-categorise as racist, and often self-categorise as liberal. As a result, these individuals are less likely to self-police their prejudices and more likely to interpret any dislike they feel towards minority individuals not as racial prejudice, but judgement of the individual.[13]

As we see in table 1, this attitude is similarly widespread in Britain. While in 2016 data in this table show fewer British people agree with the statement 'there is no racial discrimination', only a minority of British people (15 per cent) strongly reject it. By contrast, in the US more than 30 per cent strongly reject the proposition that racial discrimination does not exist—and this figure has risen sharply since Donald Trump's election, as Pew Global figures

**Table 2: Racial conservatism by voters' party support***

| % | Equal opportunities gone too far[#] | Nearest US comparator | Racial resentment | US resentment comparator | Ideological colour-blindness | US colour-blindness comparator |
|---|---|---|---|---|---|---|
| Conservatives/ Republicans | 44 | 62 | 21 | 59 | 22 | 34 |
| Labour/ Democrats | 24 | 24 | 10 | 22 | 11 | 11 |
| Liberal Democrats | 18 | - | 9 | - | 10 | - |
| UKIP | 65 | - | 22 | - | 35 | - |

*Strongly agree and somewhat agree responses combined.
[#]UK: 'Do you agree or disagree: equal opportunities for black and Asian people have gone too far, not far enough or just about right?'; US: 'Do you generally favour or oppose affirmative action for racial minorities?'

Source: UK: British Election Study Online Panel 2015, authors' data collected by YouGov, March 2018; US: Gallup, July 2015; YouGov USA, April 2018 and the Cooperative Congressional Election Study, 2016.

from August 2017 (not shown) show that the percentage of Americans agreeing 'racism is not a problem' is at an all-time low of 12 per cent, and those strongly rejecting colour-blindness is at an all-time high at 60 per cent. It thus highlights that acceptance of racism as a structural problem in the US was a response to the politicisation of race following Donald Trump's 2016 victory, rather than being fixed, unchangeable opinion. Importantly, these racial attitudes, together with the opinions on race equality discussed earlier, are polarised by party preference in Britain in a similar way to the US, where racial attitudes are one of the main differentiators between Republican and Democrat partisans (as shown in table 2) and as a result are likely to be as sensitive to current political context and politicisation.

British parties, like their American counterparts, have electoral incentives to respond to these differences in outlook by playing up or playing down race as an electoral strategy. Yet, for both parties it also creates unsolvable tensions. On the left, the emergence of a growing identity liberal electorate has presented Labour with a long-term opportunity, as demographic change builds support for the pro-diversity positions it has embraced. However, this has not been cost free in the short term. The growth of this liberal electorate has increased tensions with socially conservative traditional Labour supporters, many of whom continue to express degrees of discomfort with diversity. The result has been a vicious circle, with ambiguity over immigration, and latterly over Brexit, seemingly the only solution available to Labour—but one that is not sustainable indefinitely.

The Conservative party faces a related tension. It has traditionally benefitted from the mobilisation of nationalism and social conservatism, so a backlash against diversity could boost its support. Yet the demographic and cultural changes producing the backlash also make mobilisation of identity conservatism unsustainable in the long term, as it alienates young and ethnic minority voters even further. Already in 2017, the Conservatives discovered that embracing the pro-Brexit, nationalist identity voters was not cost free— as their gains among this electorate were offset by losses among the large and growing racially liberal electorate. As a result, as individual Conservative politicians give in to the temptation to play the race card, the party as a whole often distances itself from these attempts. A good example of this is the recent case of Boris Johnson, who likened Muslim women wearing burkas to letterboxes, and who experienced a significant backlash from his own party, including Prime Minister Theresa May.

Racially conservative attitudes in the US also drive opposition to both racial equality policies and broader welfare policies perceived as benefitting minority groups, over and above Americans' objective economic interests.[14] It is not clear whether this is an inevitable pattern, but we see from existing research on British support for welfare state policies that presenting these as being targeted at, or even just benefitting, ethnic minorities reduces public support.[15] Given that the partisans of the main parties feel differently about these issues presents another electoral incentive to politicise this area of policy making. This has not happened yet, but the temptation to politicise race remains, and even if mainstream parties do not succumb to it, a resurgent UKIP, or a party with a similar agenda could in future exploit divides over race and race conscious policy.

## Conclusions

New divides in identity attachments and social values are emerging in Britain as a result of growing ethnic diversity and the sustained expansion of higher education. We have examined two issues with the potential to mobilise such divides, producing the politics of 'culture wars': immigration and race. Conflicts over immigration had disrupted British politics for over a decade before the EU referendum, and played a major role in the choices that voters made. Yet, post-Brexit, policy makers will have a rare opportunity to craft policy in line with the public mood, which has become less hostile in the wake of the Brexit vote. Nevertheless, voters remain deeply divided over immigration, so the potential for new conflicts will remain.

While the main political parties have devoted much time and effort to wrestling with the problem of immigration, another serious and potentially growing problem has yet to attract attention: that Britain is also divided on its attitudes to race and racialised policies. While immigration is an issue where Brexit opens the door to new policy compromises, the issue of diversity is more complex and goes closer to the heart of the value divide between the identity conservative right and the identity liberal left. Any compromise on these issues aimed at winning back socially conservative white voters—a declining but still large and vital group—will risk antagonising cosmopolitan graduates and ethnic minorities, whose electoral influence is already large and will continue to grow. Politicians from all parties will need to think deeply about diversity and address the distinctions between xenophobia, racism, and racially conservative attitudes. The conflicts which emerge over these more fundamental aspects of identity politics may prove more intractable than anything they have thus far faced. The playing out of this dynamic will be a central feature of post-Brexit politics, even if immigration is (to a degree) tamed as an issue.

## Notes

1 British Social Attitudes surveys for 1997; British Election Study face-to-face survey for 2017.

2 I. Storm, M. Sobolewska and R. Ford, 'Is ethnic prejudice declining in Britain? Change in social distance attitudes among ethnic majority and minority Britons', *British Journal of Sociology*, vol. 68, no. 3, 2017, pp. 410–434.

3 R. Ford and M. Goodwin, 'Britain after Brexit: a nation divided', *Journal of Democracy*, vol. 28, no. 1, 2017, pp. 17–30; M. Sobolewska and R. Ford, 'Brexit and identity politics' in *Public Opinion and Brexit*, The UK in a Changing Europe, 2018; http://ukandeu.ac.uk/wp-content/uploads/2018/01/Public-Opinion.pdf (accessed 14 January 2019).

4 G. Evans and J. Mellon, 'Immigration and euroscepticism: the rising storm', UK in a Changing Europe blog, 2015; http://ukandeu.ac.uk/immigration-and-euro scepticism-the-rising-storm/ (accessed 14 January 2019).

5 R. Ford and K. Lymperopoulou, 'Immigration: how attitudes in the UK compare to Europe' in *British Social Attitudes: the 34th Report*, London, NatCen, 2017.

6 R. Ford, G. Morrell and A. Heath, 'Fewer but better? British attitudes to immigration', in *British Social Attitudes: the 29th Report*, London, NatCen, 2012.

7 R. Ford and A. Heath, 'Immigration: a nation divided?' in *British Social Attitudes: the 31st Report*, London, NatCen, 2014.

8 J. Gest, *The New Minority: White Working Class Politics in an Age of Immigration and Diversity*, Oxford, Oxford University Press, 2016.

9 B. F. Schaffner, M. MacWilliams and T. Nteta, 'Understanding white polarization in the 2016 vote for President: the sobering role of racism and sexism', *Political Science Quarterly*, vol. 133, no. 1, 2018, pp. 9–34.

10 S. Bowler and G. Segura, *The Future is Ours: Minority Politics, Political Behavior, and the Multiracial Era of American Politics*, Thousand Oaks CA, Sage/CQ Press, 2011.

11 D. R. Kinder and L. M. Sanders, *Divided by Color: Racial Politics and Democratic Ideals*, Chicago, University of Chicago Press, 1996.

12 E. Bonilla-Silva, *Racism without Racists: Color-Blind Racism and the Persistence of Racial Inequality in America*, Lanham MD, Rowman & Littlefield, 2003.

13 Ibid.

14 M. Gilens, S. F. Schram, J. Soss and R. C. Fording, *Race and the Politics of Welfare Reform*, Ann Arbor, University of Michigan Press, 2003; B. R. Knoll and J. Shewmaker, '"Simply un-American": nativism and support for health care reform', *Political Behavior*, vol. 37, no. 1, 2015, pp. 87–108.

15 R. Ford, 'Who should we help? An experimental test of discrimination in the British welfare state', *Political Studies*, vol. 64, no. 3, 2016, pp. 630–50; R. Ford and A. Kootstra, 'Do white voters support welfare policies targeted at ethnic minorities? Experimental evidence from Britain', *Journal of Ethnic and Migration Studies*, vol. 43, no. 1, 2017, pp. 80–101; A. Kootstra, 'Us versus them: examining the perceived deservingness of minority groups in the British welfare state using a survey experiment', in W. van Oorschot, F. Roosma, B. Meuleman, T. Reeskens, eds., *The Social Legitimacy of Targeted Welfare: Attitudes to Welfare Deservingness*, Cheltenham, Edward Elgar, 2017, pp. 263–280.

How to cite this article: M. Sobolewska and R. Ford, 'British Culture Wars? Brexit and the Future Politics of Immigration and Ethnic Diversity', in G Kelly and N Pearce (eds.), Britain Beyond Brexit, *The Political Quarterly*, Vol 90, Issue S2, 2019, pp. 142–154. https://doi.org/10.1111/1467-923X.12646

# The Divergent Dynamics of Cities and Towns: Geographical Polarisation and Brexit

WILL JENNINGS AND GERRY STOKER

THE BREXIT vote revealed a country divided by place, reflecting the diverging trajectories of economic development and politics taken by locations that have prospered in a globalised knowledge economy—predominantly cities—contrasted with places on the periphery, in towns and rural areas.[1] The same dynamics are observed in the United States, where support for the Democratic party is increasingly concentrated in urban areas, while the Republicans have lately made electoral inroads across the rural and small-town America that is shrinking or stagnating in terms of its population and jobs—creating a polarised politics that is divided by demographics and geography. In Europe, there has been a clear spatial pattern in electoral support for populist parties and candidates.[2] There are ways in which the British case has distinct features—due to its particular geography and institutions—but it largely reflects a wider trend where 'place' is increasingly consequential for political change and public policy.

While the EU referendum vote put the political divide between Britain's towns and cities into the spotlight, this divide is the product of long-term forces of social and economic changes. In this chapter, we show how geographical polarisation has and continues to reshape British politics, in the diverging trends between those places that have experienced relative decline and those that have thrived. Not only do these changes have electoral consequences for the major parties in Westminster, they pose particular challenges in terms of public policy.

Our argument proceeds as follows. Firstly, we demonstrate the trend towards geographical polarisation in voting behaviour, as the populations of big cities have voted in increasing numbers for Labour, while the residents of towns and rural areas increasingly have opted for the Conservatives. Secondly, we argue and show that this trend reflects economic as well as cultural forces: the schism between places reflects both divergent paths of demographic and economic change and related variation in the cultural and social outlooks of voters. Thirdly, we discuss the major challenge—amplified by Brexit—that this geographical polarisation presents for each of the parties as they seek to build electoral coalitions that reach beyond their existing strongholds. In concluding, we explore how the parties are presently responding to the place-based divergence of voting behaviour and policy problems.

Published by John Wiley & Sons Ltd, 9600 Garsington Road, Oxford OX4 2DQ, UK and 350 Main Street, Malden, MA 02148, USA

## Part I. The trend towards geographical polarisation

The thesis of bifurcated politics, or 'Two Englands', that we set out in previous work[3] argues that social and economic change is fundamentally reshaping electoral politics in England and Wales (with Scotland having undergone a nationalism-based realignment in the past decade). Specifically, cities are becoming younger, more ethnically diverse, more educated and more socially liberal—while towns are aging, are less diverse, more nostalgic and more socially conservative. These dynamics, we argue, have led to *tilting* of Britain's political axis towards the cosmopolitan-communitarian dimension, as both voters and places change, though a full-blown realignment has not yet materialised.[4] These processes are being inexorably driven by a number of social and economic trends.

1. *Economic divergence through urban agglomeration:* a defining feature of today's global knowledge economy is the gravitational pull that clustering exerts on creation of jobs and economic activity—increasing the geographical divide between economic winners and losers.[5] Cliffe argues that those places that have found a way to thrive typically 'have some combination of transport links, housing, natural resources, skills, international connections, open-mindedness, existing industrial clusters and political can-do'.[6] At the same time, other places have experienced the loss of skills, jobs and investment, degradation of infrastructure and the urban environment, and low levels of entrepreneurship,[7] becoming locked into a long-term spiral of economic decline—often following deindustrialisation. These economic forces have left towns and cities on different tracks.

2. *Education:* the 'great divergence' described by Moretti[8] is a function both of urban agglomeration and geographical sorting of workers on educational lines. In Britain, expansion of higher education since the 1990s has led to growing numbers of younger people leaving home and, after university, seeking employment and settling in or near cities and large towns where skilled jobs are increasingly located. Those not in higher education face a similar dilemma as to whether to move to major towns or cities where jobs and business opportunities are clustered. Economic geographers have long discussed the London and south-east 'escalator', which sucks in young people and deposits their exhausted middle-aged remains in outlying regions. Cities also tend to offer greater access to both 'highbrow' and 'emerging' cultural capital, exerting another pull factor on younger populations attracted to the bright lights, entertainment and culture. Crucially, education is also an important predictor of political values, in particular growing social liberalism,[9] and thus this demographic trend contributes to divides in the social outlooks of places as well as their demographics.

3. *Immigration and diversity:* rising immigration, in particular since the 1990s, has seen an inflow of people—heavily concentrated in cities—who are

younger and more economically active than average. Immigration on the scale experienced in recent decades has had transformative effects on the communities and places in different ways. It also has increasingly structured electoral politics.[10] At the same time, areas of low ethnic diversity have tended to see higher levels of opposition to immigration and social change. Place provides the opportunity for regular engagement with others nearby and a process of social exchange encourages a search for shared ground and a common understanding. Cultural stereotypes come to define the understanding of the place where people live. It defines who they are and what they represent. Other places and their populations become defined as different, alien and not to be trusted. Politicians can play on and reinforce this felt sense of difference to bolster their support and so place-based identity becomes politically weaponised and a symbol to drive a more polarised politics.

4. *Changing class structures and social ecology:* For many years, deindustrialisation has driven the shrinking of Britain's traditional working class, and erosion of its political representation. The perceived loss of social status among the white working class,[11] most acutely felt in those places where communities were organised around large local industries/employers, is associated with support for the radical right. At the same time, the changing structure of economic activity has seen the emergence of classes of 'new service workers' and others employed in precarious service industries (such as call centres, bar staff, fitness instructors)—with such jobs most concentrated in densely populated urban areas. Not only has the traditional working class declined, then, but the whole social class ecosystem has changed—as the old working class gradually dies out in the former manufacturing heartlands, being replaced by the new working class—the Uber drivers and call centre operators of today—most commonly located in the big cities.

In combination, these trends are gradually reshaping the geography of electoral politics—in transforming patterns of support for Labour and the Conservatives (as well as substantially impacting on spatial distribution of the Brexit vote). Figure 1 plots the Labour party lead over the Conservatives in terms of percentage vote share for all parliamentary constituencies in England and Wales in the 1979 and 2017 general elections against the population density of the constituency. This reveals that over this nearly forty-year period urban density has increasingly become associated with voting behaviour. In 1979, Labour did slightly worse (and the Conservatives slightly better) in areas with low population density—for instance, rural areas and small towns, but electoral contests were more balanced at higher levels of density. By 2017, this pattern remained at low levels of urban density, but Labour performed substantially better in areas with high population density, that is, large towns and cities, as is indicated by the steeper slope of the line-of-best-fit. As population density rises by an additional person per hectare, so

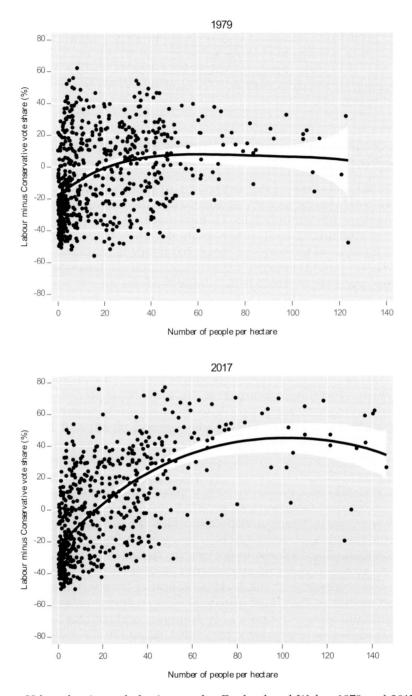

**Figure 1:** Urban density and election results, England and Wales, 1979 and 2017

Labour's lead over the Conservatives increased by about one percentage point (up until those constituencies with about sixty people per hectare, at which point the average lead levels off at around 40 per cent). This provides us evidence of a clear geographical polarisation of voting behaviour—as places change, so too does their politics (and the particular mix of problems facing policymakers).

## Part II. Economic decline, cultural values and geographic polarisation

So how does geographic polarisation lead to political difference? There has been substantial debate recently as to whether the rise of populism, and the Brexit vote, can be attributed to 'cultural backlash' (relating to anti-immigrant, racial resentment and authoritarian attitudes) or 'economic insecurity' (partly as a response to events of the global financial crisis and stagnation of the neoliberal growth model).[12] We consider this a false dichotomy, and believe that place allows us to better understand the intersection of economic change and cultural values. Our central argument is that places that have experienced relative decline have become more 'closed' on the 'open-closed', or 'cosmopolitan-communitarian', dimension. At the same time, places that have enjoyed relative growth have become more socially liberal. It is difficult to disentangle the precise mechanisms that lead to different political outlooks in different locations. The main candidates are the processes of demographic change (leading to changes in the sorts of people living in different places), self-selection (leading people to move to places where there are people who share their values) and neighbourhood effects and social contact (leading people to adopt the values of other people in their area).

If fundamental changes in the economic trajectory of places are behind this emerging divide in contemporary politics, then it should be possible to relate decline affecting places to voting behaviour. To do this, we adapt a measure of relative decline (and growth) developed by Pike et al., which uses indicators for a range of population and employment factors to determine the relative rate of decline of constituencies in England and Wales compared to one another.[13] These indicators are designed to capture the rate of population growth, economic activity and enterprise, the inflow of younger workers and students, and the level of education of the workforce—critical factors for success in the global economy.[14] As such, this measures the trajectory of particular places in terms of both human and economic capital.

In Figure 2, we plot this measure against change in the Labour and Conservative vote share between 2005 and 2017. (Parliamentary boundaries were revised in 2010, and we have the notional results for 2005 but not before, meaning our analysis cannot go further back in time.) It reveals a striking pattern where Labour has tended to make gains in areas subject to least decline and experienced losses in areas of most decline. The reverse is

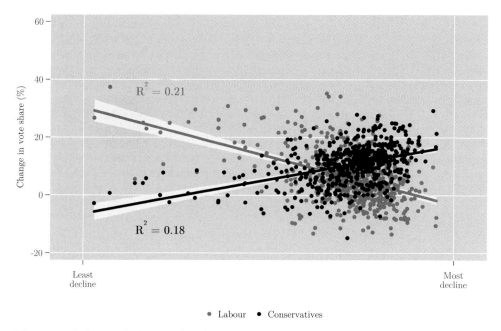

**Figure 2:** Relative decline and Labour and Conservative vote, England and Wales, 2005 to 2017

observed for the Conservatives—who tend to do better in places that have experienced relative decline in recent years. While there is plenty of noise around the trend, the findings suggest that geographical polarisation is being influenced by the relative demographic and economic trajectory of different places.

To what extent might decline also be associated with particular values or policy preferences? It is possible to consider the degree to which our measure of relative decline corresponds to the open-closed dimension. For this, we use estimates of constituency opinion produced by Hanretty et al. on the issues of immigration and same-sex marriage, using survey data from the British Election Study online panel in 2014[15] —which are standardised and combined to capture the 'open-closed' dimension (with higher values corresponding to more closed attitudes on these issues). Figure 3 plots how open or closed a given constituency is on these issues (on the y-axis) against the level of relative decline (on the x-axis). This again reveals a distinct pattern whereby areas that have experienced most decline are those that are most 'closed' (that is, opposed to immigration and/or same-sex marriage) in their attitudes. Areas subject to least decline are most open (that is, most socially liberal) on these issues. It seems, then, that the demographic and economic condition of places is linked to the particular cultural outlooks of their populations. (Although the observed relationship is correlational the temporal

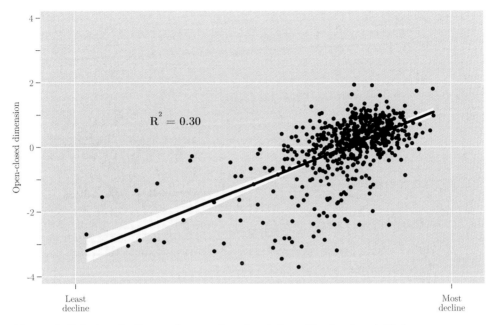

**Figure 3:** Relative decline and open-closed opinions, England and Wales

structure of our data makes it unlikely that open-closed attitudes would be a significant driver of decline over the preceding time period.)

# Part III. Implications for the future of British politics

These processes—of demographic and economic change—present both political disruption (the 'revenge of places that don't matter')[16] and major problems in terms of public policy (designing and funding the right social and economic policies for locations that have both different needs and resources).[17] This schism between places forms a backdrop to post-Brexit politics over the next decade or so that the major parties will have to confront. Labour is struggling to sustain support in smaller towns, while it piles up votes in metropolitan areas. The Conservatives, on the other hand, are losing in cities—among younger and more educated voters—and gaining in towns and rural areas. To build a broad electoral coalition, neither party can afford to ignore the places where they have been losing ground, nor wait for 'demographic destiny' to run its course. In short, our major national parties are facing tricky problems posed by this trend of geographical polarisation. How can they appeal across the divide to win votes? Can they design policy measures to deal with divergent issues faced in different locations? Should struggling places be written off, condemned to a process of inexorable decline, while a few lucky cities are selected as the engine of economic growth, or should the aim be a more equitable policy offer? Is it possible to craft political messages that speak to the distinctive local, regional and national identities of Britain's towns and cities? The early indications are that the parties are struggling to meet the challenge both politically and in policy terms.

To frame the political challenge, it is helpful to recognise that the shifting voting patterns are a tilting of the axis, not a complete realignment. Labour retains support in towns, and likewise, the Conservatives retain some electoral presence in cities. The rise of nationalism outside England has added new dimensions to Britain's electoral arithmetic and in Scotland has resulted in distinct party politics—with the SNP landslide in 2015 breaking Labour's long-held dominance of Scottish seats in Westminster. The drop in the vote share of other parties in England in the general election of 2017 marked a seeming return to the old days of two-party politics. However, a re-emergence of support for an alternative political force beyond the two main parties in England cannot be ruled out because of the continued persistence of strong negativity in public opinion towards mainstream parties and politics. Voters may yet be receptive to a 'new' offering by challenger parties or breakaways—especially in the wake of any Brexit-related chaos or perceived backsliding on the referendum. Our focus is on the prospects of Labour and the Conservatives, but they do not possess a guaranteed monopoly over the future of British politics.

For the two parties, the dilemma is whether to adopt a minimalist or maximalist approach to electoral coalition building. Should a party look to consolidate its current vote and make just enough gains to win a parliamentary majority, or should it seek a radical transformation that extends its appeal outside its base or 'core vote'. When parties are popular, they are more able to reach outside their comfort zone.[18] At the Labour party conference in 1999, Tony Blair declared 'the class war is over'. That he was able to do so reflected the impregnable position of Labour in the polls and also that the social base of the party's electoral coalition was slowly changing, masked by the success of the New Labour electoral machine. Neither party today is in a commanding position that would allow it to make such a claim, to steal the clothes of its opponents without risk of alienating its core vote. Electoral realignments come with substantial risks and transition costs for parties, not least as newer supporters tend to have weaker partisan attachments (the dramatic rise and fall of the Liberal Democrats between 2010 and 2015 serving as a good example of the potential fickleness of voters).

A further complicating factor beyond the difficulties of securing a convincing parliamentary majority in light of the geographical polarisation of electoral politics is the unprecedented level of public disaffection and cynicism about politics and politicians in Britain. In *The Good Politician*,[19] we use survey data and diaries from Mass Observation to show that negativity towards political elites and the practices of politics is more widespread and more intense that in any period since 1945. Brexit has further polarised the electorate through the emergence of new identities—of 'Leavers' and

'Remainers'. Parties must therefore find a way to widen their electoral coalitions at a time when public trust is at an all-time low and a new cross-cutting cleavage means that attempts to win over some groups risk alienating others.

For the Conservatives, the rhetorical ambition of the May government—launched with May's 'burning injustices' speech on the steps of Downing Street on 13 July 2016—was to construct a maximalist coalition that reached out to Labour's Brexit-voting heartlands (the 'tanks on Labour's lawn' strategy). This maximalist agenda survived until the disastrous 2017 general election, where results in constituencies like Canterbury and Kensington & Chelsea revealed the perils of this strategy; and even before then there had been U-turns on new policies like energy price caps and workers on company boards. Since then, the Conservatives have stuck to a more minimalist approach—with their attention dominated by Brexit and internal party wrangling over how hard or soft Brexit will be. Burnt by the experience of trying to appeal far beyond core supporters, the Conservatives will likely make token efforts to attract supporters from declining towns and may offer up occasional policies (such as those relating to the environment) aimed at the social liberalism of city dwellers. Fundamentally, however, under May's leadership the focus is on delivering a pragmatic Brexit, maintaining some semblance of party discipline, shoring up the party's core vote and avoiding economic meltdown in the aftermath of the UK leaving the European Union. Only failure on one of these fronts, and a leadership change, is likely to open up the prospects of a more maximalist coalition strategy again.

For Labour, the unexpectedly good result in the 2017 general election has also locked the party into a minimalist strategy. This continues to exploit Corbyn's projected image of authenticity and economic populism (for example, nationalisations, attacks on offshore tax havens), combined with a critique of austerity, which has particular appeal to voters in cities. The party also has been helped by its association with a softer version of Brexit (although its position remains tortuously ambiguous). Again, it would appear that only a significant electoral failure and the election of a new party leader would create conditions ripe for a more maximalist strategy that was able to recover losses in places that have drifted away from Labour.

A major problem in developing a more maximalist strategy is that neither of the parties appears comfortable in developing policy agendas that resonate with different parts of the country or speaks a language that reconciles identity politics and social liberalism. In many ways, this is not surprising given the high degree of centralisation of Britain's political system. Yet if our analysis is correct, and profound economic and social forces are generating divergent conditions in different geographical locations, then a differentiated policy response is required, with a politics to match. Different parts of the country face distinct sets of policy problems. Areas that have enjoyed relative growth tend to face demands associated with that, such as in terms of housing costs, congestion, pollution and lack of educational and other infrastructure. For areas that have experienced relative decline, the issue is how to develop innovative responses that manage to exploit a new niche for economic dynamism, but at the same time meet the health and social care needs of an ageing and relatively unhealthy population. Economic, planning, housing and social needs interventions need to be tuned to the circumstances faced in different locations but, despite recent devolution initiatives, our current system of governance is ill-equipped to deal with that prospect. Austerity measures since 2010 have greatly undermined capacity of local government across the board and cuts are continuing to impact. Failure to reform local government finance has left a local taxation system that is not progressive and not robust enough to garner the resources required in areas of either growth or decline. Yet, if anything, what appetite there was for devolution and decentralisation has weakened with the departure of Osborne from the Conservative government and the rise of a Corbyn-led Labour policy platform focused more on rekindling state direction of the economy.

Our main political parties are stuck in minimalist positions, focused on shoring up their core vote and managing internal party conflicts, unable to articulate a unifying vision in terms of policy or identity. Yet our analysis of the spatial political economy of twenty-first century Britain lends support to the idea that what is needed is the vision and leadership to deliver a more maximalist position that offers a very different type of governance and policy dynamic. In the present context—of a politics that is divided, parties and leaderships that are becalmed, a state that is under strain, and an electorate that is discontented—such an outcome seems unlikely, but not impossible. The geographical polarisation which now lies at the heart of British politics presents opportunities as well as challenges. These will be reaped by the party that is best able to offer hope for places of relative decline and at the same time can articulate a political message that is inclusive in terms of identity—bridging the divergent outlooks of the Two Englands.

As the moment of Brexit Day in 2019 approaches, we are faced with a situation where—no matter the outcome of the final negotiations—there is no straightforward path for either of the two main parties in Westminster to secure a large parliamentary majority from a divided and disenchanted electorate. That is even before any disappointment felt by voters regarding the precise form and delivery of Brexit. The parties are in an even more invidious position when it comes to the task of designing policy responses that address the disparate social and economic challenges confronting different parts of the country.

If we are correct about the new dynamics driving British politics, it will eventually reach a breaking point: based on their actions since 23 June 2016, both the Conservatives and Labour are struggling to reach a position on Brexit that is viable either in terms of satisfying their supporters or in terms of securing a deal with the EU. At the moment, both party leaderships are engaged in dangerous fantasies of the sunlit uplands that await British politics after Brexit. On Brexit, neither party is being straight with their supporters. The Conservatives remain in thrall to their eurosceptic wing, not facing up to the compromises that need to be made, while Labour is offering the meekest of opposition on Brexit, despite the majority of their voters supporting Remain. Neither party seems able to tackle the pressing challenges facing the country, instead offering a sad mix of infighting and cynical posturing. Given the tide of change in electoral politics we identify, it may take time for the parties to adjust their strategies, but time may be running out for a political class who appear so dramatically out of touch.

## Notes

1 W. Jennings and G. Stoker, 'The bifurcation of politics: Two Englands', *Political Quarterly*, vol. 87, no. 3, 2016, pp. 372–82. W. Jennings and G. Stoker, 'Tilting towards the cosmopolitan axis? Political change in England and the 2017 general election', *Political Quarterly*, vol. 88, no. 3, 2017, pp. 359–369. W. Jennings, A. Bua, R. Laurence and W. Brett, *Cities and Towns: the 2017 General Election and the Social Divisions of Place*, London, New Economics Foundation, 2017.

2 For example, A. Rodríguez-Pose, 'The revenge of the places that don't matter (and what to do about it)', *Cambridge Journal of Regions, Economy and Society*, vol. 11, no. 1, 2018, pp. 189–209.

3 Jennings and Stoker, 'The bifurcation of politics', 'Tilting towards the cosmopolitan axis?'.

4 S. B. Hobolt, 'Brexit and the 2017 UK general election', *Journal of Common Market Studies*, vol. 56, 2018, pp. 39–50.

5 P. R. Krugman, *Geography and Trade*, Boston, MIT Press, 1991.

6 J. Cliffe, 'England's cosmopolitan future: Clacton versus Cambridge', *The Economist*, 6 September 2014.

7 C. Martinez-Fernandez, I. Audirac, S. Fol and E. Cunningham-Sabot, 'Shrinking cities: urban challenges of globalization', *International Journal of Urban and Regional Research*, vol. 36, no. 2, 2012, pp. 213–225.

8 E. Moretti, *The New Geography of Jobs*, London, Mariner Books, 2012.

9 P. Surridge, 'Education and liberalism: pursuing the link', *Oxford Review of Education*, vol. 42, no. 2, 2016, pp. 146–164.

10 A. F. Heath, S. D. Fisher, G. Rosenblatt, D. Sanders and M. Sobolewska, *The Political Integration of Ethnic Minorities in Britain*, Oxford, Oxford University Press, 2013.

11 J. Gest, *The New Minority White Working Class Politics in an Age of Immigration and Inequality*, Oxford, Oxford University Press, 2016.

12 R. Inglehart and P. Norris, 'Trump and the populist authoritarian parties: the silent revolution in reverse', *Perspectives on Politics*, vol. 15, no. 2, 2017, pp. 443–454.

13 A. Pike, D. MacKinnon, M. Coombes, T. Champion, D. Bradley, A. Cumbers, L. Robson and C. Wymer, *Uneven Growth: Tackling City Decline*, York, Joseph Rowntree Foundation, 2016.

14 To construct this measure values for each of the following indicators are first standardised (i.e. rescaled by subtracting the mean ($\mu$) from the observed value (x) and dividing by the standard deviation ($\sigma$): $z = \frac{(x-\mu)}{\sigma}$) across all 573 parliamentary constituencies in England and Wales:

  i Change in the rate of economic activity (%), 2001 to 2011.
  ii Change in the number of businesses (all firms), 2010 to 2016.
  iii Change in the number of jobs, 2009 to 2015.
  iv Change in total population, 2001 to 2011.
  v Change in net inward migration of 15–19 year-olds, 2001 to 2011.
  vi Change in proportion of population with a degree, 2001 to 2011.

  The final index takes the average of the six standardised indicators for each constituency and is then inverted so that higher values indicate greater decline. (Pike et al.'s original measure uses ranks of the constituencies on each of the indicators, whereas we standardise the indicators to provide a more fine-grained measure of relative decline.)

15 C. Hanretty, B. Lauderdale and N. Vivyan, 'Dyadic representation in a Westminster system.' *Legislative Studies Quarterly*, vol. 42, no. 2, 2017, pp. 235–267.
16 Rodríguez-Pose, 'The revenge of the places that don't matter'.
17 W. Jennings, A. Lent and G. Stoker, *Place-based Policymaking After Brexit*, London, New Local Government Network, 2017.
18 J. Green and W. Jennings, 'Party reputations and policy priorities: how issue ownership shapes executive and legislative agendas', *British Journal of Political Science*, 2017, pp. 1–24, https://doi.org/10.1017/s0007123416000636.
19 N. Clarke, W. Jennings, J. Moss and G. Stoker, *The Good Politician: Folk Theories, Political Interaction, and the Rise of Anti-Politics*, Cambridge, Cambridge University Press, 2018.

How to cite this article: W. Jennings and G. Stoker, 'The Divergent Dynamics of Cities and Towns: Geographical Polarisation and Brexit', in G Kelly and N Pearce (eds.), Britain Beyond Brexit, *The Political Quarterly*, Vol 90, Issue S2, 2019, pp. 155–166. https://doi.org/10.1111/1467-923X.12612

# Brexit and the Nations

## MICHAEL KEATING

## Brexit and the union

THE CENTRAL promise of the Brexit campaign was to 'take back control'—to restore British sovereignty. Initially referring to parliamentary sovereignty, this rapidly morphed into the sovereignty of the British people, creating a binding mandate for withdrawal. That is an important move, but in both cases sovereignty was to be located in one place. This reflects the traditional 'Westminster' view of the United Kingdom as a unitary state in which competences may be devolved to local levels but ultimate power remains at the centre.

At the periphery, there is a different view, which sees the UK as a union of nations, whose position within the state is the product of a historic pact and is conditional. The alternative Scottish theory denies that the Union of 1707 created a sovereign parliament that reflected only English traditions of sovereignty. On the contrary, the issue of sovereignty was unresolved, as recognised by Lord Cooper's *obiter dictum* in the famous case of *MacCormick vs Lord Advocate* in 1953, where he stated that 'the principle of the unlimited sovereignty of Parliament is a distinctively English principle which has no counterpart in Scottish constitutional law'. This is not merely a Scottish nationalist interpretation but is present in Scottish unionist thought. Irish unionism incorporates ideas of a historic bargain and, in Northern Ireland, has been informed by the Covenant tradition in which loyalty is contingent; hence the historic coexistence of a strident 'Britishness' with willingness to break with the UK should unionists feel betrayed.

This tradition sees the UK as a plurinational union of nations lacking in a unitary people or *demos*. Rather, citizens in the non-English nations have a choice of identities and can hold more than one at the same time. Nor does the UK have a single purpose or *telos*, but is interpreted differently across and within its component parts. Rather than being a single shared notion, the union is a family resemblance concept, without shared normative foundations. This ambivalence, far from a weakness, has historically proven to be its strength. Successive UK governments' campaigns to give it firmer grounding in 'Britishness' or 'British values' have merely served to highlight divisions and, ironically, put the union itself at risk.

Unionism thus stands out in Europe as a state ideology that is not inimical to the recognition of national pluralism. The one thing it could not accept was parliamentary institutions in the component parts, arguing that, precisely because these were nations, such institutions would inevitably assume

Published by John Wiley & Sons Ltd, 9600 Garsington Road, Oxford OX4 2DQ, UK and 350 Main Street, Malden, MA 02148, USA

sovereignty rights. This position shifted at the end of the twentieth century, when unionists accepted devolution settlements for Scotland, Wales and Northern Ireland. This marked a significant constitutional moment, but left critical questions in abeyance. The issue of sovereignty was skirted. Westminster insisted it retained the power to legislate in devolved matters, but accepted a convention that it 'normally' would not. Scotland was not given the right to secession, but in practice the Cameron government agreed to an independence referendum, staged in 2014. The Northern Ireland settlement provided for secession and union with the Republic of Ireland by referendum if the demand were present. It invited citizens of Northern Ireland to adopt and express a range and mix of identities. There were north-south institutions and east-west institutions satisfying both nationalist and unionist concerns. Issues of sovereignty and allegiance to the Crown were avoided. There was no reform of the centre corresponding to the reforms at the periphery so, as it had after the unions of 1707 and 1801, it carried on as before. Devolution did not encompass England (which accounts for some 85 per cent of the population) apart from a weak provision allowing English MPs a separate vote on legislation only affecting England. The new settlement reinforced the nature of the UK as a plurinational union, whose institutions were not fixed, but in evolution.

Far from being in contradiction with the European project, this *ad hoc* union, with no defined constitutional status, no unitary *demos*, no fixed *telos* and a refusal to address the issue of sovereignty explicitly, bears a remarkable resemblance to that project. There is what scholars of European integration describe as a 'good fit'. Indeed, the EU has provided an important external support system for the devolution process, compensating for its incompleteness. In the first place, Europe provides a discursive space for ideas of shared and divided sovereignty, multiple *demoi* and constitutional pluralism, which characterise the UK's evolving constitution. Europe is understood and framed by different actors in different ways, as a free trade area, an intergovernmental body, a federation in the making or a *sui generis* polity. It has economic, social, cultural and political dimensions, stressed at different times by different actors.

Second, the EU provides for market integration and regulation at the European level, allowing for a more expansive devolution settlement within the UK than would otherwise be possible. The European Single Market has allowed an open border between the two parts of Ireland and the removal of all physical controls. It has permitted all-Ireland markets to emerge in agriculture and energy and encouraged cross-border cooperation. The Europeanisation of Ireland has coincided with the 'post-nationalist' turn in the Republic and an increasing recognition of the shared historical experiences of both islands.

Third, the EU, together with the European Convention on Human Rights, provides a rights regime detached from national citizenship and national identity, enforceable directly in the devolved territories. In Scotland and

Northern Ireland, large numbers of citizens do not regard themselves as British.[1] Making this the condition for human and civil rights would therefore be problematic. European rights, however are another matter, commanding broad consensus.

## Brexit scenarios

While England and Wales voted to leave by around 53 per cent, Scotland voted by 62 per cent to remain. Northern Ireland voted to remain by 56 per cent, but there was a big difference between the two communities. Nationalist voters supported Remain by over 80 per cent, while Unionists showed a majority for Leave (Table 1). Surveys have shown that many of the same factors worked across all three nations, but in Scotland and Wales the leadership of the nationalist parties delivered majorities for Remain among social groups that, in England and Wales, voted Leave. The Scottish National party (SNP) has long seen the EU as an important external support system for an independent Scotland. The Northern Ireland Social Democratic and Labour party (SDLP) is historically pro-Europe. Sinn Féin, now the larger nationalist party, is historically eurosceptic but supported Remain on the grounds that it did not want to 'repartition Ireland' by erecting a hard EU border. The Democratic Unionist party (DUP) supported leave, while the Ulster Unionist party (a much-diminished force these days) was for Remain but now supports leaving. English identity, which has been growing in recent years, however, is strongly associated with voting Leave.

This leaves a set of clashing mandates. The UK government insists that the verdict of 'the British people' must be respected, which assumes a single *demos*, denying the existence of a Scottish *demos* that was implicit in conceding the independence referendum. Within Northern Ireland, there are not the concurrent majorities that have been required over the years to bind both communities into constitutional reforms. Nor, however, are there clear majorities available for alternative paths, which we can characterise as: disintegration; recentralisation; and reconfiguration.

## Disintegration

In the immediate aftermath of the referendum, Sinn Féin called for a poll on Irish reunification. The SNP declared that a second independence

**Table 1: Brexit vote, Northern Ireland (%)[6]**

|  | Nationalist | Unionist | Neither |
| --- | --- | --- | --- |
| Remain | 88 | 34 | 70 |
| Leave | 12 | 66 | 30 |
| Total | 100 | 100 | 100 |

169

referendum was likely, a position that was hardened in 2017 when Article 50 was triggered. Yet there are enormous difficulties in the UK falling apart on clear lines.

Surveys in recent years have shown that there is no majority in Northern Ireland for reunification, even among Catholics, as long as the alternative of power-sharing under the Good Friday Agreement is available. Nor is there much enthusiasm in the Republic for taking on the North.[2] Brexit may create a hard border between the two parts of Ireland, but Irish unification after Brexit would create a similar hard border between Northern Ireland and Great Britain, so that the border would merely be moved.

In Scotland, the vote for Remain did not, as widely expected, translate into increased support for independence. In fact, the electorate has never made the link between independence and Europe on which the SNP independence project is based. Surveys over the years have shown less euroscepticism across all parties in Scotland than in England, but particularly among Labour voters; SNP voters are divided in the same proportions as Scots as a whole. The British Election Study has examined the relationship between voting at the two referendums to produce a matrix with four boxes, none of which contains more than a third of the electorate (Table 2).

This leaves the SNP highly cross-pressured and at the snap general election of 2017 it lost much of its support among Leave voters, forcing it to park the idea of a second independence referendum.

Brexit has also undermined the independence-in-Europe strategy of 2014, based on the idea that, with both Scotland and the rest of the UK (rUK) inside the EU, there would be no hard border. With Scotland in the EU and rUK outside, the same problem would arise on the England-Scotland border as in Ireland. Some elements within the SNP have since argued that an independent Scotland could join the European Economic Area (EEA), which would keep it within the European Single Market and allow for free movement of people with Europe. As it would be outside the EU Customs Union, it could also potentially negotiate a free trade agreement with rUK. In the meantime, the SNP moved to support the emerging soft Brexit coalition alongside the Liberal Democrats, Greens and elements of the Labour and Conservative parties. While a soft Brexit might reduce the Scottish grievance about being dragged out of the EU, it would make independence easier, by keeping open trading links with rUK as well as the EU/ EEA. Nonetheless,

**Table 2: Support for EU and independence in Scotland[7]**

|  | Yes independence | No independence | Total |
|---|---|---|---|
| Remain EU | 27 | 34 | 61 |
| Leave EU | 17 | 21 | 37 |
| Total | 44 | 55 |  |

Brexit has not triggered a process of the disintegration of the UK, as many feared likely in the immediate aftermath of the referendum result.

## Recentralisation

A second scenario is that the United Kingdom reconstitutes itself as a unitary nation-state bound by the sovereignty of Westminster. This would go against evolving understandings of the UK as a quasi-federation in which the devolved institutions are an entrenched part of the constitution. Signs of this evolution had been the failure of the UK to challenge devolved competences (except on a couple of occasions in Wales); the reluctance to test the limits of devolution in the courts; pledges given by the No side during the Scottish independence referendum campaign; and the devolution acts of 2016 and 2017 for Scotland and Wales respectively, putting the Sewel Convention into statutory (albeit not legally-binding) form.

The first test of this was the issue of those competences that are shared between the EU and the devolved legislatures, notably in agriculture, fisheries, environment and justice and home affairs. In many of these fields, there is no UK legislation or policy, so that coherence across the United Kingdom is ensured only by EU regulation. The UK government argued that, after Brexit, common UK frameworks would be needed to ensure the operation of the UK internal market, allow it to negotiate trade agreements with the EU and third countries, and deal with externalities. It further insisted that, as these matters are covered by EU laws, the devolved bodies were merely implementing EU policy rather than making policies themselves. So these competences could be repatriated to Westminster without the devolved level losing powers, as they would exercise the same amount of discretion at the implementation end. The EU Withdrawal Bill therefore proposed that all 'retained EU law' including that in devolved spheres, would revert to Westminster. UK ministers could then decide which powers to 'release' back to the devolved level. The Scottish and Welsh governments strongly disputed this interpretation and refused to give legislative consent to the Withdrawal Bill.

After some months of negotiation, it was agreed that some UK-wide frameworks would be needed to deal with matters affecting the UK internal market, trade, international obligations and common resources. The UK government accepted that the relevant parts of the EU Withdrawal Bill would be subject to legislative consent from the devolved legislatures. It gradually conceded on the principle of blanket reservation of powers, instead working on lists of competences that could be released immediately. Other matters would be subject to non-legislative frameworks through memoranda of understanding or concordats. All powers would finally be released after seven years. Only a limited number of matters would be subject to legislative frameworks. The Welsh government accepted the compromise, but the Scottish Parliament, with only the Conservatives dissenting, refused legislative consent. Yet the Withdrawal Bill was passed. Meanwhile, the constitutional legality of the Scottish Parliament's legislation has been referred to the Supreme Court by the Westminster government.

Arguably, this changes nothing constitutionally, as Westminster always retained the right to ignore the denial of legislative consent. On the other hand, the final version of the Withdrawal Bill for the first time stipulates what will happen in the absence of legislative consent for recentralisation of powers. If the devolved legislatures consent, transfer will proceed; if they do not consent, transfer will proceed; if they do nothing, transfer will proceed. Thus, a convention that was hitherto respected is explicitly repudiated. Brexit has therefore upset the pragmatic evolution of the devolution settlement, leaving a constitutional sore to fester.

## Reconfiguration

The third possibility is a reconfiguration in which the different parts of the United Kingdom would have different relationships with European institutions. The Scottish government's paper *Scotland's Place in Europe*,[3] set out a range of possibilities. The first preference was for the whole UK to remain in the EU, followed by the whole UK remaining in the Single Market and Customs Union. Failing that, it was proposed that Scotland remain in the Single Market, using a variant of the EEA mechanism. The proposal was complex, involving, for example, identifying the final destination of goods in order to distinguish those within the Single Market from those circulating only within the UK, but the UK government later suggested something similar for keeping the UK in a customs arrangement while leaving the Single Market. The Scottish government paper also proposed that Scotland remain open to EU free movement of people, reflecting a cross-party consensus in the Scottish Parliament in a favour of migration and mobility. These proposals were ignored by the UK government, which rejected any territorially differentiated Brexit, and were not incorporated into the negotiations with the EU.

The Scottish and Welsh governments returned to the issue in their Continuity Bills of 2018. As well pre-empting the EU Withdrawal Bill after the UK government had refused to amend it to leave out the reservation of retained EU law, these provided for Scottish and Welsh ministers to retain and update EU provisions. So, Scotland and Wales would effectively shadow EU policies even after Brexit. After the Welsh government came to an agreement with the UK over the Withdrawal Act, the UK government dropped its case against the Welsh Continuity Bill.[4]

The case of Northern Ireland proved even more difficult. A key item in the Good Friday Agreement (GFA) of 1998 was cross-border cooperation. Although there are not a lot of details about this in the GFA itself, the European Single Market from 1993 allowed for the removal of the remaining physical controls at the border between Northern Ireland and the

Republic of Ireland. With the UK leaving the EU, and Ireland remaining, a new, hard border would be reinstated. Aware of the sensitivity of the issue, the UK government insisted that there would be no return to a 'hard border' or 'the borders of the past' but has been short on detail as to how this would be achieved. The Irish government, for its part, took a decision to play as a loyal member of the EU-27 and use its position there to have the Irish border included as a condition for starting substantive negotiations. In December 2017, an agreement was reached, reiterated in the agreement of March 2018 on transition and the start of negotiation on the future relationship.

This was a fudge that avoided addressing the key question. Three options were stated. First, it was hoped that the future overall agreement between the EU and the UK would avoid the need for a hard border in Ireland. It is difficult to see how this can be achieved unless the UK remains in the Single Market and Customs Union, which it has said it will not do. (The UK government's Chequers White Paper would keep the UK in the Single Market for goods and agri-foods and establish a new and hitherto untried customs partnership with the EU, but this has not proved acceptable to the European Commission and member states.) If that failed, there would be a technological solution: customs formalities and regulatory controls would be done electronically, without any physical infrastructure at the border. Yet, such a virtual border would still be a border as long as there are regulatory differences between the EU and the UK. Such differences are particularly problematic for the agricultural sector, an important matter in north-south trade in Ireland and for border communities. Third, failing the other two, there would be regulatory alignment between the two parts of Ireland as far as necessary in order to keep the Good Friday Agreement working. The UK and Irish governments fundamentally disagree on what this entails. On a narrow interpretation, the GFA says relatively little about Europe and the UK has sought to define a narrow list of competences affected. On a broad interpretation, the working out of the GFA, including opening the border and all-Ireland markets and institutions, is deeply dependent on the Single Market. This Irish government therefore interpreted this as requiring full regulatory alignment. In fact, all three options would require such regulatory alignment. Unless the whole of the UK remained in regulatory alignment, this would require a differentiated Brexit for Northern Ireland, something the UK government does not accept. Nor does the DUP, which supports Brexit but opposes a hard border, and provides the UK government with its parliamentary majority. In fact, the idea of a 'border in the Irish Sea' has little support from any of the parties, as both parts of Ireland depend more on markets in Great Britain than they do on each other's markets. Reconfiguration of the UK's relationship with the EU to accommodate different forms of Single Market and Customs Union membership for the nations of the UK appears difficult, although it remains (in September 2018) the case that a differential arrangement for Northern Ireland is the EU's backstop arrangement.

## The question of England

Successive devolution schemes since the 1880s foundered on two issues: sovereignty, and the place of England. This is not for want of thinking about the English question. Schemes for regional government have been around since the early twentieth century, including the reinvention of the Saxon Heptarchy. Moves from regional planning to regional government foundered in the 1960s and were followed by metropolitan governments in the 1970s, themselves abolished in the 1980s. After 1997, there was a further move to regional government, which failed after a referendum in the North East, and then metropolitan government came back as what was misleadingly called English devolution. In fact, these schemes were about the functional needs of planning, development and service delivery and had little to do with recognition, legislative autonomy and policy divergence as applied in the devolved nations.

Englishness was historically accommodated within the broader scope of Great Britain or the United Kingdom, in which England was the predominant partner. Only after devolution to the periphery did it become apparent and politically salient. Brexit has further exposed these different understandings of nationality and identity. It has also exposed regional differences within England as London booms as a global city while the older industrial areas are marginalised. In the absence of massive payments from London to compensate for the economic effects of Brexit on these areas, the political divide is likely to widen. Yet, for all the talk of regeneration for the North, there seems little prospect for such fiscal redirection; rather, it seems, cities will have to manage more on their own.

## What future for the union?

Following the 2016 referendum, there have been renewed calls for a comprehensive constitutional reform for the United Kingdom. They are sometimes tied to the idea of a Constitutional Convention[5] or Citizens' Assembly and a written constitution. This is not going to happen.

In the first place, it would require a settlement of the most pressing constitutional issue, Brexit, on which there is no agreement or common mandate. Scotland, Northern Ireland and (in spite of its vote) Wales will seek international and European connections of various sorts. London, of course, has its own international priorities, but not the constitutional status to pursue them—and no UK government would allow its capital city such scope.

Second, a Citizens' Assembly implies a unitary *demos*, which does not exist and is even more elusive after Brexit. There are proposals for a British Bill of Rights, which some on the right want to replace the European Convention, but tying rights to Britishness is not going to work. Some have sought to underpin common British identity by grounding it in values such as democracy, the rule of law, fair play and social solidarity. Yes, these are the very values claimed by Scottish, Irish and Welsh nationalists to underpin their own national claims.

Third, there is no agreement on the foundations of sovereignty, an issue exposed in the Scottish independence debate and after Brexit, but not resolved by consensus. Scotland and Northern Ireland have, in different ways, asserted a right to self-determination and UK governments have, in contrast for example with Spain, not denied the principle, even while making its exercise difficult. When constitutional agreement is proving so difficult within Northern Ireland, it is hard to imagine that it could be achieved across the UK as a whole. Scottish and Irish nationalists will not surrender the right, even although they have been willing to put it into abeyance in the short term.

Fourth, no practical scheme has ever been designed to give effect to a written constitution that would command consensus. Federalising ideas go back to the nineteenth century, but a convincing design needs to do two things. It must constrain the sovereignty of Westminster as well as of the other national legislatures; and it must provide for England.

Short of a definitive constitutional settlement, territorial issues will continue to be part of the politics of the United Kingdom. The vagaries of the electoral system have given territorial parties the balance of power in the 1880s, between 1910 and 1920, in the 1970s and since 2017. UKIP, a party whose support was largely confined to England and Wales, could have become a parliamentary broker and a future English party cannot be ruled out if Brexit does not deliver for the marginalised parts of post-industrial England. In that case, the United Kingdom may come to resemble Spain, where periods of majority government are interspersed with minority governments dependent on the territorial parties. There may be recurrent territorial crises, while at other times, territorial brokerage works. Currently in Spain, the Catalan nationalist parties are in all-out conflict with the centre, while the Basque Nationalist party has effortlessly transferred its support at the centre, helping to oust the conservatives and to install the socialists. Territorial brokerage will be about resources and powers and, given the small size of the peripheral nations, this will not necessarily be expensive or unduly intrusive in England matters. As long as England thinks this is a price worth paying for union, the union is likely to survive. In a post-Brexit world, that cannot be taken for granted. Yet although Brexit will leave behind fault lines in the territorial politics of the UK, it may not provoke fissures sufficiently deep as to break the UK itself apart.

## Notes

1 What Scotland Thinks, 'Moreno' national identity, surveys from multiple years; http://whatscotlandthinks.org/questions/moreno-national-identity-5 (accessed 7 November 2018). Census 2011, analysis on national identity in Northern Ireland; https://www.ninis2.nisra.gov.uk/public/census2011analysis/nationalidentity/National%20Identity%20in%20Northern%20Ireland.pdf (accessed 7 November 2018).

2 Northern Ireland Life and Times survey, 2017, ESRC; http://www.ark.ac.uk/nilt/ (accessed 7 November 2018).

3 Scottish government, *Scotland's Place in Europe,* Edinburgh, 20 December 2016; https://www.gov.scot/publications/scotlands-place-europe/ (accessed 7 November 2018).

4 The understanding is that the Welsh government will repeal its Continuity Bill although that did not happen immediately.

5 UK Parliament, Commons Select Committee, *Do we Need a Constitutional Convention for the UK?*, 28 March 2013; https://www.parliament.uk/business/committees/committees-a-z/commons-select/political-and-constitutional-reform-committee/inquiries/parliament-2010/constitutional-convention-for-the-uk/ (accessed 7 November 2018). Constitution Unit, University College London, current research; https://www.ucl.ac.uk/constitution-unit/columns/researchtest/constitution-unit/research/constitutions-constitution-making (accessed 7 November 2018).

6 J. Garry, 'The EU referendum vote in Northern Ireland: implications for our understanding of citizens' political views and behaviour', Knowledge Exchange Seminar Series 2016–2017; https://www.qub.ac.uk/brexit/Brexitfilestore/Filetoupload,728121,en.pdf (accessed 7 November 2018).

7 C. Prosser and E. Fieldhouse, *A Tale of Two Referendums—the 2017 Election in Scotland*, British Election Study, 2 August 2017; http://www.britishelectionstudy.com/bes-findings/a-tale-of-two-referendums-the-2017-election-in-scotland/#.WeoCaDb9O7M (accessed 7 November 2018).

How to cite this article: M. Keating, 'Brexit and the Nations', in G Kelly and N Pearce (eds.), Britain Beyond Brexit, *The Political Quarterly*, Vol 90, Issue S2, 2019, pp. 167–176. https://doi.org/10.1111/1467-923X.12619

# The Realignment of British Politics in the Wake of Brexit

## ANDREW GAMBLE

THE REFERENDUM vote to leave the European Union on 23 June 2016 has created a deep political and constitutional crisis. The terms on which Britain would leave or whether it would leave at all were still unclear two years after the referendum vote. The only certainty is that the process of determining a new relationship between Britain and the EU will stretch long beyond the date, 29 March 2019, on which Britain is set formally to leave the EU. As Brexit unfolds, it threatens to unleash disruptive changes in British politics and political economy. Here, I examine what it might mean for the party system. Will it mark a watershed in British politics, producing lasting political realignment of both voters and parties? Or will the existing system survive?

British politics has been in turmoil since the referendum, because this was the first time a national referendum had gone against the recommendation of the government and against the status quo. It opened a split between parliamentary sovereignty and popular sovereignty. For Leave supporters, the referendum issued a clear instruction for Britain to leave the EU. But it quickly became apparent there were many different ways of doing so, and no agreement on what the best option might be, even among Leavers. A large majority of MPs had voted Remain and were opposed to any option which involved a hard Brexit, while a minority, mainly on the Conservative benches, argued that only the hardest Brexit possible would respect the referendum vote. Prime Minister Theresa May attempted to solve the problem by calling a general election in 2017 to give her the space and authority to negotiate with the EU. But instead of an increased majority, she lost the small majority she already had and to stay in office, was forced to conclude a confidence and supply agreement with the Democratic Unionist party (DUP), which narrowed her options even further.

The negotiations were slow and arduous, because Theresa May was trying to reconcile the irreconcilable, finding a formula which could satisfy simultaneously the contradictory demands of Leave voters, the polarised factions in her party, the DUP, the business community, and the EU. This created a series of acute policy dilemmas, and along the way she lost Cabinet ministers and backing from crucial parts of the Conservative coalition and the Conservative media. By November 2018, with only four months to go before Britain formally was to leave the EU under Article 50, it was still uncertain whether the deal agreed painstakingly with the EU would command a majority in

Published by John Wiley & Sons Ltd, 9600 Garsington Road, Oxford OX4 2DQ, UK and 350 Main Street, Malden, MA 02148, USA

Parliament, because of the opposition of the DUP and the hard Brexit wing of the Conservative party.

How the parliamentary impasse over Brexit is overcome could have profound consequences for the party system. Theresa May has defined the choice as between her deal, no-deal or no-Brexit. In November 2018, it seemed quite possible that there was no parliamentary majority for any of the three and that the existing party system would buckle. One or both of the two main parties would split, and a new political landscape would emerge, either immediately through a realignment of MPs within the existing Parliament to create a new parliamentary majority, or subsequently after an appeal to the people through a general election or a second referendum.

Theresa May urged her party to support her deal against the alternatives, arguing that a no-deal Brexit would cause substantial short-term damage to the British economy and long-term damage to the reputation and standing of the Conservative party, while no Brexit at all would not respect the first referendum result and lead to a populist nationalist backlash. A YouGov poll in the *Sunday Times*[1] in July 2018 suggested that 38 per cent of those questioned would support a new party promising a hard Brexit, including many (24 per cent of the whole sample) who wanted such a new party to be anti-immigrant and anti-Islam. 33 per cent would support a new centrist party offering a soft Brexit or no Brexit at all. That does not leave many supporting the two parties which have dominated British politics for the last hundred years. The risk for the Conservatives and for Labour is that in the aftermath of Brexit, they lose ground to both a new centrist pro-European party and to a new Britain First party.

Throughout her premiership, May sought to preserve the Conservative party as a party of government and to resist the new polarisation between Leavers and Remainers already apparent in the 2017 election. Her deal was a messy compromise which gave no one what they wanted, but which she and her allies presented as the only way to maintain the Conservative party as a pragmatic party of government,[2] focussed on delivering a Brexit which would cause as little damage to the economy as possible, at the same time avoiding a permanent split in the Conservative party and a resulting breakup of the party system.

## Realignments in British politics

Realignments of political parties are rare. They take place when parties split over a fundamental issue of policy, which either anticipate or follow realignments of voters and electoral coalitions. Party realignments can happen in three main ways: when there is a formal split initiated by the party leader, as in 1846 and 1931; when senior party leaders lead a breakaway from a party as in 1886 and 1981; or when one party is taken over by one of its factions, and MPs and members aligned with other factions drift away or are driven out, as in the Conservative party after 1906.

In 1846 and 1931, the Prime Minister concluded that the national emergency was so grave that it warranted splitting his party and forming a new administration with members from opposition parties. Robert Peel in 1846 proposed the repeal of the Corn Laws but was opposed by two-thirds of his MPs. A minority followed him into a new government with Liberals and independents. The Corn Laws were repealed. The Conservative party did not form a majority government again for more than thirty years. In 1931, Ramsay MacDonald formed a national government to deal with the financial crisis. Only a small number of ministers and Labour MPs followed him, but he was joined by the Conservatives and some of the Liberals. At the subsequent general election Labour was reduced to fifty-two seats.

The second type of split and realignment happened in 1886 over the issue of Irish home rule, when Joseph Chamberlain and his supporters broke with the Liberal party and created the Liberal Unionist party which supported the Conservatives and eventually merged with them, guaranteeing a long period of Conservative ascendancy. In 1981, the Labour party descended into bitter infighting over its future direction, and twenty-eight MPs left Labour and established a new party, the Social Democratic party (SDP). The SDP formed an alliance with the Liberals, before ultimately merging with them to become the Liberal Democrats. This new centrist alliance came close to breaking through in the 1983 election, but although it almost matched Labour in votes, the first past the post system meant that Labour—although heavily defeated by the Conservatives—still won more than 200 seats. The Alliance won just twenty-three.

The third type of realignment occurred in the Conservative party after 1906. The party leader, Arthur Balfour, had been trying to hold his party together in a compromise between the protectionist and free trade wings of his party. After 1906, with the party back in opposition, that compromise broke down and the party moved to a hard-line protectionist position. Local associations deselected MPs with free trade views, and many MPs and members defected to the Liberals. The parties became increasingly polarised in the run-up to the First World War.

One route to a potential party realignment would be if a Brexit deal gets through Parliament only because of support from opposition MPs, forming in effect a new parliamentary majority. Or it could come about by breakaways from one or both of the two main parties. Or it could be the third kind, a steady purging of MPs and members, creating a much more polarised political system. This is perhaps the most likely. It is very hard to displace one of the two main parties in a system which uses a simple plurality rule in single-member constituencies. The only time it has happened so far was when Labour replaced the Liberals as one of the two main parties after 1918, but there were special circumstances, particularly the enlargement of the electorate through the extension of the franchise. Other third parties have had bursts of success, but have not been able to break the stranglehold of the two main parties. The most recent example is UKIP. Despite its success in winning more seats in the European Parliament than any other party, and winning four million votes in the 2015 general election, it only won one Westminster seat, and that was a seat held by a Conservative defector. If seats had been allocated proportionally in 2015, UKIP could have expected to win more than eighty. The main impact of third parties has been to reshape the policies, leadership and electoral strategies of the two main parties, rather than to replace them. Could Brexit change this?

In the last fifteen years, both main parties have lost support to third parties. Two of the last three general elections have resulted in a hung Parliament, and the one that did not (2015) only gave the Conservatives a very small majority. That said, and even though the first post-Brexit election in 2017 gave no party a majority, it did see a swing back to the two main parties. Very unusually, both Labour and the Conservatives gained vote share at the expense of smaller parties, particularly UKIP. Together they had more than 80 per cent of the vote, the first time this had happened since 1979.

The reason why 2017 saw a turn back to the two main parties was because of voter realignment. The referendum had highlighted the new electoral coalitions which were forming in British politics. The Leave vote was disproportionately made up of voters who were older, with fewer educational qualifications, and who lived in small towns and cities and the countryside. The Remain vote came disproportionately from the young, the more educated, and people living in the big cosmopolitan and multicultural cities. The 2017 election became defined for many voters as a Brexit election, and people voted for the party they thought best represented their referendum choice. There was a big surge of Leave voters to the Conservatives: 70 per cent of Leave voters in 2016 went on to back the Conservatives in 2017 (only 56 per cent of 2015 Conservative voters voted Leave in the referendum). There was also a big surge of Remain voters to Labour, seen as the party most likely to soften or obstruct Brexit, which enabled it to win unlikely seats such as Canterbury and Kensington, while losing former mining seats like Mansfield. In the referendum, two-thirds of Labour voters had voted Remain, but two-thirds of Labour-held constituencies had voted Leave. Both party leaderships sought to hold their old and their new electoral coalitions together by being vague about what kind of Brexit they supported. As the negotiations dragged on, the compromise soft Brexit positions adopted by both party leaderships upset those who saw the Leave/Remain split as the big question on which everything else depended.

## The Conservatives

The Conservatives are most at risk of splitting over Brexit. Their civil war on Europe has been going on for thirty years. David Cameron called the referendum to manage internal party divisions and blunt the rise of UKIP. He failed. The referendum, far from ending the civil war in the party over Europe, has intensified it. While the c.100,000 members of Conservative

Associations were strongly in favour of Leave, a majority of Conservative MPs were not, and a majority of business leaders, the core interest group which supports the Conservatives, opposed a hard Brexit, especially one involving no-deal. But that is what the hard Brexit wing of the party has embraced.

Without a majority after 2017, party discipline frayed and the Conservative government became vulnerable to pressure from its different factions, as well as from the DUP. May, however, has been an exceptionally stubborn leader. Refusing to abandon her Chequers plan, she clinched agreement with the EU in November 2018 on the legal terms of British withdrawal. She left Conservative rebels with only two alternatives: either they had to swallow hard and support her deal, accepting Michael Gove's argument that the important thing was to secure British departure from the EU in March 2019, following which the Conservatives could elect a leader to deliver a real Brexit; or they had to vote down her deal in Parliament and remove May as party leader, knowing that would provoke an irrevocable split in the parliamentary party and the fall of the government.

Theresa May is a highly cautious, pragmatic politician, who will not want to be remembered for breaking up her party. But it is becoming very hard to see how the present Conservative party can be reunited again as a broad centre-right party, whether or not her deal is rejected. Its different factions cannot agree on what form of Brexit they want, in part because they cannot agree on what kind of future they want for the UK. But however the immediate parliamentary deadlock is resolved, a shift to a hard Brexit party seems inevitable once Theresa May departs, and the purge of pro-Europeans begins in earnest. Some Conservative columnists have already begun calling for deselections.[3] The hard Brexit wing feels that time is on their side because as long as the members remain so strongly pro-Brexit, then the next leadership election, when it comes, will deliver a pro-Brexit leader. The Remain faction is in a weaker position, because any Remainer candidate for leader will struggle so long as the test—in the eyes of party members—of being a true Conservative is defined as supporting a hard Brexit.

The Remain wing of the Conservative party is also the One Nation wing, and contains those most supportive of changing tack on austerity, investing in public services, and pursuing an industrial strategy to rebalance the economy. The hard Brexit wing generally favours more deregulation, a low tax economy, more privatisation, and further cuts in public spending. Their Global Britain envisages Britain more attached to countries in the Anglosphere, and especially to the United States, than to Europe.[4] These differences on economic and social policy, and on Britain's place in the world, make the chasm in the party seem very deep indeed. Both wings see themselves as representing the interests of business and the economy. But for Remainers, the business interest they support is the one that has developed over the last four decades of EU membership, while Leavers are more willing to see corporate Britain as another sectional interest, and make no secret of the fact that many existing businesses will have to adjust or disappear post-Brexit, because they have become too dependent on their links with the European economy. They favour instead businesses and entrepreneurs who are focussed on the opportunities of global, not European, markets.

If May is blocked by her party, she could follow Robert Peel and try to pass her deal, or some variant of it, with opposition votes. That would bring a spectacular realignment of British politics. More likely is the prospect that she is challenged or resigns and is replaced by a hard Brexit leader who will be unable to unite the party. The Remainers will either break away in a group or will be steadily purged. Conservative members and voters are now both strongly Leave. There would still be some tensions. A hard Brexit Conservative party would be led by believers in Global Britain rather than Britain First. Their priorities are free trade agreements and deregulation rather than the priorities of most people who voted Leave, which are immigration control and economic protectionism. If they fail to manage the expectations of their new social base, they might see support drifting away to the populist nationalist right.

## The Labour party

The Conservatives are a party of Brexiteers led by a Remainer, while Labour is a party of Remainers led by a Brexiteer. Labour was, for a time under Kinnock and Blair, solidly pro-European, but that changed with the election of Jeremy Corbyn in 2015. His election revived the long-standing conflict between the parliamentary party and the extra-parliamentary movement. Attempts to depose Corbyn by MPs after the referendum failed, and the 2017 election consolidated his position still further. Despite Corbyn being a long-standing critic of the EU and voting against every European treaty, the switch of Remain voters to the Labour party in 2017 helped him defy the widespread expectation that he would preside over a Labour rout similar to 1983.

A few MPs and some party members have begun to leave the party, but although there has been no organised attempt so far to deselect MPs, there has also been little attempt by the Corbyn leadership to maintain Labour as a broad-based party of the centre-left. The Corbyn project seeks to recreate Labour as an extra-parliamentary party of the radical, populist left rather than as a centre-left parliamentary party. The Corbyn leadership is keen to avoid a formal split, but a gradual purging of the party of its social democrats, similar to what happened to the Conservatives after 1906, seems likely.

Within Corbyn's Labour there is a tension between Labour members, 85 per cent of whom support a second referendum on the terms of Brexit, and 90 per cent of whom would vote Remain in such a referendum, and up to a third of Labour voters, particularly in northern cities, who voted Leave. The Corbyn leadership and its trade union allies want Labour to accept Britain's departure from the EU and an end to free movement in order to preserve its old social base, but that is hard to reconcile with the enthusiasm of most party members and most Labour voters for a 'people's vote' and for staying in the EU.

Labour's pro-Brexit stance may eventually disillusion many Remain supporters, and lose votes to anti-Brexit parties like the LibDems and the Greens. Labour wants to hang on to its core working class vote in Wales, the north and the Midlands, with a class message about jobs and services and a Brexit message that Labour will not go back on Brexit (particularly free movement). Combining this with a message that can win over centrist Remain voters will be extremely difficult. Large numbers of voters will feel unrepresented either by a hard Brexit Conservative party or a soft Brexit Corbynite Labour party. Many on the pro-European wing of the party may in time conclude that the party is no longer for them, while many Labour Leave voters may shift either to the Conservatives or more likely to a new populist nationalist movement if 'proper' Brexit is not delivered.

## The Liberal Democrats and the radical centre

What part might the Liberal Democrats play in any realignment post-Brexit? They are the one national UK party with an uncomplicated and unwavering commitment to Europe. They campaigned hard to keep Britain in, and ever since have been campaigning hard for Britain to stay in. But they suffered a big electoral defeat in 2015 which saw them go down from fifty-seven MPs to eight, undoing the work of fifty years. They paid a heavy price for being part of the coalition, and supporting austerity. Since 2015, there have been few signs of a Liberal Democrat recovery. Their position changed little in 2017 and they continue to flatline below 10 per cent in the polls. They seemed to be a natural haven for Remain voters from both the Conservatives and Labour, but that has not happened yet. The party's former stronghold in the south-west is full of constituencies which voted Leave. So long as Brexit dominates the political agenda, the Liberal Democrats may struggle to win them back.

Liberal Democrats want to encourage a new grouping of the radical centre to take on the extremes in both Labour and the Conservatives. They look enviously across the channel at the exploits of Emmanuel Macron, but Macron's breakthrough was only possible because France has a presidential system. In the UK, realignment to create a new centrist force is more difficult, but not impossible. But to be credible, it might require a formal split in both major parties and the formation of a new centrist parliamentary grouping. If such a realignment happened, it might reshape British politics as decisively as in 1846 and 1931.

Brexit is the catalyst that might make it happen, but there are formidable obstacles. First, such a realignment might not succeed. Even in a scenario where a new centrist grouping was to emerge and—against the odds—

managed to gain a parliamentary majority, resulting in the formation of a government, it might be swept away when it came to a general election. Second, party loyalties are still strong. Leaving their parties is the last thing most MPs want to do, for a host of personal and political reasons. That is why defections—when they happen—are quite rare and often quite small. The defection to the SDP in 1981 was in the end less than many anticipated, and the defection to UKIP in 2014 only claimed two sitting Conservative MPs. Will Brexit be different? Party leaderships will generally do everything they can to prevent a significant breakaway. Sometimes, the issues of principle and interest are too great and parties do split, but usually only after every other avenue has been exhausted first.

## Wales, Scotland and Northern Ireland

Brexit also has a territorial dimension. The UK is a union state and the three smaller nations often diverge from England. In the referendum, Wales voted Leave in line with England, despite it traditionally being a stronghold for Liberals, Labour and Plaid Cymru, all of which backed Remain. Scotland and Northern Ireland voted Remain, by greater margins than Leave won overall in the UK. In Scotland, all four main parties backed Remain. Under Ruth Davidson, the Conservatives have become a serious force in Scottish politics again, by being liberal, non-sectarian, pro-Remain, and pro-union; meanwhile Labour elected a Corbynite leader, but has so far made only limited gains. The SNP lost ground in the 2017 election, but it remains the dominant political force in Scottish politics. The chances of holding a second referendum that delivers independence have receded, but if there is a hard Brexit, this may help the SNP, because it reminds Scottish voters that Scotland is being taken out of the European Union against their will. Scotland voting differently from England in the referendum tends to reinforce the idea of Scottish identity as different from English identity. A future Conservative hard Brexit government in Westminster would make the eventual separation of Scotland from the union more certain.

Northern Ireland also voted Remain. Here, the divisions are very deep, with nationalists including the Social Democratic and Labour party (SDLP) voting Remain, along with some unionists and centrist voters. The minority Leave vote was marshalled by the Democratic Unionists. By one of those strange unanticipated quirks of politics the botched election in 2017 made the DUP the kingmakers at Westminster, allowing the Conservative government to carry on, but only by making its programme dependent on DUP approval. This has tied the hands of the government in the negotiations over the Irish border. The EU solution of a border down the Irish Sea was flatly rejected by the DUP on the grounds that it would treat Northern Ireland differently from the rest of the UK, ignoring the fact that Northern Ireland has been treated differently since the province was first set up in the 1920s. But the Irish border quickly became one of the most intractable problems of the talks, even though British public opinion, particularly among Leavers, was largely indifferent to Irish concerns. Since the referendum, polling shows the proportion of Northern Ireland voters saying they now support Remain rising to 69 per cent in May 2018,[5] and for the first time some polls show a small majority of Northern Ireland citizens in favour of a united Ireland (though other polls contradict this).[6] Northern Ireland also has a much closer cultural connection to Scotland than to England, and will be influenced by any new push for Scottish independence. One of the long-term consequences of Brexit may well be the strengthening of forces which bring closer the breakup of the UK union state.

## The populist backlash

Brexit seems likely to deliver a more polarised two-party system, and a more polarised electorate as both the centre-right and centre-left traditions are weakened. Such polarised party systems often are the product of civil war, as was the case in Ireland and the United States. Brexit has been peaceful, but it has stirred deep passions which may determine the future parties which succeed. One of its legacies may be a greater presence for the populist nationalist right. The drums of betrayal were already beating before the Chequers agreement. UKIP saw its vote collapse in 2017, and was then embroiled in leadership in-fighting, which reduced it to insignificance. But following the Brexit press treatment of the Chequers agreement, UKIP saw a spike in its support. There have also been persistent rumours of plans to launch a new populist nationalist party which would be anti-immigrant, anti-Islam and pro-Brexit, drawing on the resentments which a decade of austerity and stagnant living standards have fostered against elites and against other cultures. It would have the backing of the US alt-right and the populist nationalist right in Europe.

The two main parties have always been very successful in recruiting forces to their left and right and holding them within a coalition which has been dominated for the most part by each party's centre. But a new period may be opening in which that pattern ceases to hold. Already, the centre has lost control in the Labour party, and the centre's hold in the Conservative party is highly fragile. Theresa May represents the last hope of the centre-right in the Conservative party. If she fails, a hard Brexit Conservative party may be obliged to move right to contain the populist challenge. Populist nationalists in the UK, like populist nationalists throughout Europe, are opposed to economic liberalism as well as to social liberalism. They want a more closed society, not an ever more open one. If such a party succeeds in establishing itself, it will be a serious rival to a hard Brexit Conservative party still entertaining fantasies about English exceptionalism and global Britain,[7] as well as to a Corbynite Labour party. Both may be forced to shift their positions—particularly on immigration—to stop its advance.

Brexit is a process which will go on dominating British politics for a long time to come. If it is mishandled, it has the potential to explode the British party system, and split both main parties. It has already produced a significant electoral realignment and the forces it has unleashed may yet force a realignment of political parties. Both main political parties are divided and struggling with so far limited success to manage its destructive fall-out.

## Notes

1 'Blow for Theresa May as public believe Boris Johnson would do better job of Brexit—new poll', *Sunday Times*, 22 July 2018; https://www.politicshome.com/news/uk/political-parties/conservative-party/boris-johnson/news/97046/blow-theresa-may-public (accessed 28 December 2018).
2 M. Hastings, 'We'll all pay for the EU obsession of the right', *Times*, 19 November 2018; https://www.thetimes.co.uk/article/we-ll-all-pay-for-the-eu-obsession-of-the-right-v3b3ttqtl (accessed 28 December 2018). W. Hague, 'Toppling Theresa May risks a bitter second Brexit referendum and a Corbyn government', *Daily Telegraph*, 19 November 2018; https://www.telegraph.co.uk/politics/2018/11/19/toppling-theresa-may-risks-bitter-second-referendum-corbyn-government/ (accessed 28 December 2018).
3 A. Pearson, 'It's not a question of whether Theresa May will lose her job, but when—and thousands of readers agree', *Daily Telegraph*, 17 July 2018; https://www.telegraph.co.uk/women/politics/sorry-prime-minister-the-time-patience-good-manners/ (accessed 28 December 2018).
4 M. Kenny and N. Pearce, *Shadows of Empire: the Anglosphere in British Politics*, Cambridge, Polity Press, 2018.
5 'Brexit: Northern Ireland support to "remain" in EU soars to 69%', *Belfast Telegraph*, 21 May 2018; https://www.belfasttelegraph.co.uk/news/brexit/brexit-northern-ireland-support-to-remain-in-eu-soars-to-69-36928116.html (accessed 28 December 2018).
6 A. Preston, 'Poll: Northern Ireland voters will back united Ireland after Brexit'', *Belfast Telegraph*, 3 September 2018; https://www.belfasttelegraph.co.uk/news/northern-ireland/poll-northern-ireland-voters-will-back-united-ireland-after-brexit-37275256.html (accessed 28 December 2018). B. White, 'Polls suggest gradual shift to united Ireland', *Irish Times*, 1 October 2018; https://www.irishtimes.com/opinion/polls-suggest-gradual-shift-to-united-ireland-1.3645214 (accessed 28 December 2018).
7 R. J. Evans, 'How the Brexiteers broke history', *New Statesman*, 14 November 2018; https://www.newstatesman.com/politics/uk/2018/11/how-brexiteers-broke-history (accessed 28 December 2018).

How to cite this article: A. Gamble, 'The Realignment of British Politics in the Wake of Brexit', in G Kelly and N Pearce (eds.), Britain Beyond Brexit, *The Political Quarterly*, Vol 90, Issue S2, 2019, pp. 177–186. https://doi.org/10.1111/1467-923X.12643

# Brexit and the Future of UK Capitalism

MARTIN SANDBU

LONG BEFORE it acquired the name of Brexit, the project of making the UK leave the European Union was a solution in search of a problem. In the battles over the Maastricht Treaty, the animating motivation of opponents was the imperative of maintaining formal national sovereignty. In the quarter century that followed, the concerns have ranged from bureaucracy and immigration to the plight of fishermen and farmers, as well as a quixotic view that trade with faraway economies is more beneficial than trade with the European continent. For each of these problems, some real and some imaginary, the EU has got the blame and leaving it has been presented as the solution, largely uncritically and thanks to a perpetual press campaign with little opposition.

This EU-bashing was always based on a fantasy. But two other facts are not. The first is that the problems of the UK economic model, and its failings, contributed to the Brexit vote. The second is that while that economic model was the result of home grown political choices, the effects of these choices were shaped by the external economic conditions created by EU membership. The way in which Britain leaves the EU, too, will shape the workings of the current model and whatever changes future UK governments make it undergo.

## 'The other Brexit question'

When Theresa May took office, it looked like she wanted Brexit to be about something, not just against something. In her accession speech outside 10 Downing Street, ending Britain's membership of the EU became an occasion to profoundly transform the country's economic model so that it would 'work for everybody'. That effort quickly ran into the sand; it was left politically bankrupt after she called and failed to win the general election in June 2017. But she was right to identify a frustration with an economy that left too many behind as the core of the Brexit vote.

Hence, what I have called 'the other Brexit question'. Behind the din of Brexit politics, and the thorny trade-offs involved in negotiating Britain's future form of association with the EU, stands the question what the country should now do with itself. In the overall debate, this question has received far too little attention. But away from the limelight, thoughtful people have begun pondering it; this collection is the latest of a series of contributions.[1] These contributions largely agree on their diagnosis of Britain's predicament. We can sum up the essence of its economic model with the following observations:

First, on the demand side of the economy, the key characteristic is high consumption and a low savings rate, whose counterparts can be seen in low investment and a persistent current account deficit. This is linked to high indebtedness and high house prices driven by fast mortgage credit growth, in turn linked to a large financial system long treated with a light touch by regulators.

Second, on the structure of supply, the share of manufacturing in total output is low by rich-country standards, and share of services correspondingly high. Even more striking is the very high share of services in UK exports. Britain distinguishes itself among larger economies by exporting about the same value of services as it does of manufactures.

Then there is a starkly polarised labour market. UK economic activity is unusually labour-intensive for a rich economy, the converse of a low rate of capital investment compared to peers. This model has led to high employment numbers, but an excess of low productivity and hence low wage jobs. In other words, the problem of the jobless poor was not so much solved as transformed into a problem of the working poor. At the same time, Britain has a large number of very high paying jobs, leading to one of the highest rates of income inequality in Europe.

And finally, the UK suffers from an extreme discrepancy of economic conditions between different parts of its territory. London is among Europe's richest regions, but some areas are on a par with the poorest parts of Slovakia and Portugal.

The most deeply felt aspects of the British model and its failures are clearly housing prices, the polarised job market and regional inequality. In the words of Christopher Bickerton, 'this kind of growth has driven apart the worlds of the high- and the low-skilled and introduced new fissures into British politics ... the idea of a national economy has given way to something else, to a depoliticised space where economic transactions take place but where nationality as such is of little consequence.'[2] And we know that support for leaving the EU was higher among those living in poorer regions, those who had not benefitted from the rise in house prices, and those stuck on the bad side of the polarised labour market, that is, those with less formal education.

While some elements are more politically salient than others, all the manifestations of Britain's economic growth model listed above are tightly linked. They are not separate ills; they are rather alternate symptoms of the same disease. The rise of finance is plausibly (though partially) to blame for both the small manufacturing sector and the reliance on mortgage-fuelled consumption for demand growth. There is also evidence suggesting that an overgrown finance sector misallocates resources away from business investment. The tilt of the economy's centre of gravity from manufacturing to financial and professional services, moreover, has reinforced both the polarisation in the labour market and regional inequality.

These developments are to a large extent the results of a set of deliberate policies. The growth of finance, a flexible labour market, and a smaller state imprint on the economy than most west European countries, were all components of the decision to chart a course towards a 'mid-Atlantic' position for the UK economy, between US-style liberalisation and private enterprise and continental regulation and state control. UK regulation was obviously finance friendly; business methods intensive in low productivity labour were helped by an immigration policy that facilitated extensive growth (by encouraging low-skilled immigration) and by a tax policy (in particular tax credits) that took the edge off some of the social consequences of the low wage economy. The relatively small size of the state, meanwhile, has strained its ability to provide public goods which could have done more to mitigate rising regional inequality. The need for fiscal consolidation after the global financial crisis, and the chosen aggressiveness with which that consolidation was pursued, worsened the strain.

The upshot of this survey of the UK growth model is that to change anything, one has to change a lot. Because the model itself interlocks so many parts of the economy, and because it is a result of a complex set of policy decisions, a fundamental transformation is necessary if the status quo is no longer unacceptable. And that is just what the Brexit referendum established. Whether there is any prospect of such a transformation depends both on what form Brexit takes, and which domestic policies the UK autonomously adopts once it has left.

## What 'Brexit means Brexit' may mean

As for the form of Brexit, two things matter in particular: the future trade relationship and how it will change (or not) the productive structure of the UK economy and, to a lesser extent, the future of EU migration to and from Britain.

At the time of writing, it is still unpredictable where the negotiations on the UK's long-term relationship with the EU will end up. A withdrawal agreement and a political declaration have both been published, but they do little to pin down the eventual destination. There are, however, roughly three possibilities, all logically coherent if not equally politically likely. There could be a soft Brexit which keeps trade frictions (nearly) as minimal as they are today; this could be achieved by something like European Economic Area membership for the UK and a Customs Union with the EU. This EEA+CU model would leave external trade conditions mostly unchanged, and—provided the arrangement is credibly permanent—keep the UK economic structure looking much like it is unless there is a national decision to change it.

Alternatively, there could be a hard Brexit—a conventional free trade agreement (FTA) which would reintroduce both customs checks and regulatory barriers to trade, but not tariffs. These would be exacerbated if the UK used its departure from the EU customs and regulatory union to strike independent FTAs with other economies—notably the US—which would have to recognise those partners' product standards as admissible in the UK market. Since these would typically violate the EU's rules in many cases, the EU will insist on sufficient barriers to prevent the entrance of non-compliant goods circulating in the UK market. The EU is one of two rival regulatory superpowers (China having a chance of becoming the third) around which countries' product and technical standards are converging. This means that even before striking out on a glorious new independent trade policy, an FTA-style hard Brexit will confront UK policy makers with an unenviably steep tradeoff between markets: any serious lowering of frictions in new trade deals would automatically and significantly raise them with the biggest market across the Channel.

Finally, there is the semi-soft Brexit that has been official UK policy since the Chequers Cabinet meeting in early July 2018. As set out in the Chequers White Paper, this model aims to maintain frictionless trade in goods, but not single market trading rights in services.

The scarier alternatives of 'no deal'—a disorderly Brexit or a reversion to mere World Trade Organisation trading terms—still remain possible at the time of writing. They would, however, lead to short-term disruption rather than the long-term structural change that is my focus here. Some form of trade agreement would follow in due course.

The status quo model would obviously bring the least disruption of external economic conditions—but would, by the same token, leave the UK blocked from striking free trade agreements with other countries. The FTA model would be at the opposite extreme—it would introduce the most trade frictions with the EU, but permit a trade policy that in theory could lower them vis-à-vis other markets. Both models are acceptable to the EU (subject to a solution for Northern Ireland; see below), but would be perceived to be extreme positions that would encounter strong resistance from one or other side of the UK political spectrum.

Chequers, meanwhile, was an attempt at a compromise position. It is, at the time of writing, still facing strong objections from the EU, and it is attacked from all corners in Westminster. In its original form it is not viable, and the term 'Chequers' has been quietly dropped by the government. At the same time, the 'backstop' or fallback relationship the withdrawal agreement sets out to ensure no need for border infrastructure between Northern Ireland and the Irish Republic, defines a minimal friction arrangement for goods trade not all that far away from the Chequers proposal. For the reasons set out below, something like it has strong political economy reasons in its favour. I will keep using the label 'Chequers' for this type of model below.

## Degrees of disruption

What would be the effect on Britain's productive structure of these varying degrees of disruption? Think of the sectors in which the UK does well at the moment. The most obvious area is of course commercial services. That includes not just finance, but a range of auxiliary and other professional services. Britain excels in cultural service exports too, from broadcasting and film making to fashion design and app development. The university sector functions to a considerable degree as an exporter of education services by hosting large numbers of foreign students and international research projects.

The other area is high-productivity manufacturing, despite a relatively small manufacturing sector overall. UK industry has successfully integrated itself with European manufacturing supply chains, and as a result has significant intra-industry trade. This is most famously visible in auto manufacturing which, since the 1980s, has been based on supplying cars to the European market. Of the 1.75 million motor vehicles produced in Britain in 2017, 80 per cent were exported, mostly to other EU countries. In the same year, Britain imported 2.3 million cars from EU countries. The overwhelming share of Britain's trade in auto parts and components is also with the rest of the EU.[3]

These, Britain's most successful economic sectors, have some things in common. They provide good jobs, due to their high labour productivity—or in the case of some services, arguably high rent extraction. They are significantly export oriented. These two traits—high productivity and export orientation—are intrinsically linked. Exporting both requires and fosters high productivity. And they are linked to a third factor: both sets of sectors are deeply integrated with the pan-European economy and the EU's Single Market. In the case of manufacturing, its productivity relies on participating in continental-scale just-in-time supply chains. In the case of services, it relies on Single Market rights to cross-border business, which are greater than in any other trade agreement, and on the free movement of people across the intra-EU border. And this includes service industries that may not first spring to mind—not just finance but, for example, fashion design (which relies on EU intellectual property protection across the Single Market) and the film industry (which recruits and shoots across Europe).

The biggest point in common is that both in high-value manufacturing and services, the best performers are successful precisely because their activities pool resources from all of Europe and sell to all of Europe. They are not good British jobs as much as good European jobs located in Britain.[4] Brexit puts them at risk of moving elsewhere, and conventional trade deals (less deep than the EU Single Market) cannot bring them back. That this fact is so deeply underappreciated has seriously distorted the debate over Britain's post-Brexit economic policy choices. The strongest economic case for leaving the EU would be that the current trade structures somehow lock the UK into a suboptimal use of its particular advantages; this seems to be what some Brexit-supporting politicians have in mind in their emphasis on striking free trade deals with other countries which would somehow better realise Britain's full economic potential.

But what are these advantages? It is true that the exceptionally deep integration of EU's national economies—which has meant a unique elimination of border frictions between them—promotes trade within the Single Market more than with any non-EU market. But it seems hard to argue that the resulting success in Britain's high-value manufacturing or high-margin services is a *distortion*—or if it is, it is a distortion that a strategic trade policy would love to be able to create.

The UK's central role in EU industrial supply chains suggests that it has a comparative advantage precisely in fitting into cross-border supply chains. But high-value manufacturing supply chains are more regional than global. In Richard Baldwin's terms, most cross-border manufacturing is organised around 'Factory Asia', 'Factory Europe', and 'Factory North America', because of the continued importance of 'distance costs' combined with the rise of just-in-time production processes.[5] So, frictionless trade within the EU's regulatory and customs union has not diverted manufacturing trade that Britain would otherwise have carried out with other markets; it has enabled Britain to realise its comparative advantage in servicing continental-scale industrial manufacturing. The alternative to Factory Europe will not be integrating with Factory North America, it will be disengaging from the international supply chain altogether.

The same is more obviously true for some services. There is no equivalent anywhere to the EU's single market in services, so there is nowhere outside the EU for the jobs serving that market to go. (This would change if the EU allowed third countries the same rights to sell into Europe as member states, which it only does with the EEA members who accept its regulatory order.) Britain's Single Market membership, far from distorting anything, has allowed it to pursue its comparative advantage in financial services to a greater degree than it otherwise would have.

The most likely consequence of Brexit, then, is to increase barriers precisely to the sectors in which Britain's comparative advantage lies and which offer Britons (and high-skilled EU immigrants) the best jobs the economy can provide. Only a status quo (EEA+CU) Brexit can avoid this altogether. Even then, however, there is a risk that the isolationist attitude of leaving the EU, exemplified in the critical attitudes to immigration that sealed the vote and any more restrictive immigration policy in future, diminishes the attractiveness of the UK to foreign workers (and students). Net immigration has already fallen steeply since mid-2016.

In contrast, the FTA option would pull the rug out from under the 'European jobs in Britain'. In goods, this will happen through the introduction of border checks. Even without the introduction of any tariffs, customs checks will still be required for purposes of rules of origin. Any absence of regulatory harmonisation will necessitate checks that goods crossing borders comply with the product standards of the importing market. The regulatory divergence is likely to become harder to manage if the UK enters independent trade deals, as mentioned earlier.

For services, the FTA option will undo the treaty basis for 'passporting' which permits the direct sale of services across EEA borders as well as a variety of trade promoting measures such as strong intellectual property recognition. A stricter migration regime would of course add to the new obstacles to services trade with the EU.

Finally, a Chequers-type model aims for the *status quo ante* in goods trade, and hence in most of manufacturing, but accepts a rupture in services.

## Brexit and the British model

It is well understood by economists, though too rarely in the public debate, that the most direct effects of the international trade environment are on the economy's productive structure rather than on the macroeconomic composition of aggregate demand. It is, therefore, on the supply side, not on the demand side, that we should examine how these various Brexit options will alter the British economic model, if at all.

If export services and high-margin manufacturing are twin peaks of British productive success, there is a striking difference in how they interact with the broader economic model and, therefore, their role in the country's political economy. In terms of the bifurcated labour market, both provide the high productivity and well remunerated jobs that one would like to see more of. But while high-margin manufacturing acts as a counterbalance to polarisation, export services in many ways aggravate it.

Good factory jobs are geographically more dispersed, and more available outside the biggest cities, than are jobs in finance or other knowledge-intensive services. In terms of social access too, high-skilled factory jobs are likely to be more open to those without the cultural background, personal connections or academic pedigree that still shape recruitment to professional services. As Institute for Fiscal Studies economists have documented, male workers with low formal educational achievement are particularly dependent on jobs in the goods producing sectors which are dependent on the EU supply chains.[6]

In contrast, knowledge-based service sectors tend to concentrate in big cities—from which many people of modest backgrounds are being priced out—and employ workers with the highest levels of academic achievement. It is fair to attribute one of the chief failures of the British economic experience since the 1980s, namely the educational and territorial polarisation of socio-economic outcomes, to its accomplishment in expanding high-productivity (or high-rent) knowledge services.

So, the external forces on the British economic model that will come with Brexit are twofold. One is foregone national income overall, the reasons for which other chapters in this collection demonstrate at length. This will strain public finances and private incomes in any scenario, but the harder the separation from the EU's trading regime, the more severe the income loss. The other is the relative effect of separation on Britain's two chief exporting successes. The challenges of the British economic model are likely to respond in diametrically opposite fashion to respective changes in the fortunes of each of the two success stories. In short, the tensions that brought us Brexit are inversely related to the prospects for high-skilled manufacturing, whereas they might be soothed by a decline in finance and similar industries, even as this would reduce the country's export earnings, overall economic output, and average incomes.

In ascending order of hardness—from a status quo Brexit through Chequers to an FTA Brexit—the services export businesses are hit sooner than goods. At the same time, some of those service sectors are more resilient to new trade barriers than manufacturing. Take financial services, as the most talked-about sector at risk of losing market access in anything but the softest of Brexits. The share of revenues in the City of London that faces disruption from the loss of 'passporting' rights to sell directly to clients in the rest of the European Economic Area is typically quoted at around 20 per cent. Some of that could be salvaged when passporting ends through judicious sharing of activity between London and EU-27 units of the same firms. In any case, the remaining 80 per cent may well be able to go on much as before—and regulatory autonomy could conceivably be used to make it easier to sell some services to the rest of the world.

More generally, it is not well known that UK services exports are already more heavily tilted towards non-EU markets than goods exports. This suggests that these exports are unaffected by EU membership and thus likely to weather Brexit reasonably well even in its harder forms. For manufacturing, in contrast, the Brexit hit will be more binary. If trade frictions make UK production unattractive for just-in-time supply chains, there are no comparable supply chains to slot into as an alternative. Even were the UK to join the North American Free Trade Agreement (NAFTA) or the Trans-Pacific Partnership (TPP), there is no realistic role the UK can play in North American car manufacturing, say, that compares to its current role in European value chains.

Putting these observations together then, the likely effects on the British economic model do not nicely align with the degree of Brexit 'hardness'. While status quo Brexit will mildly challenge the productive structure across the board, going one step harder to a Chequers-style deal will protect manufacturing, but hurt services. Going harder still, to the more distant FTA-type relationship with the EU, will hit manufacturing brutally and make little further difference to services. And the independent trade policy that is the rationale for such a relationship will tilt the economy further towards services, since new trade deals will very probably seek market access for UK service exports in return for greater import competition by manufactures.

A reflection on the prospects for investment points in the same direction as the differential incentives for production in different sectors. Low capital investment is part and parcel of the intensive use of low-productivity labour by swathes of British businesses. Now Brexit itself discourages investment overall, both because of the uncertainty it creates, and because of the certainty that whatever the outcome, the effect on growth will range from 'bad to very bad', in the words of Christine Lagarde, the IMF head. But here, too, the particular form of Brexit matters.

Some will argue that a hard Brexit, which would allow an independent trade policy, could boost investment once new trade agreements are struck with other countries. Other things equal, a significantly liberalising trade agreement with, say, the US, would be a prompt to invest in the activities that might see increased export demand (offset by disinvestment in those facing greater import competition—farming and food products, for example). Since a new trade agenda will presumably prioritise access for services exports, services investment may be thought to face better prospects under a hard Brexit-cum-'global Britain' trade policy.

But as mentioned above, for a country currently situated in the EU regulatory orbit to enter a deep trading relationship with US-centred economies runs the risk of either running duplicate regulatory regimes or even cutting off market access for EU-focussed exporters. New trade deals after Brexit may therefore act not as the usual incremental boost to GDP, export earnings and the attractiveness of investing in business capital. Instead, if they require regulatory reform, they may amount to 'guillotine' moments that trigger much greater disruption elsewhere in the economy than the incremental cross-border trade opportunities can offset. The mere agenda of a 'global Britain' could itself create quite significant uncertainty, as it introduces bigger downside risks to existing economic activity than trade liberalisation typically does. This could affect the goods producing sectors particularly hard.

These reflections raise a prospect that has received next to no attention in either the expert analysis or the public debate over Brexit. A hard Brexit (on FTA, let alone WTO trade terms) will not only ensure the most loss of growth in aggregate, but stands to exacerbate the polarising characteristics of the UK's existing economic model and harshen the social tensions to which it has given rise. In contrast, a Chequers-style outcome, while it will hurt the British economy in the aggregate, is the external environment most apt to disadvantage export services relative to the rest of the economy.

A politician who sees as her chief responsibility to put a disjointed society back together again after the Brexit referendum may well give priority to factory supply chains over the City of London. Here, then, is a persuasive political economy reason for Prime Minister Theresa May's Chequers model, which does precisely that, seeking frictionless trade in goods—essential for just-in-time manufacturing, not to mention the absence of border checks on the island of Ireland—while regaining regulatory autonomy in services at the accepted price of worsened access to EU services markets. Perversely, this just could serve as a catalyst for a rebalancing of the economic structure to remedy the divisions that pain Britain's political economy.

To be clear, a Chequers-style Brexit will not by itself do anything positive for the high-value goods sector or the parts of the economy that depend on it. Those regions and population groups at the sharp end of Britain's economic polarisation have more to lose from a loss in national income that threatens both government services and public infrastructure spending. And even just to do no harm to manufacturing-reliant segments of the economy, the British government must move its policy quite a bit closer to EU preferences than the Chequers White Paper set out. (It must, in particular, sign up to an indefinite customs union and expand the scope and the automatic updating of the Single Market rules it is prepared to accept. The government has moved in this direction.) Until frictionless trade in goods is secured for sure, these sectors will be hit by withheld investment and relocation of production to continental Europe.

## Rebalancing the British model

A concerted policy programme based on the idea of favouring the UK's high-value goods producing sectors—starting with managing Brexit so as to protect those sectors above all—may be the country's best chance at a growth strategy that prioritises the neglected parts of the economy, even at the price of slower growth in the aggregate. Manufacturing jobs in general have become scarcer in all rich countries, and high-productivity (and hence high-paid) manufacturing jobs are, by their nature, always going to be limited in number. The labour-intensive manufacturing of the mid-twentieth century will never return (nor would it be able to sustain the living standards we rightly expect in advanced economies today). That does not mean it is impossible to boost modern manufacturing in a country with the right conditions and policy makers set on the task.

A recent study from the US offers an instructive example.[7] In the aggregate, its manufacturing sector has had one of the rougher experiences in the rich world in recent decades; and manufacturing-intensive areas have on average performed markedly worse than the economy at large. Yet a number of industry-heavy communities—the Grand Rapids region of Michigan is one example—have not just avoided that fate, but outperformed even the non-manufacturing-dependent part of the economy. The outperformance shows up in jobs growth that may be in manufacturing or in new (service) sectors.

These successes can be attributed to policy measures—including local infrastructure, customised job training through local educational institutions, and extension services for small to medium manufacturing firms—and to education levels in the community, also amenable to influence by policies on education and to boost the attraction and retention of highly educated residents. Such interventions interact to make private investment and hiring more profitable; the skills-related policies also contribute to local earnings growth, with further positive spill-overs in turn.

What could UK policy to do emulate such success stories and encourage investment and productivity growth in high-value manufacturing or alternative activities for the areas that currently rely on it? There is little evidence that private business investment is particularly sensitive to either corporate tax rates or the interest rates influenced by monetary policy. Among tax policies, the tax rules for capital income may be more relevant, but here, the political economy is hardly favourable. If one root cause of Brexit is the unequal distribution of the fruits of economic growth over the last generation, a policy of favouring capital income over labour income in the tax code is likely just to make things worse. By and large, it is not rentiers and capital owners who feel left behind by economic change.

A much more promising policy effort would be to tilt the relative profitability of labour-intensive and capital-intensive production models, by making the former more expensive and the latter more lucrative. This can be done by lifting wage floors and requiring better working conditions, while at the same time upgrading workers' skill levels so as to make labour more complementary to capital enhancements. Sadly, the immediate effect of the Brexit vote has been a *reduction* in businesses' spending on skills training—see Swati Dhingra's chapter in this collection.

To reverse trends headed in the wrong direction, a combined policy is required. The government must urgently secure market access for the most valuable sectors with certainty (so as to encourage private skill formation)—this means a close economic relationship with the EU; investing directly in skill enhancement, productivity and infrastructure in the targeted sectors under a long-term productivity strategy; and most importantly, doing so in a place-based fashion, conscious of the regional impact both of the existing UK growth model and of leaving the EU. This may well mean demoting commercial services in the hierarchy of policy priorities.

## Conclusion

Few of the frustrations that prompted the British public to vote Leave were caused by the EU. And yet both the political economy of Brexit, and its likely economic effects, point towards a profound reform of the growth model that did in fact cause them. While Brexit will result in a UK economy that is less prosperous overall, there is a possibility it will also start to redress some of the imbalances I set out at the beginning.

That probably requires the long-term economic relationship with the EU will be at least as close as the goal of frictionless trade in goods aimed at in the Chequers plan. A more distant relationship will intensify the contradictions built into the current economic model. That could theoretically be a reason to think it will also create greater pressure to resolve them. More likely, it is a reason to doubt any government can choose such a deep rupture. The pressure to change the model is in any case so strong now—in part thanks to the divisions laid bare by the Leave vote itself—it seems change will have to come. That change will not, of course, make itself. It will require a broad set of joined-up policies, of the kinds outlined above: greater public investment, tighter labour market regulation, and increased spending on skills and training and public goods in lagging regions.

All of this is much more compatible with a Chequers-type goods-focussed model than the alternative hard Brexit destination (though both are worse overall than the EEA-CU option). We could list more policies, but what they have in common is a view of the state that is much more comfortable with market-shaping interventions than has been the case in the UK policy making class for a generation. They are also nigh-on impossible without accepting a larger state imprint on the economy—simply put, higher levels of taxation and spending. On both dimensions, then, an economic model closer to what is found elsewhere in Europe.

At the same time, Brexit will force a starker choice between hewing close to and deviating from the EU's regulatory zone (in favour, presumably, of the US one). Even if the UK retains the extensive package of regulation required to avoid new frictions in trade with Europe, it will nevertheless have lost its influence on how that regulatory regime evolves. The likely result is that the differences between Europe and the US, which the UK has at times worked to reduce, will accentuate. The global independent trade policy pursued by some Brexiter politicians may, by their own admission, only be achievable through a deep rupture with Europe's regulatory regime —at least if an ambitious free trade agreement with the US is to be struck. But again, that very fact makes it far less likely to happen because the public support will be lacking.

The paradox of Britain's EU membership is that has enabled the UK to fulfil its plausible destiny as a hybrid between a European and a US socio-economic model. The paradox of Brexit may well turn out to be that it forces Britain to become more European.

# Notes

1 See M. Sandbu, 'The other Brexit question', *Financial Times*, 20 July 2018; https://www.ft.com/content/674f11f6-8b71-11e8-b18d-0181731a0340 (accessed 14 January 2019).
2 C. Bickerton, W. Lightfoot, G. Gudgin, J. Mills, 'Brexit and the British growth model', Policy Exchange, 23 July 2018; https://policyexchange.org.uk/publication/brexit-and-the-british-growth-model/ (accessed 14 January 2019).
3 Data from the European Automobile Manufacturers Association; https://www.acea.be/statistics/article/motor-vehicle-trade-between-the-uk-and-main-eu-partnersx; also SMTT Vehicle Data; https://www.smmt.co.uk/vehicle-data/manufacturing/ (both accessed 14 January 2019).
4 This point is well made by journalist Simon Nixon. See 'Brexit: free movement of people means free movement of jobs—to the U.K.', *Wall Street Journal*, 8 June, 2016; https://www.wsj.com/articles/brexit-free-movement-of-people-means-free-movement-of-jobsto-the-u-k-1465414470 (accessed 14 January 2019).

5 See, for example, R. Baldwin, 'The new globalisation: a manufactured crisis', *Irish Times,* 12 December 2016; https://www.irishtimes.com/culture/books/the-new-globalisation-a-manufactured-crisis-1.2902678 (accessed 14 January 2019).

6 P. Johnson, 'We must not ignore plight of low-paid men as once we ignored that of working women', Institute for Fiscal Studies, 12 November 2018; https://www.ifs.org.uk/publications/13706c; A. Norris Keiller, 'Who bears the brunt of trade barriers with the EU?', Institute for Fiscal Studies, 15 October 2018; https://www.ifs.org.uk/publications/13488 (both accessed 14 January 2019).

7 T. J. Bartik, 'Helping manufacturing-intensive communities: what works?', Center on Budget and Policy Priorities, 9 May 2016; https://www.cbpp.org/research/full-employment/helping-manufacturing-intensive-communities-what-works (accessed 14 January 2019).

How to cite this article: M. Sandbu, 'Brexit and the Future of UK Capitalism', in G Kelly and N Pearce (eds.), Britain Beyond Brexit, *The Political Quarterly*, Vol 90, Issue S2, 2019, pp. 187–199. https://doi.org/10.1111/1467-923X.12648

# Index

*Note*: page numbers in italics refer to tables and diagrams; alphabetical arrangement is word-by-word.

# PLYMOUTH
## THROUGH THE LENS

### VOLUME ONE

COMPILED BY
## BRIAN MOSELEY

**B. S. MOSELEY**
**PLYMOUTH   DEVON**
**1985**

ISBN 0 901676 06 3
First published: September 1985
Text © Brian Moseley 1985


British Library Cataloguing in Publication Data:

Plymouth: through the lens.
Vol. 1
1. Plymouth (Devon) — Description — Views
I. Moseley, Brian
942.3'580855'0222      DA690.P7

Published by B. S. Moseley, 21 Pennycross Park Road, Plymouth, and printed by Hitchings and Mason Ltd., West Hoe Road, Plymouth, Devon.

# LIST OF ILLUSTRATIONS

# ACKNOWLEDGMENTS

I should like to place on record my thanks to the following people for their help in the preparation of this volume:

Mr. J. Barber, Curator, and Mr. W. H. Scutt, Assistant Keeper of Archaeology & Local History, Plymouth City Museum and Art Gallery;

Aerofilms Ltd;

Mr. Bernard Mills;

Mr. Brian Mardon, of Hoopers News;

and Mrs. A. R. Skinner, Mrs. Lamb and Mr. J. Smith of the Plymouth Local History Library, who ably and enthusiastically continue the tradition of trying to find answers to the most impossible questions.

Finally, I would like to express my appreciation of the late Mr. Leslie Fenn, who during his work with Plymouth Corporation took photographs of many ordinary buildings which would have otherwise gone unrecorded.

*Brian Moseley*

The hub of the country bus network was the Western National Omnibus Company's office in Whimple Street, which was opened in the early 1920s by the Devon Motor Transport Company.

In 1948 the green buses left St. Andrew's Cross for Tavistock, Newton & Noss, Totnes & Paignton, Mothecombe and Upton Cross. The Plymouth Joint Services red buses went to Tamerton Foliot (82), Milton Combe (85), Dousland (86), Shaugh Bridge (89), Cornwood (90), Shaugh Prior (91) and Wembury Beach (96A). A 14lb parcel could be sent by bus to Tavistock for just 10d. but 4-gallon milk churns would be carried only by special arrangement.

When this photograph was taken in June 1955 the new Bus Station in Union Street was in use and Stafford Williams' Magnet Restaurant had been transferred to 34 Cornwall Street where he continued in business until 1981. The building on the extreme right is the Royal Insurance office.

Note how the Western National, Royal Blue and Parcels signs have simply been fixed over the windows of what had previously been a pawnbrokers shop.

*(City Museum)*

The Chimes Tavern stood at No. 5 Catherine Street although it fronted on to Princess Street. (In fact it used to be 18A Princess Street).

Bert Bowler was the licensee before the War, followed by Howard Newnham. The last named also looked after the Melbourne Inn, Cecil Street, the Regent and Criterion Inns, Stonehouse, the Madeira, Union Street, and the Fellowship at St. Budeaux.

At No. 4 Catherine Street was a Nissen hut which housed part of the City Treasurer's department, while next door to that can be seen the former Catholic Apostolic Church. This was the temporary home of the George Street Baptist Church in the post-war years.

*(City Museum)*

Plymouth Printers Ltd. began in 1899 as an offshoot of the Plymouth Co-operative Society. It was situated at 15-17 Woolster Street, next door to the Allenby Arms.

Batter Street lies between the printers and the premises of M. Thomas (Motors) Ltd., distributors of Humber, Hillman, and Sunbeam-Talbot cars and Commer and Karrier commercial vehicles, all part of the Rootes Group.

Note Percy Gollop's Austin A40 van, one of a range which included the Devon Saloon, Sports and Countryman models as well as a Pickup Truck.

The photograph is dated January 1956.

*(City Museum)*

The turnplate at North Quay, Sutton Harbour, was pictured in June 1963. The line to the right ran only to the South Wharf where, after just 6 chains, another turnplate took the line to Vauxhall Quay. It was originally intended to take this line right down to the Barbican itself. The line on the left ran for 9 chains along North Quay towards Friary Goods Yard.

An amenity block for the yacht marina was built on this site in 1974.

Note the tug being broken up alongside the China House.

*(Brian Moseley)*

The Great Western Railway's line on to North Quay came off its Sutton Harbour Branch. It was opened for traffic on November 6th 1879 and was originally built to the Broad Gauge. Where it crossed Sutton Road a signal cabin was provided to control the gates and a signal for each direction. The post visible to the left of the track was the base of the signal controlling movements from the Quay back towards Laira. There was a speed limit of 15mph.

Traffic ceased to use the line after the War; indeed by 1944 no GWR freight trains were scheduled to go beyond the Sutton Harbour Branch. It was officially closed in the late 1960s. This photo was taken in June 1963.

Vehicles with a 20ft. or longer wheelbase were prohibited due to the sharp curve giving access on to the Quay.

*(Brian Moseley)*

Great plans had been laid for Sutton Harbour in the early nineteenth century. New wharves were to be built and the success of the Plymouth & Dartmoor Railway pointed to other possibilities. North Quay was constructed in 1850 but railway development was a bit slower as the age of steam took another 19 years to reach the Harbour. In February 1879 the London & South Western Railway opened Friary as a goods station and laid one of the tracks just right to be extended under Exeter Street and on to North Quay. This it did in October 1879, beating the Great Western by two weeks. It was built to the standard gauge. However, it was too late as the GWR had already started to develop Millbay Docks as Plymouth's commercial port.

In 1948 there were still two trains scheduled by the Southern Railway to journey down the 1 mile 2 chains long branch, one at 9 a.m. and the second at 6.15 p.m. Both were due to be back at Friary inside half an hour.

This crossing was also controlled from a signal box which stood just behind the wall on the right. It was removed about 1962. The track on the Friary side of the tunnel was lifted in 1956.

*(Brian Moseley)*

Notte Street was still cobbled in January 1953 when this photograph was taken. It shows Numbers 15 and 16 on the south side, facing Finewell Street. Hoe Street is on the left.

Kate Tenney continued to run her fathers greengrocers shop; they had been at these premises for over 50 years by this time.

Next door was Wilfrid Hope's snack bar which had previously been a wardrobe dealers. On the end of the block, at the junction with Zion Street, was Sherrill's Dairy.

*(City Museum)*

The narrow pre-war streets created many a bottle-neck in the post-war years as more motor vehicles appeared on the roads. One such black spot was the junction of Woolster Street with Vauxhall Street, pictured here at 4.30 p.m. on September 14th 1954. On the left is the Old Ring of Bells public house.

Number 4 Vauxhall Street (Monsen's) was built around the end of the seventeenth century. The fine doorway opened on to a rectangular courtyard from which another door led into the shop. For most of the time this was a general dealers.

A. E. Monsen's now occupy the premises next door. This Grade III listed building also dates from around 1700 and has been described as being of "a painted brick front to a rubble structure." The carved head keyblock above the door is thought to be of a pirate but its origin is a mystery. The premises appear to have been occupied by shipbroker Henry Bellman for a long time although in the 1880s it seems to have also housed the Sutton Harbourmaster.

Both buildings were listed in 1943 as desirable for preservation as a whole but Number 4 has since been replaced by flats.

*(City Museum)*

These buildings, which stood around the corner from the Old Ring of Bells, had an interesting history.

The one in the centre of the picture dated from around 1700 and by 1850 was a beer house called the Steam Packet Inn. The building on the right was the Prince George which was noted as the place where Prince William Henry became a Freemason in 1786. They were then known as Numbers 13 & 14 Vauxhall Street. By the end of the 19th century they had ceased to be public houses and they had also been renumbered.

A further re-shuffling of numbers took place in the 1920s when they became Numbers 1 and 3, which they remained until they were demolished in 1957. This photo was taken in June 1955.

Considering that the old Prince George building was let as private rooms and possibly later as a warehouse, it is surprising to note that even as late as 1952 the building was recorded as having the only surviving Elizabethan plaster ceiling in Plymouth.

*(City Museum)*

When in 1810 King George III reached his Jubilee, Plymouth celebrated by constructing a new road from the Old Tree at Bretonside towards the newly built Embankment. This was known as Exeter Street and the Jubilee Hotel dated from that year. To the right of the Hotel is Sutton Road.

The road from St. Andrew's Cross was widened as far as this point in 1957 when Eastern Approach was built.

After 170 years of serving thirsty travellers, the Jubilee was demolished in March 1981.

To the left of the Firestone Tyres advert was Salem Street and the entrance to Friary Goods Yard. Note the Austin van advertising "Plymouth's First Garage", an honour claimed by the Mannamead Garage in Elm Road. The picture was taken in October 1958.

*(City Museum)*

Just up Exeter Street from the Jubilee Hotel was the coach and motor body builders, Brailey and Toms.

Before the War, Ernest Brailey had been in business in Hawkers Avenue, between Exeter Street and Sutton Harbour. Afterwards, the company took over these premises, pictured in October 1958, which had previously been run by Service Garages (West of England) Ltd.

In 1953 they built a 29 seat coach body on to a Bedford OB chassis for the Embankment Motor Company.

*(City Museum)*

This "Olde Worlde" structure is typical of those buildings which are fascinating to look at but must have been miserable to live in.

Known formally as No. 2 Teat's Hill Cottages, it was given the name "Ivy Cottage" and was situated on the old ropewalk which ran from Teat's Hill Road to the Barbican East Pier.

The cottage was thought to have dated from the 17th century. It was partly slate-hung and apart from its rather obvious massive chimney stack it also boasted a pole staircase. The west facing wall was at one point almost four feet thick at ground level.

On the ground floor was a porch giving access to a closet and then the living room. There were two other rooms also. Access to the first floor was up either a conventional stairway or the pole one. Here two rooms had been made into one large bedroom and there was a small chamber over the porch. This is shown in the picture above.

Access to the attic was by means of the pole staircase only and this room had its own fireplace which was served by the chimney stack over the porch. Many of the windows in the cottage had been blocked up or removed over the years.

At the end of last century the cottage was occupied by a labourer and from the 1930s until demolition it was the home of Mr. John Dawe.

Both photographs were taken in April 1959.

*(City Museum)*

It is difficult to imagine that a six-lane dual-carriageway cuts right across this scene today! This is what Ebrington Street looked like in June 1958, some six years before it was sliced in two.

On the left is Green Street and the corner of the Lanyon Almshouses. Also just visible are the Coburg Memorial Hall and the Norley Inn which stood on the corner of Norley Place.

The corner of the Ham Street Wine and Spirit Vaults is the white building on the right. Bollom's the dry cleaners are on the corner of Gibbon Street. Above them, Harry Vere had his dental surgery. In the same block were Syd Ogden the tobacconist, Alpines the drapers and H. Scanes, ladies hairdresser. The RSPCA and veterinary surgeon Ken Morgan occupied the first floor. The Beford van is just emerging from Park Lane.

Western National 94A is on its way to Elburton, Yealmpton and Newton Ferrers, a journey which cost 1/9d. A return ticket could be had for 2/10d.

*(City Museum)*

This block in Armada Street, pictured in October 1956, is now the site of Mount Street Primary School.

To the left of the picture can be seen the corner of the old Mount Street School. This was built in three stages, 1873, 1877 and 1887. The last section, a higher grade school for some 113 boys, was transferred in 1897 to a new building in Regent Street. This in 1926 became Sutton Secondary.

At No. 9 was R. G. Morrisey's cooked meat shop; note the extended chimney to carry away those pleasant pasty smells! Next door was a Plymouth Co-operative Society shop which had been opened in 1888. At No. 11 Isabel Leach had her drapers shop and next door to her was a confectioner, which doubtless acted as the school tuck shop.

It may be noted how the street is devoid of parked cars, a scene very different from today.

*(City Museum)*

19

This picture of the Portland Inn at 29 James Street, Plymouth, was taken in March 1956.

The Cullum family were licensees here for some 40 years but Charles Hocking ran it after the War. The Ind, Coope & Allsopp brewery was in Weston Park Road and in Bath Street previous to that.

James Street still connects North Road East with Cobourg Street.

*(City Museum)*

This fine and study building was the Co-operative Wholesale Society's warehouse on the corner of York Street (to the right) and Morley Street (to the left).

Opened in May 1922, it was built on the site of the old Trinity Baptist Chapel. The chapel had ceased to be used as such around the turn of the century and by 1920 had been replaced by a butchers, a wholesale fruit merchant and the St. Andrews Mission Hall.

It was as early as 1905 when the Plymouth Co-operative Society asked the CWS to open a warehouse in the Town so when it did arrive, some 17 years later, they held a Shopping Week to celebrate.

On the corner of the building was a plaque which read: "Co-operative Wholesale Ltd. Reg'd Office 1 Balloon Street, Manchester. Bankers, Manufacturers, Merchants, Shippers, Insurers, Farmers. CWS Productions obtainable only from retail Co-operative stores throughout the Country".

The building was pulled down when Princess (later Mayflower) Street was being developed in the early 1960s. It stood where the multi-storey car park is behind Cornwall Street, just to the west of Armada Way.

*(City Museum)*

Numbers 3 to 5 Morley Street faced up Richmond and York Streets towards Cobourg Street. To the left of the picture was Russell Street and on the opposite corner was William Trevor's newsagents shop pictured in "Vanishing Plymouth".

Next door to Adams was Walker's the chemists and then the greengrocers Dodd & Berriman. Just before the War the two floors over the chemists were known as Morley Chambers and were the home of the Plymouth Council of Social Services and the Plymouth & District Cripples Aid Society.

The photo was taken in February 1956.

*(City Museum)*

The New George Street frontage of the Plymouth Co-operative building gives a clue to the position in our modern City Centre of Numbers 1 to 3 King Street. This is now the junction of New George Street and Raleigh Street.

Whilst the tiny No. 1 had always been a newsagents, Ivor Dewdney's was, at the end of last century, a beer house. Presumably the "Hot Pasties" sign is hung where the name-board used to be. The adjacent premises were occupied at that time by the Church Extension Association.

Thomas Lloyd also operated Tonoids Ltd., manufacturing "The Tonic for Those Over Forty".

Note the Daimler car, which appears to be a 1949 Straight Eight.

Opposite this group of shops was the Old Barley Sheaf Public House, on the corner of Cambridge Street. The photograph is dated May 1957.

*(City Museum)*

This row of shops stood on what is now the New George Street end of Market Avenue. Queen Street ran through to Union Street.

William Luckie was the landlord of the Woodman Inn, a rather unusual name for a pub in the centre of a City. Next door was Ernie Stephen's the pork butcher, followed by a branch of Pooley's the bakers, and then Perilla's fish and chip bar. Number 4 was a tobacconists and snuff shop with Bert Hooper's betting shop above. The shops on the far end are pictured on the previous page.

It may be correctly assumed from the architecture that the building seen here in May 1957 occupied by Pooleys and Stephens was at one time all the same shop.

Note the Double Diamond advert — it makes a change from all those Guinness ones.

*(City Museum)*

These premises stood on the south side of King Street, facing up Tracey Street. Giving every appearance of having been tacked on the end of the row, the T/V Radio Company's little shop was in fact the middle of 12 shops between Queen Street and Summerland Place. Edmund Daniel's dairy had stood beside it in 1939.

But look more closely. Either side of the first floor window are two emblems apparently cut into the stonework. The one on the left reads "For Truth in Therapeutics" encircling a central motif of "NAMH Ltd". The one on the right shows a jumble of letters rather like some mysterious formulae: the meaning of this is not yet clear.

These were the premises of William Dawes, medical herbalists, who declared himself to be a "Fellow of the National Association of Medical Herbalists". His adverts for Dorzone Constipation Herbs — "bring brightness and joy to life" — and Dorzone Blood Wine at 1/6d or 2/9d appeared frequently to support his claim "Get Back to Nature and Live".

Searle's premises were a grocers and second-hand bookshop in the early 1930s and a drapers before that. Just visible is the window of Jimmy Hughes the outfitters.

The photo is dated May 1957.

*(City Museum)*

In an age when all shops seem to look the same it may seem odd to see four very different facades within the same row. John Wride's wallpaper shop was probably different again but there is not much of it left in this picture from January 1958.

The sign above Alfred Deacon's Cycle Works in King Street will doubtless bring back happy memories to many, advertising as it does Rudge and Robin Hood machines. Was the latter as "Light on the Purse" as it was "Easy on the Road"?

At No. 25, the Victoria Restaurant, Carlo Valente cooked his fish and chips; note the date on the building. The sign on the end shop reads "Johnnies of Plymouth" although just before this photo was taken it was Higman's fish shop. The John Bull Stores had stood next to it.

*(City Museum)*

King Street railway arch, looking west towards Stone-house, pictured in January 1956.

R. & M. Tall, the fruiterers and florists, were situated on the corner of Harwell Street, with Steve Constantinou's restaurant next door. Mrs. Mary Wakeman's tobacconists shop was up by the arch, just by the Forum Cinema's advert for "Seven Brides for Seven Brothers" (starring Jane Russell).

On the left of the picture is Stanley Mallett, fishmonger, while the Wellington Inn is just out of sight.

The arch itself was erected in 1848 to carry the South Devon Railway into Millbay and was still used until the 1960s. Demolition came in 1974.

*(City Museum)*

King Street boasted five pubs, the Woodman Inn, the Wellington, the Bull's Head, the Caxton Arms, the Old Barley Sheaf, and lastly the Galatea, pictured here in January 1960. All of them survived the war-time blitz but only one, the Bull's Head, has managed to survive the post-war blitz.

The Galatea occupied numbers 81 and 82. Its unusual name comes from Greek Mythology, Galatea having been the girlfriend of a Sicilian shepherd. Landlords have included A. Mullins, Fred McKenzie and Albert Uren before the War and Bert Luckie afterwards. The grocers shop next door was run by Ernie Skidmore.

Note the Ford Escort Van, a type which had been introduced just a couple of years earlier.

*(City Museum)*

The bulldozer looks like it is poised to demolish this row of shops in King Street.

David Greig's the grocers had the nearest shop, on the corner of Well Street. Next to Mrs. Crittenden's Caxton Arms Public House was draper Sam Caplan, butcher George Horne and then Radio Rentals Ltd. Dingle's ladies hairdressing business had already moved to the new building on Royal Parade.

At the end of this line of shops was W. H. Box, the herbalist, who had occupied this site for over 50 years.

Note the "fan" design over the first floor windows. The photograph is dated October 1957.

*(City Museum)*

This small but impressive building was not surprisingly designed by John Foulston. Situated on the north side of Princess Square, it opened in 1822 as the Plymouth Subscription Classical and Mathematical School. It was also known as the New Grammar School.

When in 1866 the Reverend Harpley resigned as Head Master, the school was combined with the Corporation Grammar School and it continued to be known as such until 1885. Then it was combined with the Park Grammar School in Park Street, Plymouth, and took the Corporation name with it.

The building then housed the Plymouth School of Art until 1911 when it became a billiard hall and charabanc booking office. It was later rebuilt internally and in 1934 became the City Auction Galleries of Woolland Son and Manico, Auctioneers and Estate Agents.

Note the 1951 Austin A70 Hereford and the 1949 Triumph Mayflower. The picture was taken at the end of July 1957.

*(City Museum)*

A familiar sight on the walk from Plymouth to Stonehouse were the Savoy Grill and the Central Restaurant, on the City Centre side of the Union Street railway arch.

The Hill family had taken over Jonathan Parkyn's Great Western Coffee Tavern at the beginning of the century. For over fifty years they served breakfasts, morning coffees, lunches and teas in these premises at 158 Union Street. Before the War the premises next door had been Snawdon's furnishing emporium and before that Pengelly's Gramophone Stores.

Note the advert for Cadbury's Lucky Numbers, "the new all-chew assortment". The picture is dated February 1960.

*(City Museum)*

This aerial picture shows Stonehouse during the reconstruction works of twenty years ago.

The block of three premises just east of St. Mary Street housed the Stonehouse Branch Post Office, Wilson's shell fish shop and the Prince Arthur Public House. Further east, on the corner of Battery Street, is the Royal Sovereign pub next door to what until recently was Louis Paul's wholesale news warehouse. Just across the other side of Battery Street the old Grand Theatre is seen being demolished.

After Union Place comes Clarence Place with the Royal Naval Hospital Inn by the entrance gate to the Hospital itself. This was begun in 1758 and completed in the early 1770s. It was surrounded by a high wall to deter deserters!

Opposite the Hospital is the Clarence House Reception Centre in the old 1801 workhouse, and the Church St. Matthew, which was demolished in 1970.

The photo is dated July 1963.

*(Aerofilms Ltd.)*

At the rear of the old Stonehouse Branch Post Office was the Robin Hood Public House. St. Mary Street is in the foreground with Union Place on the left.

Sam Day was the landlord here in the early 1930s and Charlie Bate just before the War.

The picture was taken in January 1961.

*(City Museum)*

At the beginning of the century this was Vincent Elliott's mineral water factory. The houses on the right were part of Windsor Place which ran along Union Place, Stonehouse, to the Plymouth, Stonehouse and Devonport Tramway Company's depot almost on the corner with Manor Street.

By this time Bowering & Company had already taken over Isaac Latimer's printing works in George Street, Plymouth. They moved into 18 Union Place, Stonehouse, around 1900. After the Second War, the road was renumbered on the odds/evens system and this became number 26.

The photo was taken in May 1958. By 1960 the Press was located at Friary Yard, Knighton Road, St. Judes, and continued in business until the death of Mr. J. C. Bowering, when it was sold to Messrs. Clark, Doble & Brendon.

*(City Museum)*

High Street, Stonehouse, is pictured here in August 1955.

The railings of High Street Primary School are on the left and next door was the School Clinic. Between Harris's newsagents shop, just receiving its delivery of thirst quenching soft drinks, and the greengrocers, was Tweedside Place. Down that lane was the engineering works of Woodrow Metals Ltd.

At the end of this block, on the north side of High Street, can be seen the Royal Naval Hospital Inn. On the right-hand side, behind the van, can be seen the corner of St. Mary Street.

*(City Museum)*

Entrance to the three residences known as Wesleyan Cottages, Stonehouse, was by means of an alley from East Street. This passed between No. 7 East Street and the Methodist Sunday School which stood on the empty site in the foreground. They must have been very dark places to live.

The church itself had been erected in Edgcumbe Street in 1813 but it was not until about 1885 they took over the Stonehouse Board Infants School for use as a Sunday School. The infants just moved across the road.

February 1956 was when the photo was taken.

*(City Museum)*

It will be correctly deduced from this October 1956 picture of 1 and 2 Newport Street, Stonehouse, that the one nearest the camera was a public house.

When Mary Wills kept order here in the 1850s there were two other bars in the street, one of which was the Steam Packet Inn. However, the Commercial Inn, as No. 2 was known, lasted only until the beginning of the First World War.

*(City Museum)*

The west side of Chapel Street, Stonehouse, looks a real shambles in this photograph taken in October 1956. These buildings ran from the top of the slope at Emma Place down to Newport Street and Stonehouse Bridge.

At this time only two of these shops were occupied. Chemist Frances Packer was at No. 31, originally a boot and shoe shop but a chemists since the late nineteenth century. Two doors away Mr. Williams was still serving portions of fish and chips.

Before the blitz did its damage No. 32 had been a doctors surgery; No. 34 was a greengrocers run by Percy Skinner (who also had the chip shop at that time) while Harry Luscombe was the newsagent at No. 35.

*(City Museum)*

The Red Lion Public House in Stonehouse stood on the corner of Chapel Street and George Street. It dated from the early 1800s and stood next to Monague Gosling's general shop, formerly a tailors. Note the Sunblest bread displayed in the window.

Mrs. Dorothy Crocker, who kept the shop at No. 15, had by this time moved to Brownlow Street. The photo is dated April 1957.

*(City Museum)*

St. Stephen's Church, Clowance Street, Devonport, was designed by Mr. James Piers St. Aubyn (1815-1895) and was consecrated on September 21st 1858, almost two years after its designer became a Fellow of the Royal Institute of British Architects. The Church had three aisles and considerable ornamentation.

All but the tower was destroyed in the War and services were then held at St. Aubyn's, Chapel Street. The Church was finally demolished in 1959.

Until 1864 the curate, the Reverend George Proctor MA, lived with his naval surgeon son at 10 George Street. Then, on November 18th, the foundation stone of a new parsonage was laid. The day was dogged by bad luck. The man who was going to perform the ceremony, Colonel Owen of the Royal Engineers, had an accident the day before so was unable to attend. Instead, the vicar of St. James, Plymouth, the Reverend Bliss, obliged.

And it rained. Indeed it poured down. In fact it was so bad that the Reverend Arthur Dixon and his guests got drenched and quickly made for the old billiard room in Pembroke Street where the speeches were given and lunch taken.

This fine Vicarage was situated at 27 George Street, opposite the Church. It was also designed by Mr. James Piers St. Aubyn, and built by a Mr. Jeffery of New Passage, at a cost of some £1,400. After the bombs destroyed St. Stephens, the Vicarage was apparently used as a private residence.

The photograph of the Church was taken in October 1959 and that of the Vicarage in November 1961.

*(City Museum)*

This picture shows 29 to 35 Clowance Street at the junction with St. Stephen's Street, on the left. St. Stephen's Church is out of sight on the left. The photo was taken in September 1955.

Number 31 was a general dealer's shop occupied during the 1930s by a Mrs. Ellis, a Mrs. Kathleen Lakeman and in 1939 by Mrs. Jeanette Sparrow. After the War the shop was run by a Mrs. V. Wilcox.

The shop next door had been a bakers and was run since the end of last century by various members of the Davey family. The last of this line was Mrs. Janie Davey who ran the shop just before the War.

At the end of the block of buildings, out of sight to the right of the photograph, stood the Clowance Tavern on the corner of Stanley Street.

St. Stephen's School stood in the gap after No. 35.

*(City Museum)*

St. Stephen's National Schools in Clowance Street, Devonport, opened in 1870, about 70 years after the Town's first public school was started. It had boys', girls' and infants' sections although later it took only girls and infants. The head mistress before the War was a Miss C. A. Bailey.

At the time the School was opened there were no less than 142 schools in Devonport with about 6,500 children attending. In the St. Aubyn area there were some 80 children per school while up at Stoke there were about 30 to each school. The average figure of about 44 per *school* is interesting as this is now about the size of a *class* in a school!

The photo was taken in September 1955. Note the school bell in the roof apex.

*(City Museum)*

43

Christmas decorations adorn the baker's window in this picture of George Street, Devonport, in December 1961.

At the turn of the century Solomon Stephens had his bakers shop in Ham Street, Plymouth. Thirty years later, after joining with Risdon, he had eleven shops. This one, at No. 66 George Street, was previously Henry Hurrell's.

Next door had been a Co-op chemists. Now, as the Fairfax Cafe, as well as selling Faggots & Peas, Fish & Chips and Hot Grills, it was also offering self-drive cars for £2 a day. The Vauxhall Victor parked outside introduced the panoramic windscreen and when introduced in 1957 it cost £485 plus £243.17s purchase tax.

Mrs. Lily Scott was landlady of the White Swan in the fifties and Mrs. Lily Sloman ran the drapers shop next door.

*(City Museum)*

John Wesley (1703-1791) opened his first Methodist Chapel at Bristol in 1739. Only seven years later he made his first visit to Dock. In 1786 the Methodists opened their first place of worship in Dock, in Ker Street, where Wesley himself later came to preach.

When the Devonport Central Hall was opened in 1926 the Chapel went out of use. By the outbreak of the Second World War it was being used as a Drill Hall for the 164th Heavy Brigade of the Territorial Army Royal Artillery. The officer in charge was Major E. M. Gard RA(TA), who was previously a Captain of the 158th Heavy Battery stationed at Lambhay Hill in Plymouth.

The building was to be demolished in November 1960 but received a reprieve until 1962. At least it gave time for this photo to be taken in January 1961.

*(City Museum)*

The photographer's official car, Ford Anglia GDR 739, is seen here parked in Duke Street Ope while he recorded for posterity Numbers 23 to 26 Duke Street, Devonport. They faced the Forester's Arms and the Duke Street Inn, the corner of which is on the left of the picture. The photo was taken from the steps of St. John's Church in August 1956.

Number 22 had not always been a private house; it was a bakers shop in 1850, a century after Duke Street came into existence.

Frank Jackman's fish and chips shop had previously belonged to Edwin Truscott and before that was a haberdashery. In the early 1930s, Number 25 was occupied by a shoemaker by the name of Broad. The roofless No. 26 had been Elsie Gomer's general stores.

*(City Museum)*

The Bakers' Arms, pictured here in May 1957, was at 44 Duke Street in Devonport. Ker Street and George Street were out of picture to the left while St. John's Church was further up the road to the right.

Fred Parker pulled the handles at the Bakers right through the 1930s while Fred Glanville was licensee after the War. Mrs. Maud Bates kept the shop next door, where she evidently sold Burton's Ice Lollies.

*(City Museum)*

One could be forgiven for thinking that Number 29 Chapel Street, Devonport, was an ice cream shop but in fact it was Percy Smith's hairdressing salon. Could this be Mr. Smith having a breath of summer air one sunny day in August 1959?

At the end of the 19th century the business belonged to a Mr. Jabez Smith but by 1900 Albert Smith had taken over and it was known simply as Smith's Haircutting Rooms. Then it had two other owners, John Foss (1907) and G. Baker (1928) before Percy Smith appeared on the scene in the early 1930s. He remained here certainly until 1940 and was obviously back at Chapel Street by 1959 but in between it is believed the premises became a pie shop.

Chapel Street was built around 1770 just about the time that Stonehouse Bridge was being constructed. Just out of the picture to the left was Stanley John's general store; his son now owns a bookshop near the City Museum. Further up the Street was the Brown Bear Public House, which still survives today.

Incidentally, Neilsons (Ice Cream & Frozen Foods) Ltd. were a Canadian Company who had just arrived in Plymouth following the acquisition of a Cornish manufacturer. They had been operating in England for about three years.

*(City Museum)*

Devonport's Forum Cinema is on the left of this picture of No. 49 Princes Street. This was on the corner of St. Aubyn Ope which led down to Fore Street. The spire of St. Aubyn Church can be seen on the right behind the rear of the old Devonport Post Office.

Harry Clarke's shop stood almost opposite the Hippodrome Cinema. John and Elsie Rowe ran it as a general dealers before the blitz while Mr. Clarke was wielding his scissors at No. 12 Lambert Street. The Rowes had taken it over from Miss Johns whose father, William, owned the shop in the 1890s.

The photo was taken in September 1957.

*(City Museum)*

Standing four-square and alone in Princes Street, Devonport, is the Barnstaple Inn, pictured here in October 1958.

Mrs. Ethel Phillips was its landlady before the War. Mr. E. G. Roberts took it over in the 1950s. Note the pulley system for raising and lowering the inn sign.

Visible on the left of the photo is the Morice Street Wine and Spirit Vaults.

*(City Museum)*

This was the Granby Street Salvation Army Hall, which was demolished along with the Barnstaple Inn to make way for Granby Way.

The Morice Town Salvation Army Corps was formed in 1880, two years after one was started in Plymouth. Their first meeting was held outside the Market where their leader, Captain Joseph De Bau, was arrested during a disturbance led by Mr. Greenslade Medland, landlord of the Butchers Arms, Cross Street, and butcher Mr. Thomas Canniford.

Situated just two doors away from the Devonport Soup Kitchen, the Hall was opened in 1900. It was demolished sixty years later. The photo was taken in October 1958.

The clothes line on the right is at the rear of the Barnstaple Inn, Princes Street.

*(City Museum)*

William Street had only six months to live when this picture was taken in July 1959. Early the following year it ceased to carry traffic to Devonport via New Passage Hill.

Bill Merrin's chip shop can be seen on the left. The "Road Closed" sign stands in Mooncove Street which ran along the rear of these buildings and joined Albert Road.

The Morice Town Wine & Spirit Vaults probably dates from the 1850s. It occupied only the corner premises until the mid-1930s when it took over No. 39 next door which had been William Cook's stationery shop. This then joined the H. & G. Simonds owned pub to the slightly older Plymouth Brewery's Royal Standard at Number 38. Fred Baldwin looked after the Morice Town in the fifties.

Laurie (Malta) Ltd., one of the Street's many Naval Outfitters, occupied the shop next to the Royal Standard; it had previously been a newsagents.

*(City Museum)*

Advert hoardings rather dominate this picture of Ferry Road at its junction with New Passage Hill to the left and William Street to the right.

Number 1 William Street had had a varied life. Formerly a drapers and a cycle shop, it became William Merrin's fish and chip shop just before the War.

A Vauxhall Velox car is parked outside the Steam Bridge Inn, Moon Street. At the back of the Inn, behind the Co-op milk float, was the Ship Inn, John Street.

In the gap where the Cleveland Petrol advert stands was the Spiritualist Church and next to that a general store run by Ernest Jane. A fish and chip shop stood on the corner of Moon Street.

The photo was taken in September 1959.

*(City Museum)*

At the rear of the Steam Bridge Inn stood the Ship Inn, 38 John Street, Devonport.

John Street dated from the 1790s when this area was opened up by the commencement of the ferry service to Torpoint. Like most pre-war streets it had several general shops plus a couple of grocers and even a baker. There were only 38 premises in the street so they were certainly well served for shops!

Francis Wilson was landlord of the Ship in 1939 with Mr. Frederick Ellis following him in the fifties. At the time this picture was taken in September 1959 a Mr. Dibble was the tenant. The Corporation paid less than £100 for the premises in readiness for it to be demolished to make room for the Dockyard extension.

Only two other buildings survived in John Street in the fifties, the Freemason's Arms and a single house (No. 11) on the west side of the Street.

*(City Museum)*

The Keyham Wine and Spirit Vaults still stands today on the corner of Albert Road and Charlotte Street — but it looks nothing like this! Charles Hunt was in charge at 13 Albert Road when this picture was taken in March 1958.

In those days Charlotte Street continued across the other side of Albert Road. On the left side had been the Morice Town Council School, of which Mr. Fred Dunn was the head master with Miss Mabel Mortimer and Miss E. R. Beer looking after the girls and infants respectively. On the right had stood the Methodist Chapel.

Also in the picture is Norman Cook's newsagents shop on the end of the houses to the rear of the pub.

*(City Museum)*

The Crimean War of 1854-56 brought a lot of work to the Naval Dockyard just as other wars have continued to do. The prosperity which came with it combined with the recent extension of the Yard to North Keyham, brought about the streets between what are now Albert Road and St. Levan's Road.

Pictured here is the east side of Charlotte Street, photographed in March 1958. Haddington Road is just to the left of the parked cars. Note how wide the street was and how an attempt had been made to make it more pleasant by lining one side with trees.

Cedric Venus's chemists shop at the far end of this row had already disappeared but Stan Rundle's shop is just visible above the cars. At No. 99 was Percy Lang's betting shop in what had for many years been Algar's dairy and before that a lamp oil shop.

Boot repairer Fred Moore occupied No. 101 which had previously been a general store run by William Hatherby.

In the immediate post-war years when people from Keyham still loyally shopped at what was left of Devonport, the crooked spire of St. James the Great was a familiar landmark on the walk from St. Levan's Gate to William Street.

Started in 1849 and designed by Mr. James Piers St. Aubyn, the Church was intended for use by men working in the nearby Keyham Steam Yard. It was damaged during the air raids of 1941 and was never re-opened. It was demolished in the mid-1960s.

At the beginning of the century the houses in the picture did not exist. This area, between St. James Place and Barlow Place, was occupied by North and South Clarence Villas.

They had large private gardens which ran right to the edge of the church grounds. By 1920 Atherton Place, of which the post office was No. 1, and the five houses of St. James Terrace were built on the site.

In the mid-1930s the post office was at the corner of Keat Street. By 1939 it had transferred to William Trethewy's grocers shop which was later taken over by Herbert Peachey.

The photo is dated April 1956.

*(City Museum)*

"Dockyard Specials" are here lined up alongside the wall in St. Levan's Road ready to speed the workers homewards. The photo was taken in July 1955.

In those days there was a break from noon until 1.30 p.m. The hooter would sound at 1 p.m. to remind those men who had gone home to lunch that it was time to return to work.

The wall on the right was moved back in February 1957 so that a bus bay could be created which helped to ease the chaos that occurred here particularly at the evening out-muster.

All the houses on the left are still in existence with the exception of the "Fortune Cafe", behind the lamp-post.

Bus 70 (CJY 10) was one of the wartime wooden-seated vehicles and was withdrawn in 1956. The bus in the middle of the road, one of the post-war Weymann-bodied Leylands, is just arriving; the conductor is busy changing the side indicators. The fare to the City Centre was 4d.

*(City Museum)*

This September 1956 photograph shows Alvin Gamble's "Fortune Cafe" at 57 St. Levan's Road. This was situated between Keyham Road and Sennen Place, between the two blocks of houses which are still standing today. The wall of the gas works is behind the building.

Immediately after the War this one-time dwelling was used by Mr. S. S. Peard, naval and civilian tailor. By 1955 Mr. Gamble had added it to his mini-empire of a snack bar in New Street, Plymouth, and an antique shop in Union Street, Stonehouse.

What the significance of the word "In" is to the left of the door is not clear — unless the back door was marked "Out" of course! The wording to the left of that again appears to indicate that a sweet or a tea cost 3d each.

*(City Museum)*

Ford Station on the old Southern Region was situated at the eastern end of Station Road, Keyham Barton.

The line through Ford, from Lydford to Plymouth, was built by the Plymouth, Devonport and South Western Junction Railway in order to give the London and South Western Railway an independent route into Plymouth. At that time they were using a third rail on the broad-gauge GWR Tavistock Branch.

This new line was officially opened on May 30th 1890 and the first public passenger train called at Ford on June 2nd. It was quite an important station for Dockyard workers and until the end of February 1947 it even boasted a signal box.

All the Southern Region lines west of Salisbury were transferred to the Western Region from January 1963 and within months it was announced that Ford (Devon) and Devonport (King's Road) would close as from January 6th 1964. In the event the last trains called on September 6th, the day on which this photograph was taken.

At the time of its closure Ford was served on weekdays by thirteen trains to Plymouth plus an extra one on Saturdays. On Sundays only three trains called, the first at 12.05 p.m. There were earlier trains on Sundays to Tavistock and Exeter. The only through train from London Waterloo to call was the 01.15 passenger and news at 7.18 a.m. and the only train right through to London left at 12.05 p.m.

The single fare in 1959 for the 228 miles journey to London was £1 17s 4d.

*(Bernard Mills)*

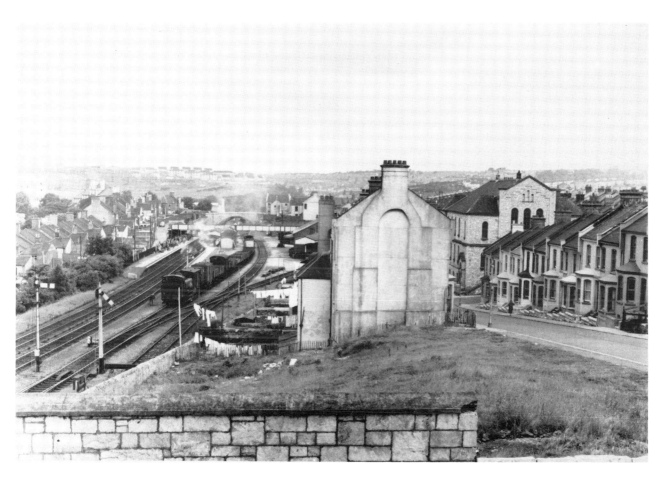

It looks like the days washing is about to get smothered in soot in this picture of Keyham Station taken on a Friday in July 1957. The signals are "off" to permit the 0-6-0 Pannier Tank to take its wagons forward to Devonport and thence to the sidings at Tavistock Junction.

The train is assumed to be the local Dockyard freight, probably the late afternoon one which would have used the loop line in order to let an up Saltash to Plymouth rail motor pass. A down train, an unadvertised workmens train to St. Austell, would have been due about the same time which may account for the waiting passengers on the Cornwall-bound side.

In Admiralty Street will be noted the Methodist Church which was erected in 1906 and had a large hall and stage in the basement.

*(City Museum)*

The junction of Tavistock Road, Plymouth, with its namesake from Devonport has seen many changes over the years. For hundreds of years nothing much happened to it, then in about 1934 Fred Webber opened his motor petrol station in Hartley Vale. At that time it was possible to catch a Western National bus from Crownhill to Devonport, via Peverell (Co-op Stores) for the princely sum of 4d.

Probably the biggest change came in 1943 when the American Army descended in force and in just two months constructed a 250 bed Naval Hospital on the land previously used by an archery club. The huts were later used as a Ministry of Works hostel: the layout and paths can be seen in this photograph taken in September 1961.

Then in 1946, Manadon Hill was widened into a dual-carriageway and the access road to the houses was created. Mind you, at that time the only property here was Hill House, the one on an angle. The ground between it and the Church had been allotments. The area shown here was still outside Plymouth until 1950.

Great destructive things began to happen in 1966/67 when what had been Dock Lane was widened and an enormous roundabout wiped out the old junction. Now, in 1985, the area has again changed beyond recognition with the opening of the Parkway.

*(Aerofilms Ltd.)*

During the motoring boom of the 1930s many small "motor spirit service stations" were opened. They sold petrol and oil but offered no repair facilities. One of these was the Embankment Filling Station which was opened around 1933 by Mr. Edgar Bearne. It was situated just off the old Laira Roundabout.

By the outbreak of the War the business was in the name of Mrs. Winifred Bearne, as it was in September 1954 when this photograph was taken. The river Plym and Saltram Park can be seen in the background.

Wartime petrol rationing had ended only four years before and branded petrol had only been on sale again for some 18 months. Rationing was soon to be introduced again, however, following the Suez Crisis of 1956.

Note the boundary stone just to the right of the telegraph pole. Plymouth extended its boundary to this point in 1896. When built the petrol station was in the parish of Eggbuckland but soon came within the City limits when in 1938 the boundary was extended as far as the bridge over the Plym at Marsh Mills.

*(City Museum)*

"Briarleigh", pictured here in January 1961, was situated at Estover, just off Plym Bridge Lane near Mainstone Farm. It was known until the mid-1920s simply as "Rock".

The house dated from around 1780 and was believed to have been a farm house. This picture shows the south front which remained almost unaltered for some 180 years. The wooden porch had its original door and a Doric Triglyphed frieze above it. The entrance was approached by a small flight of granite steps.

Internally the entrance from the south door had been blocked off. The room to the left of the porch still had its original wooden mantlepiece and carved rosettes. Similarly the rooms above had their original mantlepieces, doors and door frames. There were three attic rooms behind the curved window.

In 1961 it was proposed to turn the estate in to a caravan site. The house itself was occupied until 1965 when the Corporation bought the land. They proposed to demolish it in October of that year but discovered that it was scheduled as of architectural importance. Twelve months later it was decided that "because of its present state the building should be demolished". This was done in 1967. Its existence is remembered by Briarleigh Close at Mainstone.

*(City Museum)*